The Latin American Left

The Latin American Left

From the Fall of Allende to Perestroika

edited by
Barry Carr and Steve Ellner

Westview Press
Boulder • San Francisco

Latin America Bureau
London

This book is included in Westview's Latin American Perspectives Series

Published in 1993 in the United States of America by Westview Press, Inc., 5500 Central Avenue, Boulder, Colorado 80301-2877

Published in 1993 in Great Britain by Latin America Bureau, 1 Amwell Street, London EC1R 1UL

Library of Congress Cataloging-in-Publication Data
    The Latin American left: from the fall of Allende to Perestroika/
    edited by Barry Carr & Steve Ellner.
       p. cm.
    Includes index.
    ISBN 0-8133-1200-0. — ISBN 0-8133-1201-9 (pbk.)
       1. Latin America—Politics and government—1948–   2. New Left—
    Latin America—History.   I. Carr, Barry.   II. Ellner, Steve.
    F1414.2.L3286   1993
    320.98—dc20   92-28615
                                                                            CIP

British Library Cataloguing in Publication Data
    A CIP catalogue record of this book is available from the British Library.
    ISBN 0-906156-73-4 (cloth); ISBN 0-906156-72-6 (paper)

Printed and bound in the United States of America

      The paper used in this publication meets the requirements
(∞) of the American National Standard for Permanence of Paper
      for Printed Library Materials Z39.48-1984.

10   9   8   7   6   5   4   3   2   1

Contents

Acknowledgments

The editors would like to thank the staff of the Research Commission of the Universidad de Oriente (Anzoátegui campus) and the History Department of La Trobe University for the generous support they have given this project over a period of two years. Special thanks are owed to Carol Courtis (La Trobe) and Lucas Alvarez (Universidad de Oriente), without whom this project could never have been completed.

Barry Carr
Steve Ellner

1

Introduction: The Changing Status of the Latin American Left in the Recent Past

Steve Ellner

The transformation of the Latin American Left since the early 1970s—the result of revisions in policy and strategy and a radically altered political landscape—can be explained in terms of international trends and national experiences in addition to profound socioeconomic and political changes. Latin American leftist parties were not exempt from the influence of Eurocommunism, which reached its apex in the 1970s, and perestroika in the following decade. Nevertheless, Latin American leftist leaders have always fervently denied that they uncritically embrace models from abroad and that their movements are replicas of others. Although the veracity of this claim has varied historically from country to country, it has undeniably been true in the recent past. Even orthodox communists have argued against the mechanical application of policies derived from perestroika, considering it an instance of the discredited practice of slavishly defending lines set down by the socialist metropolis.

Perhaps the most important set of national experiences influencing the Left was the military government of nearly all Latin American countries in the 1970s and early 1980s. During this period, repression reached new extremes as the state perfected the means of covering up the systematic elimination of the militant opposition, including clerics and other elite members who had previously been largely spared inhumane treatment; the regime's apologists actually justified these campaigns of exter-

I am grateful for critical comments from Susan Berglund, Barry Carr, and Brian Loveman.

mination along ideological lines.[1] At the time, the Left might have been expected to draw the conclusion that military coups vindicated the thesis of the dictatorship of the proletariat and the nondemocratic road to power. In fact, most leftists arrived at the opposite judgment: the weariness and hardship of years of torture, jail, and exile convinced them that the "formal democracy" that they had previously disparaged was a veritable conquest worth defending at all costs and building on.

The diversity of new forms of struggle, strategies, and challenges makes any scholarly examination of the Latin American Left a much more formidable undertaking than were books written in the past about allegedly monolithic Marxist parties, the main contribution of which was their description of universal trends and periodization.[2] Not only have communist parties now definitively lost their claim to near-monopoly status on the Left but they are subject to greater internal differences than at any time in the history of international communism. Other novel developments and challenges abound, further complicating the effort to depict the Left as a whole and to synthesize tendencies: the growth of new social movements that enter into a dialectical relationship with the Left while preserving their autonomy; uncertainty as to whether the decline of the industrial working class in the 1980s merits a reconsideration of strategy or is a temporary phenomenon induced by neoliberal policies; and the danger that leftists will be seen as accomplices in the international drug trade because of their effort to come to the defense of peasant cultivators and oppose foreign military intervention under the auspices of the Drug Enforcement Administration (DEA).

Latin American leftists are of course not alone in facing a diversity of unanticipated challenges. In one of the most provocative recent works on leftist strategy, Ernesto Laclau and Chantal Mouffe argue for recognition of the growing complexity of social relations and political conflict in developed capitalist, underdeveloped, and socialist societies. They relegate simple worker-management conflict to a secondary plane and point to the penetration of capitalist relations into new spheres that sets off untested forms of struggle. They conclude that the novelty and complexity of recent developments require the Left to rely more than ever on creativity and imagination.[3]

Examining the Latin American Left as a distinct topic rather than as an element in the context of individual national studies is plainly justified by the dramatic leftist inroads in organized labor, national elections, and armed struggle since the 1970s. As a result of these gains, the Left has broken out of its traditional ghetto and become a major protagonist in politics. Up until the 1980s, nonruling leftist parties (with the exception of Chile's) had never enjoyed widespread acceptance among voters and emerged as important actors only in moments of intense political crisis.

A few examples illustrate the Left's change in status. For decades the Peruvian Left, which was virtually synonymous with the Communist party, was uninfluential at the national level and had but a modest following in organized labor. In the 1970s the leftist-controlled Confederación General de Trabajadores del Perú (General Confederation of Workers of Peru—CGTP) eclipsed the labor confederation run by the Alianza Popular Revolucionaria Americana (American Popular Revolutionary Alliance—APRA), and in the following decade the united Left elected the mayor of Lima, who subsequently came in second in the 1985 presidential elections. In Brazil the nonpopulist Left never had more than a modest following up until the 1980s, with the rise of the Partido dos Trabalhadores (Workers' Party—PT). Contrary to the predictions of pundits that the populist Leonel Brizola would draw most of the leftist votes in the 1989 presidential elections, the PT's Luís Inácio (Lula) da Silva came within just four percentage points of winning. Fraud allegedly robbed the proleftists Cuauhtémoc Cárdenas and Juan Bosch of the presidencies in dubious electoral contests in Mexico in 1988 and the Dominican Republic in 1990. Cárdenas's 31.1 percent of the vote was particularly significant because it was the first time that the opposition had mounted a serious challenge to the ruling party since its founding sixty years before. While Cárdenas's makeshift Frente Democrático Nacional (National Democratic Front—FDN) has since attempted to transform itself into a party (a task to which Marxist leaders are committed), Bosch's Partido para la Liberación Dominicana (Dominican Liberation Party—PLD), founded in 1973, has emerged as the best-organized and most disciplined party in the Dominican Republic. Impressive electoral breakthroughs occurred in Colombia, with the election of ex-guerrilla Antonio Navarro Wolff of the Movimiento 19 de Abril (19th of April Movement—M-19) to the Constituent Assembly with 27 percent of the national vote in 1990, and in Uruguay, where a Marxist representing the leftist coalition Frente Amplio (Broad Front) was elected mayor of Montevideo in 1989. Up until then, as Dick Parker points out in this volume, the Uruguayan Left had been unable to parlay its dominant position in the nation's labor movement into support at the polls.

These electoral successes hardly mean, however, that Latin America is on the verge of sweeping revolutionary change. In the first place, it is open to question whether some of the above-mentioned parties are fully committed to a program of radical socioeconomic transformation. In the second, several of them have lost considerable ground after their initial electoral gains. As Barry Carr shows in his chapter on the Mexican Left, both qualifications are applicable to the movement led by Cuauhtémoc Cárdenas, particularly in light of the fact that the role of the former members of the defunct Mexican Communist party is unclear.

Ironically, the major exception to this continental trend of leftist advances is Chile, the one nation in which the Marxist Left had maintained an important institutional and electoral presence since the 1920s. The overthrow of Salvador Allende was a watershed not only for the Chilean Left but for that of Latin America as a whole (and, to a certain extent, that of Europe). Chile was the only country in which the wave of military takeovers in the 1960s and 1970s was directed against a prosocialist government. That the democratic tradition in Chile was the most firmly established in the continent only heightened the impact of the coup. Subsequent analyses pointed out that Allende's plurality in 1970 had not gone significantly beyond the one-third of the electorate that had supported him in the previous two presidential elections. Most (although not all) leftists who reflected on this experience reached the conclusion that a mandate for revolutionary change required nothing less than a large majority of the vote. Given the fragility of the Chilean Left's position in 1970, the Allende government should have adopted a more cautious approach that affirmed its commitment to established rules, made a greater effort to win over the middle sectors, eschewed indiscriminate nationalization, and rejected the statist model based on extreme centralism.[4] In contrast, the Partido Communista de Chile (Chilean Communist party—PCCh)—after first having accepted most of this self-criticism—by the 1980s had begun to point to the excessive legalism of the Allende government and its failure to attempt to win over the armed forces to its program of radical change.[5] At the same time, for a variety of reasons discussed by Brian Loveman in his chapter, it opted for armed struggle and, by the latter half of the decade, spurned the highly selective democratic openings of the Pinochet regime. As a consequence, it found itself isolated from other democratic sectors that were more receptive to Pinochet's political concessions and used them to their advantage. In the 1989 elections the PCCh, which participated in a congressional slate with orthodox socialists, failed to elect any of its candidates.

The Impact of Perestroika and Neoliberalism

In spite of leftist gains during the past decade, the Left in the early 1990s is more disoriented and lacking in credible options than ever before. One aspect of this paradox is amply demonstrated in Parker's chapter. On the one hand, leftist trade unionists have succeeded in gaining a dominant position in the labor movement in Peru, Uruguay, and Ecuador and made important inroads in Brazil, Colombia, and elsewhere. On the other hand, the industrial base of organized labor has been weakened by the economic contraction of the 1980s, modifications in multinational investment patterns, and the growth of the informal economy. As a result, the key role that the orthodox Left assigns to industrial workers has been placed in doubt.

Events in Eastern Europe, the resultant shift in the worldwide balance of power, and neoliberalism have been even greater blows to the ideological and doctrinal positions of the Latin American Left. For all of perestroika's attractiveness, the upheavals in the nations of the Communist bloc have called socialism's viability into question. The undisputed political and military hegemony of the United States also weakens the position of prosocialist movements. It is particularly distressing for the Left in Latin America because of the continent's historical status as a U.S. "sphere of influence." Two developments that greatly strengthen the hand of the United States and discourage leftist movements are the international isolation of Cuba and the upset defeat of the Sandinistas in the February 1990 presidential elections. In addition, President George Bush's initiative in favor of drastic hemispheric reductions in tariffs has struck a responsive chord because of the general consensus on the need to promote nontraditional exports and thus seemingly disproves the Left's standard depiction of imperialist behavior. In still another area of reversal for the Left, the widespread acceptance of neoliberal economics has undermined support for the statist model traditionally embraced by leftists. This has been especially crushing for the Left in Latin America, where statist strategies have a strong appeal due to the danger of multinational control of basic industry and the inability or unwillingness of local capitalists to invest in those sectors.

Leftist parties, even highly heterodox ones such as Venezuela's Movimiento al Socialismo (Movement Toward Socialism—MAS), which had always been a harsh critic of Soviet socialism and orthodox models based on centralism, have been negatively affected by these occurrences. Discussing MAS's response to perestroika and neoliberalism, the party's main theoretician Teodoro Petkoff told me, "We MASistas will eventually have to sit down to analyze previously held assumptions and reformulate our version of Utopia." In short, instability in the socialist bloc, U.S. ascendancy, and neoliberalism have been adverse not just to the growth of a certain brand of socialism but to socialism per se, in spite of the concerted efforts of a renovation current on the Left to disassociate itself from the system's negative features.[6]

The response of the Latin American Left to neoliberalism and perestroika has been far from uniform. With regard to the former, almost all leftist spokesmen have opposed the elimination of social welfare programs and, as did Lula in Brazil, Cárdenas in Mexico, and Bosch in the Dominican Republic, favored lengthy moratoria on payment of the foreign debt. Nevertheless, there is no consensus on privatization and the redefinition of the role of the state in promoting economic development.

On the one hand, Loveman shows that left-leaning think-tank organizations in Chile in the 1980s questioned the statist model and that socialists in the government of Christian Democrat Patricio Aylwin accepted the continuity and orthodoxy that marked his economic policy. Similarly, Juan Bosch in his presidential campaign advocated privatization of inefficient public enterprises as a means to counter corruption. Orthodox Communists and other leftists in Venezuela accepted privatization of nonstrategic sectors under certain circumstances. At the other extreme, as Donald Hodges shows in his chapter, opposition to privatization and other International Monetary Fund (IMF)-imposed policies moved the main leadership of the peronista (Peronist) Confederación General de Trabajo (General Confederation of Labor—CGT) to the left.

Argentina is typical of a number of nations in which yesterday's radical populists were transformed into champions of neoliberalism in the 1980s and, in the process, turned their backs on the virtually sacred symbols of their movement's legacy. Most of the public companies that the government of peronista Carlos Menem slated for privatization, such as railroad and telephone firms, had been nationalized by Juan Perón in the 1940s. Those CGT leaders and other peronistas who opposed Menem's economic policies were apparently truer to their idol's memory. Similarly, privatization in Mexico and the pressure to open the oil industry to foreign capital (as part of the proposed North American Free Trade Agreement—NAFTA—taking in the United States and Canada) were viewed by many as a violation of the spirit of the Mexican Revolution. The proposal was particularly criticized by Cuauhtémoc Cárdenas, the son of Lázaro Cárdenas, who had nationalized the petroleum industry in 1938. Similarly, in Venezuela, President Carlos Andrés Pérez reversed the radical thrust of his first administration of 1974–1979 by accepting IMF policies upon assuming the presidency for the second time, in 1989. Finally, the neoliberalism pushed by President Víctor Paz Estenssoro (1985–1989) in Bolivia went against the grain of the 1952 revolution that he had led.

These developments opened up possibilities for tactical alliances between the Left and those traditional politicians and labor leaders who resisted neoliberalism, as Hodges shows in the case of Argentina. Perhaps the most dramatic convergence of erstwhile adversaries is the apparent decision of Venezuelan leftists in the early 1990s to support the 1993 presidential candidacy of former president Rafael Caldera, who earlier in his career had been an ultraconservative and has now emerged as an outspoken defender of legislation favoring the popular sectors. Some leftist theoreticians pointed out that alliances between socialists and nonsocialists were grounded in the discontent felt by sectors of the bourgeoisie that were weighed down by neoliberal policies such as the drastic reduction of tariffs and the onerous terms of the payment of the foreign debt.[7]

Perestroika also produced varied reactions on the Left, but in general it dampened militant leftism and influenced Communists to abandon efforts to achieve socialism in the short-term future. Richard Gillespie points out that the conciliatory thrust of perestroika led some Communists (in nations such as Chile and Argentina) to reconsider the positions in favor of armed struggle that they had formulated in the wake of the Sandinista triumph in 1979. In the same vein, Hodges comments that Soviet policymakers under Mikhail Gorbachev prevailed upon Argentine Communists to tone down their rhetoric, even at the cost of socialist convergence. In contrast, some leftists were wary of perestroika and drew closer to the increasingly isolated regime of Fidel Castro. They feared that the Gorbachev administration's decision to cut off military aid to the Sandinista government in order to encourage a negotiated solution in Central America signaled the forsaking of Soviet commitments to the Third World.[8] Both Gillespie and Hodges note that these shifts contributed to a "polarization of the socialist Left" between those who identified with the Cuban leadership and called for a purer approach to socialism and those who attempted to forge broad-based alliances.

The Left's search for allies in the moderate camp in response to neoliberalism and perestroika appeared to be a throwback to the policy of popular-frontism that guided the Latin American Left from the 1930s to the 1960s. Nevertheless, in contrast to popular-frontism these recent alliances and agreements lacked a strategic justification and were usually viewed as conjunctural or, in some cases, merely expedient. Popular-frontism in Latin America had been underpinned by the thesis that autonomous industrial development would result from a "national democratic revolution" in which the "progressive bourgeoisie" would play a leading role and, in alliance with popular sectors, would confront imperialism and the traditional economic elite. This theory was rooted in the emergence of radical populist regimes (such as Perón's first government in Argentina and that of Getúlio Vargas in Brazil) that practiced import substitution policies to foster industrialization and often clashed with the United States and its allies.

By the 1970s, however, it was generally recognized that the stage of import substitution that promoted incipient industrial growth had reached its limits and that radical populist movements, which called for redistributive policies in favor of the underprivileged sectors, were absent from the political landscape in most of Latin America. In many countries, a new polarization pitted the Left, united in its commitment to socialism, against the status quo.[9] Although few important leftist parties raised the banner "Socialism Now," most of them discarded the "strategy of stages" in which socialism was relegated to a distant second stage. Most of them saw the revolutionary process as a continuum leading inexorably to socialism, with the working class playing a central role from the outset. While small and medium-sized business interests were seen as potential allies, the term "progressive bourgeoisie" was largely dropped from the Left's lexicon.[10]

Broad-based alliances and support for reformist governments in the 1970s and 1980s were designed to achieve more limited objectives: guaranteeing the transition to or consolidation of democracy and facing powerful right-wing adversaries. The advantages derived from these arrangements for the Left were extremely modest and the liabilities and potential pitfalls considerable. The only case in which the Left came out on top was during the government of General Juan Velasco Alvarado (1968–1975) in Peru. The Velasco regime accepted popular mobilization and organizing efforts but, because of the conflicting objectives and strategies upheld by the military officers in power, failed to convert this activity into institutional gains. The main beneficiaries of the massive unionization of these years were the CGTP, controlled by the Partido Comunista Peruana (Peruvian Communist party—PCP), and independent unions led by small parties to its left. The military, which for historical reasons viewed the APRA as its main foe, was anxious to undermine the strength of the confederation it controlled but failed to ensure the hegemony of the official Confederación de Trabajadores de la Revolución Peruana (Confederation of Workers of the Peruvian Revolution—CTRP), whose influence was mainly limited to small establishments. Nevertheless, even during this period the PCP paid a price for its support of Velasco and (although in more qualified form) of his conservative successor, General Francisco Morales Bermúdez. The PCP's condemnation of strikes of teachers and miners as the work of *apristas* and Maoists intent on creating problems for the government led to the party's nearly complete loss of influence among the workers in both sectors, to the advantage of its ultraleftist rivals. The party was also reluctant to support the general strike of July 1977 against Morales Bermúdez's austerity measures and did so only in the face of rank-and-file pressure and disobedience within its own ranks. Party leaders later publicly recognized that they had erred in uncritically backing Velasco and in attempting to put the brakes on several of these worker conflicts.[11]

The Left's most important experience of participation in a nonsocialist government was in Bolivia under Hernán Siles (1982–1985) and had disastrous consequences. On the one hand, their role of broker between popular sectors and the cabinet of which they formed part during a period of runaway inflation discredited the Partido Comunista de Bolivia (Bolivian Communist Party—PCB) and the Movimiento de la Izquierda Revolucionaria (Movement of the Revolutionary Left—MIR, which subsequently moved to the center). On the other hand, the intransigence of the Central Obrera Boliviana (Bolivian Workers' Union—COB) in refusing to join the government and calling several two-to-three-day general strikes in favor of its "ultimatumist" program played into the hands of conservatives, as James Dunkerley discusses in this volume. Siles's replacement by Paz Estenssoro led to sharp cutbacks in tin production at the behest of the IMF, which greatly weakened the tin miners' movement, the COB's backbone. Later, the PCB was able to recover its labor support and actually occupied the presidency of the COB for a short period, thanks to the rectification of its policies in the form of frontal opposition to the Paz government.[12]

The Communists also paid a price for their tacit support of military governments in Brazil and Argentina. The Partido Comunista de Argentina (Argentinian Communist party—PCA) was favorably disposed to the repressive regime of Jorge Videla (1976–1981) because of its promotion of commercial relations with the Soviet Union. This attitude was later repudiated at the PCA's "Left" congress in 1986, which purged much of the party's top leadership.[13] During the same period, Brazilian Communists approved of the military government's timid steps in the direction of democracy, a process that they feared would be endangered by the militant worker protests, originating in the automobile industry, out of which the PT emerged. The Communists developed cordial relations with social democratic and even conservative parties as part of a "pragmatic convergence" based on a nonmobilization strategy to reestablish democracy. Nevertheless, they were severely criticized by leaders of the fledgling PT for compromising the autonomy of the workers' movement, a practice that they claimed was the Communist party's major historical blunder, dating back as far as the 1940s.[14]

The Emergence of New Social Movements

The role of the Left and popular struggles in the reestablishment of democracy in the 1970s was the source of considerable debate. The fear expressed by Communist leaders in Peru and Brazil that labor strife would jeopardize the transition to democracy in their nations was shared by politicians and political analysts to their right. Indeed, several outstanding nonleftist political scientists who wrote on redemocratization in Latin America at this time cautioned against optimistic forecasts and maintained that the best that could be hoped for was a "restricted democracy" that precluded mass participation, popular protests, and significant socioeconomic change. At the other extreme, some proleftist scholars considered this focus a cover for "normative preference for the maintenance of the status quo" and criticized its omission of the influence of "radical democrats" who strove to go beyond the restoration of mere formal democracy in an effort to achieve a more authentic, participatory democracy. These leftist writers highlighted the role of popular mobilization, the armed struggle, and social movements in forcing the military to accept a return to civilian rule with no strings attached.[15] In doing so, they took issue not only with the nonleftist "redemocratization" political scientists but with several leftist ones as well. One writer, for instance, objected to the failure of fellow leftist James Cockcroft to recognize that the guerrilla movement indirectly contributed to the military's withdrawal from power by forcing it to concentrate its energy on the armed opposition, thus opening space for militant antigovernment labor movements.[16] In the same vein, another leftist, James Petras, was criticized for underestimating the effectiveness of pressure from below and instead explaining the military's abandonment of power as a stratagem designed to convert politicians into "fall guys" for the pressing economic problems of the 1980s that they had inherited.[17] By the early 1990s, the issue of military strategy and motives in returning to the barracks was far from resolved; nevertheless, the consolidation of democratic regimes was well under way in all major Latin American nations, and only in Chile and, to a lesser extent, Uruguay did the model of "restricted democracy" still prevail.

One facet of the debate regarding redemocratization had to do with conflicting depictions of new social movements in Latin America and their relationship to leftist parties and objectives. Many of these organizations were founded in response to the severe repression under military rule, when political parties were outlawed and the activity of organized labor was circumscribed. The family members of victims of state terrorism, for instance, turned to the church and human rights groups, which were able to act with greater liberty than traditional political organizations. In addition, neighborhood associations and Christian base communities channeled popular discontent over the austerity measures promoted by military regimes and the economic contraction that began in the 1980s. Some of the new social movements included many former leftist party militants. In Chile, for instance, members of the Christian leftist parties returned after 1973 to the church, where they acted in a political capacity. Furthermore, the movement of the urban poor in Santiago was strongest where the community leadership had been closely linked to individual leftist parties prior to Pinochet's seizure of power.

Alain Touraine and other sociologists who have written about the new social movements in a worldwide context have attempted to show that they are incompatible with traditional leftist politics. They point out that such movements as those that defend women's and gay rights, world peace, and ecological concerns and oppose nuclear energy are horizontally structured and suspicious of all national authorities at the same time that they are wary of leftist infringement on their autonomy. Furthermore, they do not share the Left's faith in material progress and in socialism as a panacea for the types of problems they are confronting. They question the statist model that orthodox Marxism embraces and view the technocratic state and not capitalism as the main enemy. In addition, in contrast to traditional leftist movements, they have largely nonmaterial goals based on principles that are not easily negotiable.[18]

It is open to question to what extent the concepts and paradigms formulated by Touraine and others in their writings on the new social movements are applicable to Latin America. Touraine implies that there is little affinity when he postulates that the new social movements are to postindustrial society what organized labor is to industrial society in that they embody the defense of popular and progressive interests.[19] Not only is Latin America far from achieving postindustrial status, but the influence of the groups that Touraine is concerned with, such as those pursuing women's liberation and environmental protection, pales in comparison with that of their counterparts in Europe and the United States. Finally, the conservationist creed and antimaterialism that form the basis of "deep ecology" have little resonance in Latin America, where the struggle against poverty and underdevelopment overshadows philosophical and abstract issues.

In spite of these differences, the thesis that the new social movements prefigure a new type of democracy—whose salient features are the autonomy of civil society and rank-and-file participation in decision making at all levels—is as important for the Latin American Left as it is for that of Europe.[20] Contrary to predictions, these movements did not fade into the background once democracy was reestablished in the 1980s, nor have they been subjugated by political parties. María Helena Moreira Alves shows that in Brazil the PT, which emerged out of a wave of worker and community protests, contains important contingents of labor and neighborhood activists and has maintained a special relationship with social movements. In fact, the PT's emphasis on the autonomy of unions and other popular organizations represents a departure from traditional leftist discourse in Brazil. Although other leftist parties in Latin America have raised these same issues,[21] the PT has done so more persistently, perhaps because corporatist relations in Brazil were historically so deeply entrenched.

That the Latin American Left has begun to appreciate the importance of the autonomy of civil society, however, does not mean that viable strategies and definitive models have been forthcoming. The narrow range of concerns of many of the new social movements, which often do not transcend local issues, discourages the Left from linking up with them in constructive ways.[22] Nigel Haworth, in his chapter on Peru, maintains that the allegiance of members of youth, women's, and community organiza-

tions to any particular leftist party or perspective is extremely tenuous—
a characterization that contrasts with that of the political behavior of organized workers. Similarly, Marc Chernick and Michael Jiménez, in the concluding section of their chapter on the Colombian Left, predict that the
efforts to transform local struggles around local issues into a national
movement will meet with little success. The argument that the new social
movements do not fortify leftist parties but do contribute to political culture by teaching people how to act collectively and enhancing their sense
of efficacy[23] is of little consolation to most Latin American leftists, who,
after all, are striving to attain nothing less than state power. Furthermore,
the banner of autonomy is not, in itself, necessarily progressive, as
Pinochet and other reactionaries have identified with it in their effort to
impose an apolitical model on organized labor in the face of staunch
worker resistance.[24]

Social movements in the developed nations concerned with human
rights, ecology, the spread of nuclear weapons, and immigration have
attempted to establish international networks in order to compensate for
the limited resources and coordination of their Third World counterparts.
Ecology groups argue that this expanded scope of action is a necessary
response to the internationalization of capital and the weakening of the
nation-state.[25] Their own success in forcing their governments to enforce
environmental standards has paradoxically damaged the developing
nations in that it induces multinationals to export toxic waste and relocate
high-pollution industries abroad.

The dependence of ecology and human rights groups in the Third
World on foreign governments and organizations has been cynically
exploited by powerful interests in the developing countries under the
cover of nationalism and opposition to outside interference in their internal affairs. On this basis, for instance, the Brazilian government of José
Sarney emphatically rejected aid or debt relief with strings attached
designed to limit development in the Amazonian region. Naturally, the
most effective environmental movements are those, such as that of the
Amazonian rubber tappers, that have developed a working-class or community base and are thus not overly dependent on foreign support. As I
show in my essay on Venezuela, the Left is sometimes placed in the awk-
ward position of having to risk being branded antinationalist in order to
come to the defense of environmental causes. At the same time, however,
the Left must be wary of conservationist groups that oppose all forms of
infrastructure development—especially in sparsely populated regions
near national borders—and that sometimes actually serve the interests of
multinationals themselves seeking concessions to exploit the same areas.

The Latin American Left faces a similar, perhaps even knottier predicament with regard to the international drug trade. In his chapter in this

volume, James Dunkerley indicates that the support of the Bolivian Left for peasant coca cultivators in the face of U.S.-backed military campaigns fortified its position in several respects: it was able to assert its credentials as a defender of national sovereignty; it allied itself with peasant organizations, which were historically anti-Left, as well as with the nation's only labor confederation; and its defense of the allegedly innocuous indigenous tradition of coca consumption served to "introduce into its own politics a recognition of ethnic culture." At the same time, Dunkerley notes that the Left found itself in the uncomfortable situation of being on the same side as rightist sectors that were inextricably tied to drug interests.

This same convergence was evident in Colombia, where the Left opposed extradition of cocaine smugglers on the ground that the problem involved multinationals and not just individual kingpins. Leftists such as the Sendero Luminoso (Shining Path—SL) and the Colombian novelist Gabriel García Márquez advocated the industry's legalization, the major argument being that the state would be able to capture some of its profits. Gillespie points out that in Colombia and Peru leftist guerrillas have entered into agreements with traffickers by providing them with protection in return for handsome remuneration; although the allegation is denied by the SL and other leftists, it has been well documented by Americas Watch.[26] Nevertheless, in Colombia this pact broke down as members of the cocaine cartels bought land and began to exploit areas that had previously been leftist preserves, unleashing a campaign of terrorism against the nonclandestine Left that cost hundreds of lives. One scholarly work on Peru maintains that the guerrillas protect small coca producers from both government officials and powerful drug interests that are themselves bound together in an uneasy alliance.[27]

The Armed Struggle

The guerrilla movements that were operating in Peru, Colombia, El Salvador, and Guatemala in the early 1990s were different in fundamental ways from those that abounded throughout the continent in the 1960s. In all four nations, the guerrillas were able to establish a solid foothold in certain areas over an extended period of time. The decision to avoid national projection initially in order to work secretly and patiently to win over the peasants in those regions accounted for their relative success. Their broad social base contrasted with that of the guerrillas of the 1960s and early 1970s, whose predominantly middle-class origin facilitated their detection in slum dwellings where they attempted to carry out political work.[28] Other factors that explain the greater staying power of the guerrillas in these four countries are their abandonment of the *foco* (focus) strategy, in which political objectives are subordinated to military ones, as well as (particularly in the case of Guatemala) their greater sensitivity to the preservation of Indian identities and traditions.

The original guerrilla movements of the 1960s, influenced by the experience of the Cuban Revolution, had presumed that the struggle for power was a short-term proposition, an illusion that was not easily overcome. By the early 1990s, it was evident that the guerrilla movements and government forces in Colombia, El Salvador, and Guatemala had reached a stalemate and that the insurgents could not hope to achieve power in the short- or medium-term future. The guerrillas discarded plans for an immediate mass insurrection, which had been successfully applied in 1979 in the months prior to Anastasio Somoza's overthrow and unsuccessfully in El Salvador two years later. Instead they adopted the "prolonged popular war" approach. Thus, for instance, Colombia's M-19, whose dramatic actions were intended to trigger immediate change in the power structure, had its fighting power reduced to a bare minimum, while the Fuerzas Armadas Revolucionarias de Colombia (Revolutionary Armed Forces of Colombia—FARC), by far the largest guerrilla organization, followed a more cautious, long-term strategy. The protracted nature of these struggles was recognized by U.S. strategists linked to the State Department, who abandoned the idea of completely subduing the guerrillas in favor of "low-intensity warfare" designed to wear down the enemy over a period of time.[29]

Recognition of the impasse led both official sectors and guerrillas to revise their demands for a negotiated solution. Previously, the guerrillas had viewed peace settlements as either a ploy to achieve a respite or an ultimate recourse tantamount to capitulation. Their demands for the establishment of a provisional government, the complete integration of guerrillas into the armed forces, and thorough socioeconomic transformation were unrealistic and may have been formulated for propagandistic purposes only. By the early 1990s, these radical proposals had been largely replaced by the call for the elimination of paramilitary groups, the purging of military officers responsible for the flagrant violation of human rights, reductions in the armed forces, and judicial reforms. The guerrilla movements were mainly concerned with avoiding a repetition of the Colombian experience under President Virgilio Barco Vargas, when hundreds of members of the Unión Patriótica (Patriotic Union—UP), established to facilitate the incorporation of the FARC into the political life of the nation, were gunned down; the Left amply demonstrated the linkage between death squads, which acted with impunity in these cases, and the armed forces.[30] Another, more limited demand was the implementation of democratic reforms. Thus, for instance, the Colombian government convoked a Constituent Assembly that encouraged the M-19 to accept an amnesty agreement that the FARC also considered signing. A third proposal, put forward by various armed groups and accepted by the Colombian government, was the carrying out of developmental programs in areas controlled by the insurgents and the granting of a minimum salary to former guerrillas along with credit to allow them to purchase farmland. Gillespie shows that in recent years armed actions were generally designed to force the government to the bargaining table rather than to topple it. Salvadorian guerrillas even attempted to convince Washington by word and deed that a long-drawn-out war would be exceedingly costly for the United States at the same time that they pledged not to endanger its vital interests once a solution had been reached.[31] The radical change in the strategy pursued by Salvadorian guerrilla leaders as a result of their determination to put an end to over a decade of civil war is amply documented by Tommie Sue Montgomery in her chapter in this volume.

The extended duration of the armed struggle presented guerrilla organizations with unforeseen difficulties. On the personal side, individual guerrillas grew accustomed to a certain life-style, and, as Gillespie argues, were unequipped for the radically different challenges of an aboveground existence. At an organizational level, the transition represented unknown and risky terrain, as was fully demonstrated by the UP experience in Colombia. Rosa Luxemburg and other socialists have pointed out that a prolonged legal existence can foster the development of a bureaucracy within leftist parties that has a vested interest in maintaining the status quo and is unprepared for clandestine activity when circumstances require it.[32] Conversely, guerrillas who have spent most of their adult lives engaged in armed struggle may be reluctant to seize the opportunity to achieve legal status, even in situations in which such a move is highly beneficial to the revolutionary cause.

The Struggle to Deepen Democracy

Just as the terminologies "Left" and "Center" have been turned on their heads in the socialist countries as a result of perestroika, the continued relevance of these terms has been questioned in the rest of the world. Parties such as the MAS in Venezuela have attempted to discard the leftist label on grounds that it unnecessarily polarizes public opinion and reinforces damaging stereotypes and, in any case, is obsolete. This assertion, although perhaps accurate from a pragmatic viewpoint, fails to take into account the profundity of differences between those who advocate far-reaching structural change to overcome underdevelopment in Latin America and those who are mainly concerned with policy reforms. Because of the fading out of radical populism in much of Latin America, the Left is no longer divided between prosocialist and propopulist wings.

Nevertheless, consensus with regard to definitions and long-term goals has hardly been achieved, in large part because recent events in Eastern Europe have discredited traditionally accepted models of socialism. In recent years, leftist theoreticians and party leaders have placed greater emphasis on novel forms of democracy and participation than on public ownership of the means of production.[33]

Some leftists have challenged the notion—posited by the French school of "new philosophers" headed by André Glucksmann—that socialism and Marxism are inherently totalitarian by arguing that only under the socialist system can authentic democracy prosper. This assertion has gained credibility in Latin America as a result of the leading role that leftist parties have played in the deepening of democracy following the restoration of democratic regimes in the 1980s. Leftist parties such as the Núñez Socialist party in Chile and Venezuela's MAS were the first to implement primaries for the selection of party authorities combined with a mixed system of nominal voting options and proportional representation of minority slates. In her essay's section entitled "The Novelty of the PT" and in other works, Moreira Alves discusses in considerable detail the structural and electoral reforms of the PT and the labor confederation it controls.[34] The PT and other Latin American leftist parties were in the forefront in calling for decentralization and similar mechanisms to foster popular input into decision making. At the Constituent Assembly in Colombia in 1991, for instance, the M-19 became the foremost proponent of transferring authority from the nation's "presidential monarchy" to a unicameral legislature that was to be more receptive to popular interests.[35] Finally, leftist parties have supported the model of worker participation in companies (known as *cogestión*) embraced by organized labor in Venezuela, Bolivia, and elsewhere. The traditional reformist parties, which for decades had arrogated to themselves the image of paladins of the democratic cause, have been reluctant to follow the lead of the leftists in actively backing these concrete proposals and initiatives (see, for example, my chapter on Venezuela).

Complementary to the Left's greater commitment to democracy was its receptivity to pluralism, which found expression in intra-Left party unity. The renunciation of the monolithic model by Communists and other leftists opened the possibility for unity encompassing a larger number of parties and ideological currents than had ever converged before. In the past, successful revolutions had been conducted for the most part by single organizations, as was the case in Cuba and Nicaragua. In the 1980s, in El Salvador, Guatemala, and Colombia between four and six guerrilla groups attempted to overcome years of bitter infighting by establishing single commands. In El Salvador they went so far as to carry out integrated military actions and to make plans for coalescing into a single party.

At the same time, electoral coalitions encompassing a host of leftist parties were successful in electing candidates in important cities and states in Venezuela, Peru, and Uruguay. Nevertheless, the Left was unable to establish a tradition of electoral cooperation as, for instance, the communists and socialists in Chile had on the basis of support for the presidential candidacies of Salvador Allende prior to 1973. Perhaps the greatest obstacle to electoral unity was the sheer number of parties involved. In Venezuela, the MAS attempted to gain hegemony on the left in the form of a veritable veto power by arguing that numerous minuscule parties would never be able to reach consensus on major issues and thus represented a liability for those who were seriously interested in challenging the status quo. Peru was the nation in which the failure to sustain unity did the most damage by condemning the Left's efforts to come to power by electoral means. According to polls at the outset of the 1990 presidential campaign, Alfonso Barrantes of the Izquierda Unida (United Left—IU) had the inside track, but the alliance ended up splitting in two. Voters generally blamed Barrantes for the split, and as a result he drew fewer votes than his less well-known rival on the left. The case of Peru illustrates the potential benefits of unity and the disastrous consequences of the failure to achieve it. This issue looms as the Left's most compelling challenge in Latin America.

Concluding Comments

Both optimistic and pessimistic scenarios for the Latin American Left can be constructed on the basis of an analysis of past events. Ronald Chilcote, in the concluding section of his chapter, argues that the recent swing of the pendulum to the right as a result of events in the socialist world will reverse itself in favor of "an eventual resurgence of Marxist thinking adapted to new and changing conditions." That the problems of dire poverty and extreme inequality in Latin America have been intensified by the economic crisis of the 1980s and early 1990s suggests that the Left may recover from its ideological disorientation by reasserting an anticapitalist critique and defending a revised vision of socialism. A second prediction, less favorable to traditional Marxism, is that important sectors of the Latin American Left will fill the void left by the virtual disappearance of radical populism. Discouraged by the setbacks on the world scene, these parties could conceivably follow the example of the Sandinistas by ceasing to call themselves socialist, at least publicly, and pursue a vague Third Worldist approach.[36]

Three salient characteristics of Latin American leftist movements of the early 1990s that distinguish them from the Left prior to 1973 are worth underlining: the importance the Left attaches to the struggle to achieve democracy and deepen democratic structures and practices; the diversity of currents of opinion and organized groups on the Left, which do not see their differences as irreconcilable; and the legitimacy attained by leftists, which has allowed them to overcome their marginal status. These developments are partly the result of changes in the socialist countries following Gorbachev's assumption of power, which marked the definitive end of the Cold War and the myth of monolithic communism. Perestroika and related occurrences in Eastern Europe encouraged the Latin American Left to upgrade the importance of the struggle for democracy and to accept a pluralistic vision of ideological diversity; at the same time, the negative stereotypes that had condemned the Left to a ghetto existence for much of its history were largely effaced.

Nevertheless, these three characteristics cannot be attributed exclusively to events in a worldwide context. The wider acceptance of the Left and its enhanced legitimacy, for instance, reflect the erosion of support for the reformist political parties that compete with it for the same constituency. The popularity of reformism in Latin America had been underpinned by the strategy of import substitution, which was a viable model until the exhaustion of its "easy" stage in the 1960s. More recently, the leaders of many of the reformist parties, such as the Acción Democrática (Democratic Action—AD) in Venezuela and the peronistas in Argentina, have opted for neoliberal formulas. The attractiveness of neoliberalism, which in Latin America is a throwback to a previous period when foreign capital was welcomed with open arms, is limited in comparison with that of import substitution, which conveyed great hope because of its nationalist overtones and the redistributive policies it promoted in favor of the popular classes. These economic and political transformations in Latin America strengthen the position of the Left in that they undermine the appeal of its historical rivals.

The editors of this anthology have attempted to stress the diversity of the Latin American Left by providing as many as twelve chapters on individual topics, thus sacrificing some of the detail that would have been included in a volume with fewer chapters of greater length. A discussion of the Left in power in Cuba and Nicaragua was not included because it would have exceeded the space limitations of a single volume.

A negative side has been included in this brief overview of the Latin American Left. The worldwide questioning of socialism per se due to the disruptions in the socialist nations has obscured the Left's long-term objectives and placed in doubt whether it could count on international financial or even political backing in the event that it came to power.

Furthermore, the Left's newly adopted Gramscian, democratic strategy, based on its gradually fortified position in the institutional life of the nation, fails to take into account the political instability and military intervention that have plagued Latin America since independence.

While the turmoil in the socialist bloc has had a disorienting effect, the Latin American Left's survival and growth demonstrate that it is not, as has been widely assumed, dependent on foreign models and assistance. What should be clear from this introductory overview of the Latin American Left is that it can no longer be understood solely on the basis of foreign influences, ideology (itself largely shaped from abroad), and performance in organized labor. Support for the Left has extended beyond its historical constituency of organized workers and intellectuals at the same time that leftist parties have succeeded in identifying themselves with established traditions that they had previously belittled. In short, in much of Latin America leftist and proleftist organizations have become intimately tied to the institutional and cultural life of their respective nations and thus need to be analyzed in those contexts.

Notes

1. Marysa Navarro, "The Personal is Political: Las Madres de Plaza de Mayo," in Susan Eckstein, ed., *Power and Popular Protest: Latin American Social Movements* (Berkeley: University of California Press, 1989), 244.

2. One standard work in this genre is Robert J. Alexander, *Communism in Latin America* (New Brunswick: Rutgers University Press, 1957).

3. Ernesto Laclau and Chantal Mouffe, *Hegemony and Socialist Strategy* (London: Verso, 1985). Socialist scholars have heavily criticized this work for abandoning class analysis and long-term socioeconomic objectives altogether. See Norman Geras, *Discourses of Extremity* (London: Verso, 1990).

4. For a discussion of the influence of the Allende experience on the Latin American Left and that of Venezuela in particular, see Steve Ellner, "The MAS Party in Venezuela," *Latin American Perspectives*, 13, 2 (Spring 1986):102–104.

5. "XV Congreso del Partido Comunista: Adiós a la armas," *APSI*, 291 (February 13–19, 1989):11–14.

6. Teodoro Petkoff, interview, Caracas, March 7, 1991. The Left, of course, faces this same predicament throughout the world; see Daniel Singer, "The Last Superpower," *Nation*, January 7–14, 1991, 13.

7. Roger Burbach and Orlando Núñez, *Fire in the Americas: Forging a Revolutionary Agenda* (London: Verso, 1987), 84.

8. "In Third World Nations, the Legacy of Marx Takes Many Different Shapes," *New York Times*, January 24, 1989, A-1, A-11.

9. Important exceptions are the M-19 in Colombia, the Montoneros of Argentina, and the Tupamaros of Uruguay, who did not embrace socialism as a major goal even (as did the Sandinistas) in private. For a discussion of these populist strains, see Richard Gillespie, *Soldiers of Perón: Argentina's Montoneros* (Oxford: Oxford University Press, 1982).

10. For a discussion of recent modifications in the theory of the "bourgeois democratic revolution" in developing nations, see Donald Hodges and Ross Gandy, *Mexico 1910–1976:*

Reform or Revolution? (London: Zed, 1979), 99–121; Steve Ellner, *Venezuela's Movimiento al Socialismo: From Guerrilla Defeat to Innovative Politics* (Durham: Duke University Press, 1988), 25–31.

11. Fernando Rospigliosi, "La paradoja del velasquismo: La oposición del movimiento sindical a la dictadura militar," *Apuntes* (Lima), 23, 2 (1988):57–159.

12. Robert Alexander, "Bolivia," in *Yearbook on International Communist Affairs* (Stanford: Hoover Institution, 1987), 52.

13. Mark Falcoff, "Argentina," in *Yearbook on International Communist Affairs*, 1987, 48; *La lucha por el socialismo con democracia: Conversaciones con Nahuel Moreno* (Buenos Aires: Ediciones La Chispa, 1986), 69.

14. The PT's former secretary-general Francisco Weffort has developed this critique in a series of scholarly works analyzed by John D. French in the introductory chapter of *The Brazilian Workers' ABC: Class Conflict and Alliances in Modern São Paulo* (Chapel Hill: University of North Carolina Press, 1992). See also Silvio R. Duncan Baretta and John Markoff, "Brazil's Abertura: From What to What?" in James M. Malloy and Mitchell A. Seligson, eds., *Authoritarians and Democrats: Regime Transition in Latin America* (Pittsburgh: University of Pittsburgh Press, 1987), 56.

15. Jorge Nef, "The Trend Toward Democratization and Redemocratization in Latin America: Shadow and Substance," *Latin American Research Review*, 23, 3 (1988):150. Terrie R. Groth argues that the position of these political scientists, many of whom previously defended a corporatist framework, was "conditioned largely by the paradigm of their previous work." Groth, "Debating Latin American Democratization: A Theoretical Guide," paper presented at the Latin American Studies Association congress in New Orleans, March 1988, 26.

16. Hobart Spalding, "The New Cauldron to the South," *Monthly Review*, 41, 11 (April 1990): 51.

17. Paul Cammack, "Resurgent Democracy: Threat and Promise," *New Left Review*, 157 (May–June 1986):121–128.

18. Alain Touraine, *Anti-Nuclear Protest: The Opposition to Nuclear Energy in France* (London: Cambridge University Press, 1983), 34–57.

19. Touraine, *The Voice and the Eye: An Analysis of Social Movements* (London: Cambridge University Press, 1981), 24; Ron Eyerman and Andrew Jamison, *Social Movements: A Cognitive Approach* (University Park: Pennsylvania State University Press, 1991), 26, 146.

20. Scott Mainwaring and Eduardo Viola, "New Social Movements, Political Culture, and Democracy: Brazil and Argentina in the 1980s," *Telos*, 61 (Fall 1984):21–22. Judith Adler Hellman argues that new social movements in Latin America have the potential to exert a profound influence on leftist parties, as has occurred in Europe on such issues as nuclear energy and sexism. Hellman, "The Study of New Social Movements in Latin America and the Question of Autonomy," *LASA Forum*, 21, 2 (Summer 1990):7–12.

21. Ellner, *Venezuela's Movimiento*, 175–176.

22. Spalding, "The New Cauldron," 50–51.

23. Tilman Evers, "Identity: The Hidden Side of New Social Movements in Latin America," in David Slater, ed., *New Social Movements and the State in Latin America* (Amsterdam: CEDLA, 1985), 43–71.

24. Jacqueline Roddick, "Chile," in Jean Carrière, Nigel Haworth, and Jacqueline Roddick, eds., *The State, Industrial Relations, and the Labour Movement in Latin America* (New York: St. Martin's Press, 1989), 1:210–211; Daniel H. Levine and Scott Mainwaring, "Religion and Popular Protest in Latin America: Contrasting Experiences," in Eckstein, *Power and Popular Protest*, 203–240.

25. Kathrine Yih, "The Red and the Green," *Monthly Review*, 42, 5 (October 1990):26–27.

26. Cynthia McClintock, "Peru's Sendero Luminoso Rebellion: Origins and Trajectory," in Eckstein, *Power and Popular Protest*, 84. Americas Watch published a 123-page report entitled

The Killings In Colombia; see George Winslow, "Credibility: A Casualty in the War on Drugs," *In These Times*, May 17–23, 1989, 19.

27. Edmundo Morales, "The Political Economy of Cocaine Production: An Analysis of the Peruvian Case," *Latin American Perspectives*, 17, 4 (Fall 1990):105–108. Certainly the term "narco-guerrillas" used by some journalists is misleading; see, for instance, Georges A. Fauriol, "The Shadow of Latin American Affairs," *Foreign Affairs*, 69, 1 (1989/1990):118.

28. Gabriel Puerta (former leading Venezuelan guerrilla, member of the Bandera Roja), speech delivered in Cumaná, March 22, 1989; Marco Moreira Alves, *A Grain of Mustard Seed: The Awakening of the Brazilian Revolution* (Garden City: Anchor Books, 1973), 181.

29. Leftists debated whether these struggles could be considered "low-intensity warfare." See the series of articles in *NACLA: Report on the Americas*, including William M. LeoGrande's "Central America Counterinsurgency Revisited," 21, 1 (January/February 1987).

30. *Voz* [Colombian Communist party newspaper], November 12, 1987, 4.

31. These remarks were made by Salvadorian guerrilla leader Joaquín Villalobos in an article published in *Foreign Policy*. See William Bollinger, "Villalobos on 'Popular Insurrection,' " *Latin American Perspectives*, 16, 3 (Summer 1989):46.

32. This same dilemma was noted by the sociologist Robert Michels in *Political Parties*, first published in 1911.

33. Robert Barros, "The Left and Democracy: Recent Debates in Latin America," *Telos*, 68 (Summer 1986):50–52. See also the essays in the third part of Julio Labastida Martín del Campo, ed., *Hegemonía y alternativas políticas en América Latina* (México: Siglo XXI, 1985).

34. María Helena Moreira Alves, "Trade Unions in Brazil: A Search for Autonomy and Organization," in Edward C. Epstein, ed., *Labor Autonomy and the State in Latin America* (Boston: Unwin Hyman, 1989), 60–62.

35. *New York Times*, December 9, 1990, 3.

36. For a discussion of "new populism" see Michael L. Conniff, "Urban Populism in Twentieth Century Politics," in Joseph Tulchin and John Chasteen, eds., *Problems in Modern Latin American History* (Wilmington: Scholarly Resources, in press).

2

The Political Left in Chile, 1973–1990

Brian Loveman

Overview Prior to 1973

Nowhere in Latin America have Socialist, Communist, Marxist-Leninist, and radical Catholic political parties and movements had more political influence than in twentieth-century Chile. From 1932 to 1973 the Socialist and Communist parties achieved consistent electoral successes, permanent participation in the legislature, periodic representation in government coalitions, and, in 1970, the election of a Socialist president. Ideological and organizational predominance in the labor movement, a significant presence in poor urban neighborhoods, shantytowns, and even the countryside, and a network of newspapers, party journals, and cultural activities made the Socialist and Communist Left an active force in Chilean politics.

Diversity on the Left increased from the late 1960s to 1973. Groups favoring faster and more radical change splintered from the Christian Democratic party, thereby adding several radical Catholic parties to the traditional Marxist Left. These included the Movimiento de Acción Popular Unitaria (Movement of Popular Unitarian Action—MAPU), the MAPU Obrero-Campesino (Worker-Peasant MAPU—MOC) and the Izquierda Cristiana (Christian Left—IC).[1] In addition, in the mid-1960s the Movimiento de Izquierda Revolucionaria (Movement of the Revolutionary Left—MIR) and other smaller groups supported the Cuban model of armed revolution.

The political evolution of the Chilean Left occurred *within* the legal framework of Chilean formal democracy. Although some socialists professed revolutionary Marxism and the Communists' ultimate objec-

23

tive was overturning capitalism in favor of socialism, the Left usually behaved as a legal opposition as in European multiparty systems such as those of France and Italy. Although leftist groups were sometimes repressed or outlawed, as, for example, were the Communists from 1948 to 1958, the political Left was effectively incorporated into the political system. It usually participated fully and accepted the "rules of the game" in practice while condemning formal democracy and capitalism in principle.[2] The Left and the Christian Democrats took democracy for granted. They had forgotten that civil liberties and rights, the party and industrial relations systems, the labor movement, and military subordination to civil authority were exceptions in Latin America that Chileans had won through political struggle.

The coup that overthrew the Unidad Popular (Popular Unity—UP) government of Salvador Allende in 1973 and what followed altered the meaning of "democracy" for the Chilean Left, dramatized the danger of denigrating "bourgeois rights," and eventually taught that democracy and constraints on government authority were worthy ends in themselves rather than instrumental values useful for the transition to socialism. As had their counterparts in Eastern Europe and their socialist–social-democratic compatriots in Western Europe, most of the Chilean Left proclaimed by the mid-1980s that there could be no socialism without democracy, that many of Marxism-Leninism's fundamental tenets had been erroneous, and that it was Spanish and French socialism, Italian communism, and even German social democracy rather than the *socialismos reales* of Eastern Europe that provided proper direction for Chilean development.[3]

Ironically, these discoveries were more consistent with the history of the Chilean Left and, especially, of the Socialist party and the Catholic Left, than were the revolutionary bombasts of the 1960s and 1970s that had led to disaster. For the first seventy years of the twentieth century the political Left had helped to forge Chilean democracy. From 1970 to 1973, however, it sought to impose on the majority a vision shared by a minority, using the instruments of the state in a fashion that allowed local and international opponents to mobilize against the Allende coalition. That peaceful revolution or deep reform requires a formidable consensus on values and objectives was a lesson the Chilean Left had not yet learned.

Dictatorship and the Chilean Left

Sixteen years of dictatorship followed, with brutal repression of the leftist parties, the labor movement, and community organizations identified as "Marxist" or "subversive." Surviving, interpreting the causes of

Popular Unity's defeat, responding to the dictatorship's policies and their consequences, reconstituting effective party organizations, redefining socialism, and battling to restore Chilean democracy became the agenda of the Chilean Left after 1973.[4]

The military government sought to legitimate repression with the declared fiction of "internal war." Institutional innovations by the military junta also anticipated an effort to establish a new political system, later called "authoritarian democracy" or "protected democracy," that would severely curtail democratic politics as conventionally understood and seek to outlaw Marxist parties and movements. The military junta consolidated the authoritarian system in a 1980 plebiscite to approve a new constitution. Implemented in 1981, the constitution provided guidelines for the transition from junta dominance to a permanent form of authoritarian "protected democracy."[5] The government also adopted the most radical version of neoliberal economic innovations in Latin America, thereby undermining the social foundations of the traditional Left—the labor movement—and drastically reducing the role of the state in public enterprises, the regulation of the private economy, and the overall direction of Chilean development.

Initial Response to the Coup

The military junta moved quickly against the Popular Unity political parties, the labor movement, and other opposition. Military tribunals condemned "traitors" to death, and many leftists were killed without benefit of the kangaroo courts, joining their compatriots in mass graves. Thousands more were brutalized and incarcerated. Despite the revolutionary proclamations of the MIR, some Socialists, and other coalition parties, the Left was not organized to offer effective resistance to the coup or the military junta.[6] From 1973 to 1976 survival took precedence, with the MIR, the Communist party, and the Socialists taking numerous casualties in military raids characterized euphemistically by the government as "battles" or "confrontations."

Debates over tactical and ideological culpability for the coup and methods of resistance to the military government's repression dominated the Left.[7] The exile of thousands of leftists and other Chileans further complicated the picture as internal and external directorates of the main leftist parties differed over tactics, the desirability of collaboration with nonleftist parties and movements, and long-term objectives. In 1975 representatives of all the Popular Unity parties except Acción Popular Independiente (Independent Popular Action—API) met in Berlin and called for a broad front, including the Christian Democrats, to end the dictatorship. After four years of frustration and fragmentation, however, the

Popular Unity dissolved in 1979, this action coinciding with the formal division of the Socialist party (1979) and a dramatic change in political line on the part of the Communists (1980).

The Communist Party, 1973–1986

The Communist party, despite its relatively moderate role in the Popular Unity coalition, suffered fierce repression by the military junta. Party officials, union officers, and peasant and community leaders were arrested, tortured, murdered, and "disappeared." In response, the party sent key leaders into exile and established a clandestine directorate in Chile. Funds from the Soviet Union, East Germany, Italy, and other external sources supported its resistance to the dictatorship.

In assessing the coup from 1973–1975, the Communists noted the role of U.S. imperialism, the intervention of the CIA, and the strength of internal reaction. It reserved its harshest criticism, however, for "opportunists," petty-bourgeois pseudorevolutionaries, and "ultraleftists"— meaning the MIR, some Socialists, and scattered Catholic radicals whose tactics alienated the middle classes and pushed the military toward the coup.[8] Basically, the Communists' first *autocrítica* (self-criticism) consisted of reaffirming its positions and lamenting its inability to impose its gradualist line on the Popular Unity coalition. The Communists defined the military regime as fascist, a "product of counterrevolution, of the violent interruption of the revolutionary process."[9] To confront this challenge, they proposed an "antifascist front" with both tactical and strategic objectives: to create a broad coalition to oust the dictatorship and to sustain the coalition to form a government and promote democratization of the political system.

Most non-Marxists resisted participation with the Communists in such a coalition. Whereas the Catholic church, especially the Vicariate of Solidarity, proved willing to shelter individual Communists, denounce human rights abuses, and call for relaxation of the government's campaign of terror against the Left, it maintained an emphatic official distance from the Popular Unity and the Communist party. The Christian Democrats, especially those identified with former president Eduardo Frei, insisted on their historical rejection of the Communists and sought an opposition coalition that excluded most Marxist-Leninists. This doomed the Communists' effort to be a principal voice in a broad opposition front to the dictatorship—even had the opposition been able to mount such a front.

By 1979–1980, the political consolidation of the Pinochet regime, the plebiscite that imposed a new constitution, and the economic recovery that bolstered the neoliberal model confronted the Communists with insoluble dilemmas. Elements of the Communist Youth and some members of the party directorate rejected the antifascist-front concept and the party's unwillingness to support the MIR in armed struggle against the government. Similar dissent among community organizations and residents of the peripheral urban shantytowns and slums, combined with the obvious failure of the party's previous tactics either to weaken the regime or to enhance relations with the Christian Democrats and Center-Left groups, required reconsideration of its positions. In any case, the formal division of the Socialist party in 1979 and the movement of many socialists away from orthodox Marxism made insistence on the broad antifascist-front line futile.

International events also influenced redefinition of the Communists' tactics and strategic line. At the twenty-sixth congress of the Communist party of the Soviet Union, Leonid Brezhnev remarked that "revolutions must know how to defend themselves," referring indirectly to the Popular Unity experience but also to the Cuban, Nicaraguan, and African socialist regimes. The victory of the Sandinistas over the Somoza dictatorship in Nicaragua and intensified conflict in El Salvador also encouraged some Communists to add a military component to their resistance to the Pinochet government.

On September 4, 1980, the tenth anniversary of Allende's election, Luis Corvalán, speaking from Moscow, marked a critical turning point in Communist strategy and party evolution: "To defeat the fascist dictatorship there is no other path than confrontation on all fronts, making use of all forms of combat."[10] In November, speaking in Sweden, Corvalán added: "The right of rebellion against tyrants figures in the Bible and in the doctrine of the Fathers of the Church and the theologians of the Middle Ages. It was recognized before Plato . . . and inspired all the bourgeois revolutions, the independence movements in Latin America, the proletarian revolutions, and the movements of national liberation. . . . There is no other way to recover liberty for Chile than by fighting.[11]

The official line of "antifascist-front" was changed to that of "popular rebellion" culminating in "popular insurrection." This decision by the Communists, however well justified by the government's repression and the inability of the opposition to cast off the junta, did not mean an end to the traditional political work of the party but did represent a dramatic shift in emphasis and image. It produced further isolation of the Communists from the Center and the Center-Left, a pretext for increased government repression, and, eventually, serious divisions within the party. It also meant a tactical alliance with the "ultraleftists" earlier blamed for the coup and with the more orthodox Socialists and a number of Catholic radicals who shared the commitment to armed struggle. Strategically, it also underscored the Communist assessment that a negotiated transition from dictatorship according to the terms of Pinochet's 1980 constitution would leave Chilean politics permanently militarized, authoritarian, and seriously constrained in overcoming the new socioeconomic model installed by the junta.

In 1980 the Communist party lacked significant military capabilities to implement the new line of popular rebellion. Gradually, contacts with the MIR, the formal establishment in 1983 of the Frente Patriótico Manuel Rodríguez (Manuel Rodríguez Patriotic Front—FPMR) with linkages to the party, and efforts to train, equip, and activate armed elements gave operational meaning to the strategy announced in 1980.

From 1983 to 1986 Communist cadres, the MIR, the FPMR, and other leftist resistance fighters carried out a number of actions, including sabotage of power lines (apagones), bombings, attacks on police, kidnapping of military personnel, and even destruction of Pinochet's helicopter. These acts brought hope to some, provoked rage in others, and raised serious objections to the "overmilitarization" of the party, lack of control by the directorate over armed cadres, deemphasis on traditional political work, and lack of discussion and consultation concerning policies within the directorate. This produced discomfiture for many militants accustomed to the party's historical style and tactics.

In its 1985 report, the central committee of the Communist party recognized the importance of the popular protests, strikes, reactivation of the labor movement, and mass mobilization that had occurred since 1983, pointing to the importance of "the introduction of new methods of struggle, methods that permit the growing use of revolutionary violence by the people against the violence imposed by fascism." Making clear the party's line regarding the end of the dictatorship, it declared: "The end of fascism will not be the fruit of one battle, nor of the action of only one sector of the opposition, but the result of a series of great and small struggles of the Chilean people, until a state of national rebellion is created that makes the situation unmanageable for the tyrant and makes possible steps toward ending the fascist dictatorship and returning to democracy."[12] Iteration of this line evoked admiration among those suffering the regime's brutality and fostered pride in the party's resolve and courage to overcome the pervasive fear engendered by years of state terrorism.

The Communists apparently intended to intensify the armed struggle, providing weapons and training to cadres and others willing to confront the dictatorship in the countryside, mines, and urban centers. This strategy suffered severe reverses in 1986 with the government's discovery of large arms caches in northern Chile and an unsuccessful assassination attempt on Pinochet. These setbacks further alienated the Communists and other groups within the Movimiento Democrático Popular (Popular Democratic Movement—MDP) from Christian Democrats, renovated

Socialists, the church, and other non-Marxist opponents of the government. The junta also used these events to validate its internal-war thesis and justify intensifying attacks on party members and other leftists. As it became clear that the military government had survived the wave of protests and popular mobilization (1983–1986) and that armed struggle by leftist cadres could not topple the regime, the Communists and other advocates of popular rebellion and insurrection found themselves ever more politically isolated.

Divisions within the MIR, the FPMR, the Almeyda Socialists, and the Communist party itself followed, with some militants retreating from insistence on a military ouster of the dictatorship. By 1988, formal separation of the FPMR from the more intractable FPMR-Autónomo, the emergence of at least three distinct factions within the MIR, and adherence by the Almeyda Socialists to the Coalition of Parties for NO in the plebiscite campaign left Chilean Communists with fewer allies and more divided internally than at any time in the past half-century.

The Socialist Party, 1973–1986

Unlike that of the Communist party, the official Socialist party line since its twenty-second congress in Chillán in 1967 had been that "revolutionary violence is legitimate and inevitable."[13] Despite the official rhetoric, the Socialist party had hardly armed itself from 1967 to 1973. The military junta's postcoup repression decimated the ranks of Socialist leaders, killing some, jailing others, and forcing many into exile. A clandestine directorate headed by Ezequiel Ponce and Carlos Lorca attempted internal resistance; in exile, Socialist leaders headed by Carlos Altamirano attempted to reconstitute the party first in Cuba and then in East Germany.

In 1974 the internal directorate issued the so-called Document of March accusing the party of responsibility for the defeat of the Popular Unity because of its lack of Leninist principles and organization, its petty-bourgeois composition, and its incapacity to defend the revolutionary process. This document virtually proposed fusion with the Communists.[14]

Internal reaction to this document spawned the Coordinadora Nacional de Regionales (National Coordinator of Regionals—CNR), a loose coordination of regional units that was to recover the nationalist, autonomous, non-Leninist legacy of historical socialism. Both internally and in exile, however, the Socialist party was divided over tactics, organization, objectives, and coalition strategies. Personalist animosities and ambitions added to the fragmentation. By 1978, opposition to the former firebrand Altamirano, now accused of right-wing opportunism, conflicts over the extent of collaboration with the Christian Democrats, and the expulsion from the internal directorate of "moderate" leaders such as Erich Schnake, Adonis Sepúlveda, and Alejandro Jiliberto fractured the party.

A faction headed by Clodomiro Almeyda insisted on a Marxist-Leninist definition of the party and on strengthening traditional ties with the Communists and the MIR. It also came to favor armed struggle against the dictatorship. Altamirano complained about East German intervention favoring the Almeyda faction; in 1979 a party plenum shifted the secretariat to Chile, replacing Altamirano with Almeyda. The Socialist party decomposed into numerous personalist and ideological factions,[15] a process from which Almeyda emerged "victorious." Former leaders such as Aniceto Rodríguez and Raúl Ampuero formed minifactions, each with its own view of the Popular Unity defeat, tactics for confronting the dictatorship, alliance strategy, and goals. Repeated efforts to reunify the party, initially under a Comité Permanente de Enlace (Permanent Linkage Committee—CEP), failed, after the CEP's 1983 initiative to encourage collaboration with Christian Democrats was rejected by some Socialists. Carlos Briones, secretary-general of the party from 1984 to 1986, declared that the Socialists were neither social democrats nor Communists but rather "revolutionary socialists, an original creation of the Chilean people."[16]

In practice, this meant confusion and cleavage from 1979 to 1986, with Socialists joining each of the three major blocks formed after 1983 to challenge the Pinochet government: the Alianza Democrática (Christian Democrats, some Socialists and the Republican Right), supporting civil disobedience and peaceful negotiations for a democratic transition; the MDP (the Communists, the MIR, and the Almeyda Socialists), supporting armed struggle, popular mobilization, protests, and rebellion and calling for the immediate deposition of Pinochet, abrogation of the 1980 constitution, and disavowal of the accords with the International Monetary Fund; and the Bloque Socialista (Socialist Bloc—BS) (some Socialists, the MAPU, the IC), opposed to armed struggle but attempting to bridge the differences between the MDP and the AD to encourage a unified opposition to the Pinochet government.[17]

Prior to 1986, the Socialists were unable to overcome the personalist, ideological, and organizational splits that had plagued them since the 1973 coup. Nevertheless, they had achieved tentative consensus on internal pluralism, intellectual toleration, and the importance of democracy for Chile's future. They adopted a new political lexicon and a new view of their relationship to the working classes and other groups in Chilean society. They rejected "vanguardism," "dictatorship of the proletariat," and any preconceived future utopia.[18] These changes facilitated collaboration with the Christian Democrats and allowed the gradual development of a Center-Left coalition to challenge the dictatorship in the plebiscite of 1988.

Recognition that Pinochet intended to perpetuate his administration into the 1990s and to insist on the terms of the 1980 constitution elicited a proposal from the Socialist Ricardo Lagos in January 1986 that would also affect the future of Chilean socialism. Noting the risk of complying with the electoral and political party laws proposed by the dictatorship, Lagos suggested formation of an instrumental umbrella party, the (Partido por la Democracia (Party for Democracy—PPD), in which all opponents to Pinochet could register and vote against the junta's candidate in any future plebiscite as prescribed by the constitution.[19]

This "instrumental" party proposed by Lagos survived the plebiscite and also the elections in 1989 to become a major actor in the new Chilean Congress. The domination of the PPD by Socialists raised the dilemma of dual memberships, the rationale for continuation of the PPD, and the relationship between Socialists, PPD members, and the Catholic Left after March 1990.

The Catholic Left, 1973–1986

The MAPU, the MOC, and the IC represented diverse constituencies of the Catholic Left. Each had a narrow popular base but was led by influential intellectuals who played a key role in opposition to the Pinochet government from 1973 to 1986 and in the Aylwin coalition government that assumed office in March 1990. Close connections to church organizations offered some leaders of the Catholic Left a partial shield from repression unavailable to the Communists and the MIR. This did not prevent some from being murdered, imprisoned, or exiled.

A trend after 1983 toward ideological convergence with the renovated Socialists brought important intellectuals of the Catholic Left into personal and microorganizational alliances that ultimately resulted in their merging with the Socialist party. By 1985 the MOC had amalgamated with the Socialists, and shortly thereafter prominent MAPU and IC academics and politicians joined the Socialists' non-Almeyda wing. Many preferred the PPD in 1987. Others identified with the Almeyda Socialists and in 1988 joined the instrumental party created by Communists, left-wing Socialists, and the IC—the Partido Amplio de la Izquierda Socialista (Broad Party of the Socialist Left—PAIS).

These talented and influential intellectuals, along with independent socialists and a few former members of the MIR integrated into the Socialist party after 1986, were to contribute both to the coalition that won victory over Pinochet in the 1988 plebiscite and to the technical commissions that developed the program of the coalition that elected Patricio Aylwin president in 1989.

The Invisible Left: Nongovernmental Organizations, 1973–1990

After the 1973 coup, the daily struggle for survival made the Left more pragmatic and eclectic. With international cooperation from public and private sources, a network of nongovernmental organizations emerged that became a shadow political opposition and an organizational base for a new opposition coalition. Emerging first under the umbrella of the Catholic church and the Vicariate of Solidarity, human rights organizations, research programs, and private development corporations responded to the repression and neoliberal policies with nontraditional programs and community organizations. These included community kitchens, consumer cooperatives, alternative legal and health services, and workshops producing artisan products to support families affected by the military government's policies.[20]

These organizations, novel in politics, contributed to the professionalization, technification, and sophistication of opposition political elites at a time when political parties, the labor movement, universities, student and community organizations, and other traditional political forces were suppressed by the dictatorship. Staffed primarily by leftist (or, less frequently, Christian Democratic) academics, former government officials, and professionals, they also allowed reconsideration of the role of the state in Chile by intellectuals of the Left and Center. The increasing emphasis on grass-roots, local and autonomous initiatives in the development process was a dramatic departure from the traditional state-centered vision of the Chilean Left.

Equally important, the personnel of these organizations received firsthand experience in private international cooperation efforts (called "informal diplomacy" in the years of the dictatorship), familiarized themselves with the foreign policies and assistance programs of European, North American, and Asian agencies and foundations, each with its own orientation, favored clientele, and approach to development assistance, and developed a sophisticated vision of Chile's international role. These developments altered the sometimes insular attitudes of the Chilean Left toward Eastern and Western Europe and the United States. Not by chance, key personnel of these organizations appeared as high-ranking officials in the Aylwin government's foreign relations bureaucracy and as ambassadors after March 1990.[21]

The nongovernmental organizations helped shape a new political agenda for the Left that included a new emphasis on human rights, the basic needs of the poor, the role of women in society and politics, and the environmental deterioration that resulted from neoliberalism's intensification of pressures on natural resources and the human habitat. It also injected a new pragmatism into antiregime thinking and a new recognition of the value of entrepreneurship and nonstate enterprise and the inherent limitations of bureaucratic administration. These "discoveries," combined with the experiences of leftist leaders in exile, altered the intellectual foundations of the Chilean Left.[22] Although these organizations also increased in number elsewhere in Latin America in the 1970s and 1980s (for example, in Uruguay and Brazil), nowhere did they play the crucial role of shadow political movements and think-tanks for intellectual reconstruction of the Left to the extent that they did in Chile.

The Left, the 1988 Plebiscite, and the Elections of 1989

Adoption of the 1980 constitution was a benchmark for the dictatorship and also for the opposition. It established the legal foundations of the authoritarian regime, discarded Chilean democracy, proscribed key leftist actors and ideologies from politics, and detailed procedures for a transition from junta government to full implementation of the 1980 charter. What appeared to be the high point in the Pinochet administration, however, rapidly gave way to economic recession and renewed political challenges. Intensification of the economic disaster brought antiregime protests and a broader base of political opposition than at any time since 1973. Strikes, public rallies and demonstrations, and mass protest movements gave the appearance that the dictatorship was losing some of its control. By mid-1984 hopes were high that the military government could be ousted.

From 1983 to 1986 the Left and Center opposition looked for a minimal coalition that could at least achieve Pinochet's replacement by a more flexible ruler and a quicker transition to more democratic politics. By August 1985 moderate elements of the opposition supported by the Catholic church had elaborated a National Accord for Transition to Full Democracy, that called for immediate restoration of civil liberties and rights, an end to exile, and constitutional reform. This accord attracted support from former officials of the military government and elements of the political Right, signifying some erosion of the regime's social base.

Pinochet skillfully played opposition factions against one another, reminded Chileans of the dangers of returning to the chaos of 1973, and pointed to the overt threat of violence by the Communists, the MIR, and the FPMR. He used old-time rightist *políticos* to negotiate with opponents, allowed some exiles to return, and permitted more latitude to the opposition press and selective renewal of political party activity. On retention of the 1980 constitution, the institutions of "authoritarian democracy," his own permanence in office, and repression of protesters he yielded nothing. Between 1983 and 1985 government suppression of public dissent left over one hundred dead and hundreds more injured.

Between 1983 and 1988 resuscitation of overt political activity on the Left and ideological renovation of the Socialist party permitted the construction of a coalition that used the military regime's own institutions to achieve victories in three key political contests: the plebiscite of 1988 (rejecting Pinochet's continuation in office), a plebiscite on constitutional reforms in mid-1989 that set the stage for presidential and parliamentary elections, and the elections of December 1989.

Pinochet's dictatorship drove the Chilean Left to painful introspection concerning its fundamental nature and purpose. After sixteen years of dictatorship and unsuccessful efforts to oust Pinochet through armed struggle by the MIR and, from 1980 on, by the FPMR and the Communist party, most of the political Left joined the Christian Democrats and other antijunta forces in a broad coalition. The coalition agreed to use Pinochet's own constitution and new laws on voter registration, political parties, and elections (1986).

Adopting this tactic for transition implied both short-term risks and long-term impediments to democratization in Chile. In February 1987 the government opened up voter registries for a new registration system. Initial resistance to participation in this system by most of the political Left and the Christian Democrats meant that by June 1987 only 1,200,000 of approximately 8,000,000 eligible citizens had registered. In the meantime, protests and violence had marred a papal visit to Chile, and the opposition continued to call for free, competitive elections instead of a plebiscite. Pinochet steadfastly insisted on implementing the constitution's provisions.

A loosely organized leftist coalition decided not to register under the restrictive conditions of the new law. The political Right, in contrast, organized voter registration drives, as did, eventually, the Christian Democrats. By December 1987 over four million voters had registered— enough to make the plebiscite respectable and, if the Left insisted on its tactics, to ensure a Pinochet victory. Recognition of this possibility stimulated agreement among most opposition groups, left and right, in February 1988 to form a coalition to prevent Pinochet's victory.[23]

This decision was difficult, for it also legitimated the 1980 charter that most opposition forces considered the product of a fraudulent plebiscite. The signed declaration uniting the thirteen (later sixteen) parties of the coalition called for free elections at the earliest possible time, constitutional reforms, and respect for human rights but acknowledged that the government's obstinacy made it imperative to participate in the plebiscite.

The Communists, the MIR, and some Socialists delayed the decision to participate in the plebiscite, being reluctant to validate Pinochet's new political system or to believe that fair electoral procedures would prevail. For some the decision to participate meant capitulation. For the non-Marxist-Leninist opposition the plebiscite, scheduled for October 1988, was a long shot to catch Pinochet in his own "trap." Whatever the outcome, acceptance of the 1980 constitution's framework for transition meant acquiescence in a gradualism in overturning the dictatorship's authoritarian institutions that would prove painful and frustrating long after 1988.

Opposition victory in the 1988 plebiscite with 55 percent of the vote, a minor miracle achieved under the scrutiny of the international news media and on-site poll watchers, refocused Chilean politics. The attention of the Left and all Chileans turned to the one-year transition period during which Pinochet would remain in office and organize the presidential and congressional elections stipulated in the 1980 constitution.

After preliminary political skirmishing, most of the Left adhered to an expanded coalition supporting Christian Democrat Patricio Aylwin as the presidential candidate for the December 1989 election. The plebiscite outcome, Aylwin's election victory, and the governing coalition of Socialists and Christian Democrats further isolated the Communists, the MIR, and other orthodox Marxist-Leninists. It also exacerbated internal divisions within the Communist party and the MIR, leading to damaging resignations, expulsions, and public debates.

Although the Communists had belatedly supported the opposition forces in the plebiscite, Christian Democrats and some Socialists rejected a formal coalition with them for the 1989 elections. Whereas the Communists supported Aylwin's candidacy, they failed to elect any deputies or senators on a separate slate with orthodox Socialists (PAIS) from the coalition. In part this was a result of their still-illegal status, combined with the effects of the military government's electoral law and their serious internal conflicts. It left them without direct representation in the legislature, without participation in the cabinet, and without influence in the party coalition that governed Chile after 1990. Combined with the loss of external support, the impact of perestroika, the demise of socialist regimes in Eastern Europe, and the lack of a political line to replace "popular rebellion, popular insurrection," the isolation of the Communists—despite relegalization in 1990—brought political crisis.[24]

A formal effort to "refound" the party took shape in 1990–1991 as former Communists severely criticized Stalinism within the organization, attacked "militarist deviations" resulting from the "popular rebellion" line, called for renovation, and established an entity called the Asamblea de Renovación Comunista (Assembly of Communist Renovation—ARCO). The sharp criticisms of these dissidents reflected the crisis of the party and the challenges facing it in the context of the 1990–1994 political transition specified in the 1980 constitution.

Overall, the share of legislators elected by the Left in 1989 had declined from the approximately one-third of the early 1970s to about one-fourth. Though perhaps a consequence of the unique electoral laws adopted by the dictatorship to favor the Right and the slates elaborated by the opposition coalition for the 1989 elections, there was concern on the Left that this outcome reflected the successful institutionalization by the military regime of several adverse trends: fear of socialism and redistributive policies, fear of military reaction to renewed popular mobilization, and a shift of the electorate to the political Right.

The Left and the Aylwin Government, 1990–1991

After years of human rights abuses, political persecution, exile, and institutionalized dictatorship, a coalition that both Christian Democrats and Socialists had rejected since the 1960s—and one that might have prevented the years of agony—supported the newly installed Christian Democratic president Patricio Aylwin. Aylwin had vociferously opposed the Allende government's policies and initially supported the 1973 military coup. Socialists and Communists had characterized Aylwin and the Frei wing of the Christian Democratic party as halfhearted reformers at best. Changes in the political Left and the Christian Democratic party from 1973 to 1989 now permitted the creation of a coalition in support of a program and policies that would have been ridiculed as reactionary by leaders of both Frei's revolution in Liberty and Allende's Popular Unity.

Piecemeal reform had become respectable, democracy essential, pragmatism desirable, and moderation a virtue. The political culture of much of the Chilean Left had been transformed. Prudence—or understandable fear of direct confrontation with Pinochet and the military—permeated public discussion and government initiatives. Fear of "another September 11, 1973" had been internalized; seeking consensus rather than imposition of revolutionary programs was the new motif.

Whereas small groups of revolutionary leftists still preferred Cuban socialism and sustained the anticapitalist, anti-imperialist rhetoric of the 1960s and 1970s, the Aylwin government, including former ministers of the Popular Unity government, applauded the billion dollars of new foreign investment in 1990, adopted an orthodox economic adjustment program to curtail inflation shortly after assuming office, and insisted on the priority of maintaining "macroeconomic equilibrium." This was the case despite sharp criticism by the Left and the Christian Democrats of the military's economic model and the IMF-style adjustment programs prior to 1988. Macroeconomic and political stability and "successful transition" took priority. The coalition leadership stressed the need to legitimate democracy through responsible fiscal and monetary policy as well as caution in civil-military relations.

The Chilean Left that returned to office with the Aylwin government exhibited important continuity of leadership from the 1970s. However, with few exceptions, the continuity in personalities also entailed a more reformist, sometimes social democratic Left matured by exile, sobered by repression, and transformed by intellectual renewal and daily struggle against the dictatorship.

For some, this "new" Left was neither leftist nor revolutionary.[25] Renovation required jettisoning basic Marxist tenets, such as the leading role of the proletariat and the vanguard party, the state-centered character of socialism in the passage to communism, and elimination of private property in the means of production. Renovation also implied reliance on markets and individual initiative in the economy rather than administrative allocation and acceptance of foreign investment rather than attacks on "neocolonialism," "dependency," and imperialism. The renovated Left no longer insisted on the necessity to destroy the "bourgeois state," with its formal democracy that "disguised class dictatorship."

For others, the renovated Left was a movement that had recovered its historical roots, particularly those of the Socialist program of 1947 and the legacy of Allende's commitment to socialism and democracy as requisites one for the other. Viewing the Leninization of Chilean socialism as a recent (1960s and 1970s) detour from a more nationalist, pragmatic, and democratic past, the *renovados* saw in Eurocommunism and democratic socialism signposts for a new *vía chilena*.[26]

The formation of this new Left had been difficult, uneven, wrought with painful sacrifice and personal introspection. In 1990–1991 the new Left remained without a clear long-term political and economic project, allied with Christian Democrats in administering the economy bequeathed by the dictatorship, accepting much of the neoliberal model, and constrained by the constitution of 1980. Hesitant to mobilize popular forces to demand redistribution of income or to support calls for institutional reforms, the renovated Left would ultimately face the dilemma of prolonging the coalition by continuing its moderation or following a more independent path that entailed constructive opposition to the Aylwin government. In either case, the old question of whether liberal democracy in Chile could stimulate economic growth and successfully address demands for socioeconomic justice remained unanswered.

For the hard Left, the orthodox Left, and those wishing to confront more directly the legacy of the Pinochet government—human rights abuses, authoritarian institutions, militarization of politics, and a lingering fear of another coup that constrained political initiatives by the Aylwin government—the transition had already proved disappointing by the end of 1990. Small groups resorted to armed attacks on military officers, police, and judges held responsible for human rights abuses. The assassination in early April 1991 of the rightist senator Jaime Guzmán, principal author of the 1980 constitution and political ally of Pinochet, raised tensions and focused the attention of the Aylwin government on "fighting terrorism." It also further isolated the Communist party and others on the Left who objected to the creation of a new security apparatus and more severe antiterrorist legislation.

The underlying question whether authentic democracy could be constructed on the foundation of concessions to military threats and a permanent tutelary role for the military in politics was the basic challenge for the Chilean Left—and for Chilean democracy—as President Aylwin completed his first year in office in March 1991.

Notes

1. For an overview of these parties and movements see Carlos Bascuñan Edwards, *La izquierda sin Allende* (Santiago: Planeta, 1990), 105–158.

2. See Benny Pollack and Hernan Rosenkranz, *Revolutionary Social Democracy: The Chilean Socialist Party* (London: Frances Pinter, 1986); Carmelo Furci, *The Chilean Communist Party and the Road to Socialism* (London: Zed, 1984).

3. See Ignacio Walker, *Socialismo y democracia: Chile y Europa en perspectiva comparada* (Santiago: CIEPLAN-Hachette, 1990). On "Leninización" of the Left see Tomás Moulián, "Evolución histórica de la izquierda chilena," in *Democracia y socialismo en Chile* (Santiago: FLACSO, 1983). For comparative discussion of the development of the Left in Latin America during this period see Steve Ellner, "The Latin American Left Since Allende: Perspectives and New Directions," *Latin American Research Review*, 24, 2 (1989):143–167.

4. In exile, Chilean socialists became more familiar with the work of Norberto Bobbio and Antonio Gramsci, as well as the experience of Spanish and French socialists. See Walker, *Socialismo*, especially Chapter 5, for details.

5. A short discussion of these innovations can be found in Brian Loveman, "Government and Regime Succession in Chile," *Third World Quarterly*, 10 (1988):260–280.

6. In personal conversations, members of these parties affirmed this repeatedly. Indeed, many Communists maintain that despite the "transition," the party should never again be caught "unarmed" as in 1973.

7. Perhaps the least acrimonious and most positive view of the past is found in Sergio Bitar, *Chile: Experiment in Democracy* (Philadelphia: ISHI, 1986). More illustrative is Carlos Altamirano, *Dialéctica de una derrota* (Mexico: Siglo XXI, 1977).

8. "Los acontecimientos en Chile: Visión de los comunistas," *Revista Internacional* (July–August 1974); "Informe al pleno de agosto 1977 del Comité Central del PC rendido por su secretario general, Luis Corvalán"; "Ultraizquierdismo, caballo de troya del imperialismo," public declaration, Santiago, September 1975.

9. "Ultraizquierdismo"; Bascuñan, *La izquierda*, 28–40.

10. Luis Corvalán, speech from Moscow, September 4, 1980.

11. Luis Corvalán, speech from Sweden, November 18, 1980.

12. Central Committee of the Communist Party, *Informe*, 1985. For an overview of the role of the Communists within the party system from 1973 to 1988 see Carlos Huneeus, "El sistema de partidos políticos en Chile: Cambio y continuidad," *Opciones*, 13 (January–April 1988):63–197.

13. Cited in Bascuñan, *La izquierda*, 64.

14. "Documento de Marzo," March 1974.

15. For a synoptic view of the numerous factions and efforts at reunification from 1973 to 1986 see Jorge Arrate and Paulo Hidalgo, *Pasión y razón del socialismo chileno* (Santiago: Ornitorrinco, 1989), Chapters 8 and 9. Richard Friedmann, *1964–1988 La política chilena de la A a la Z* (Santiago, 1988), includes brief historical sketches of the Socialist factions.

16. Cited in Walker, *Socialismo*, 196. An effort to assess the Socialist renovation is Manuel Antonio Garretón, "¿En que consistió la renovación socialista? Síntesis y evaluación de sus contenidos," in *La renovación socialista: Balance y perspectivas de un proceso vigente* (Santiago: Ediciones Valentín Letelier, 1987), 17–43.

17. See Brian Loveman, "Antipolitics in Chile, 1973–1987," in B. Loveman and T. Davies, Jr., eds., *The Politics of Antipolitics: The Military in Latin America*, 2nd ed. (Lincoln: University of Nebraska Press, 1989), 426–455. In January 1985 the Tribunal Constitucional declared the Almeyda faction illegal, along with the MDP, the Communists, and the MIR, for violating Article 8 of the 1980 Constitution.

18. Arrate and Hidalgo, *Pasión y razón*, 108. An insightful article on the importance of language regarding democracy, markets, private property, and conflict is Tomás Moulián, "El lenguaje sobre la democracia: Mercado y guerra," *Opciones*, 16 (May–August 1989):45–51.

19. Ricardo Lagos, "Partido por la democracia," *Convergencia*, 12 (December 1987):18–19.

20. A useful overview of these organizations is found in Taller de Cooperación al Desarrollo, *Una puerta que se abre: Los organismos no gubernamentales en la cooperación al desarrollo* (Santiago, n.d.). See also Francisco Vio, *Primero la gente: ONG, estado y cooperación internacional en el tercer mundo* (Santiago: CEAAL, 1989).

21. A partial list of these appointments is found in Brian Loveman, *Organizaciones privadas para el desarrollo y cooperación internacional: Chile 1973–1990* (Santiago: EFDES, 1990).

22. Perhaps the bluntest expression of these changes is Hernán Vodanovic, *Un socialismo renovado para Chile* (Santiago: Editorial Andante, 1988).

23. For a collection of articles detailing the evolution of the opposition and the creation of the coalition see Paul Drake and Ivan Jaksic, *The Struggle for Democracy in Chile 1982–1990* (Lincoln: University of Nebraska Press, 1991).

24. See various authors, "La crisis del partido comunista: Una reflexión necesaria," *Segunda Reflexión*, January 1991; Luis Guastavino, *Caen las catedrales* (Santiago: Hachette, 1991); Volodia Teitelboim, "Intervención," Acto de clausura de la campaña de legalización, Teatro Caupolican, 28 October, 1990. In 1987 the FPMR divided into an "autonomous" and a Communist-linked faction.

25. "Tan distintos como dos gotas de agua," *Punto Final*, October 1989, 9. In 1987 the MIR divided into two factions, the MIR-Pascal, favoring armed struggle and alliance with the FPMR and the Communist party, and the MIR-Político, led by Nelson Gutiérrez, which suspended armed struggle. By 1990, a third and more radical faction emerged, the MIR–Comisión Militar, which approved of execution of leftist "traitors."

26. See interviews with Oscar Waiss, "Partido Socialista de Chile (Fracción Núñez) and Ricardo Núñez Muñoz," in Patricio Tupper, ed., *Opciones políticas en Chile* (Santiago: Ediciones Colchagua, 1987), 320–343.

3

Radicalization and the Left in Peru, 1976–1991

Nigel Haworth

In July 1977, popular mobilization against Peru's military government occasioned President Francisco Morales Bermúdez to announce the return to barracks of the military and the calling of elections to reestablish democratic government. In 1978 elections were held for a Constituent Assembly from which emerged a new constitution; in 1980 general elections produced the return to power of a Belaúnde-led Acción Popular (Popular Action—AP), the same civilian party and president brought down by the military in 1968. Since then, Peruvian democracy has seen six further major electoral contests—municipal elections in 1980, 1983, 1986 and 1989; general elections in 1985 and 1990.

Democratization seems, therefore, to have become fully established in Peru as elsewhere in Latin America. However, one aspect of the process differs markedly. Out of the popular mobilization of the late 1970s emerged, for the first time in Peruvian history, a Left engaged in electoral politics. Elsewhere in Latin America the Left has been an active constituent of democratic activity for a generation or more; in Peru this has not been the case. The Left began to emerge as a coherent political force only in the 1960s and was denied a chance to develop an electoral tradition by the 1968 military coup. Thus, in the reactivated democratic process of the late 1970s and the 1980s, the Left has had to come to terms with the complex politics and procedures of liberal democratic organization and its

The Department of Management Studies and Labour Relations, Faculty of Commerce, and the Research Committee of the University of Auckland together made the research for this paper possible by providing generous funding. Their support is gratefully recognized.

associated contradictions without any previous experience upon which to ground its strategy.

Simultaneously, it has had to respond to the popular demands that provoked the fall of Morales Bermúdez and that have lodged great expectations in the Left, and if this were not enough, it has had to confront the challenge of the armed struggle waged by the Sendero Luminoso and other guerrilla movements sworn to oppose participation in the democratic process. Inevitably, therefore, the past fifteen years have seen the Left's fortunes ebb and flow as circumstances have changed. Whatever the dilemmas it faces, the emergence of the Left into national politics is a remarkable development.

The Demise of the Morales Bermúdez Government

The rise of popular opposition to Morales Bermúdez and the consequent retreat to barracks have their origins in the reforms introduced by Velasco after 1968.[1] During the so-called first phase of military rule (1968–1975), a dramatic reform process was set in motion. It included a serious attempt at agrarian reform; measures to increase popular participation in agrarian, industrial, and social decision making; reform of the media; the restructuring of the relationship between Peru and the international economy; the restructuring and strengthening of the state; the destruction of the traditional power of Peru's famed "oligarchy"; and the implementation of a third development path, "neither communist nor capitalist." As a model, it was both unexpected and contradictory and soon ran into major economic problems.

One consequence of its implementation was the deliberate fostering of popular organization and expectation. Myriad organizations were charged with developing a social base for the "Peruvian Revolution." Simultaneously, leftist parties were, albeit grudgingly, permitted space to develop and found roots in peasant, *barrio*, youth, and worker organizations alongside the mobilizing agencies of the first phase. In particular, trade union growth was dramatic.

The importance of trade union growth to popular mobilization has roots in the 1960s.[2] Until then, the Left was effectively marginalized in popular politics by the powerful presence of the Alianza Popular Revolucionaria Americana. The APRA and the Left disputed the popular leadership role in the late 1920s and early 1930s and the APRA won, condemning the Left to relative obscurity. However, in the 1960s, popular sentiment moved away from the APRA, primarily because of the ever more pragmatic pursuit of political power that led it into ill-considered alliances with parties of the oligarchy. Erstwhile APRA supporters rejected the politics of compromise, particularly within the labor movement. In 1968, the Confederación General de Trabajadores del Perú—

broadly linked to the pro-Moscow Partido Comunista Peruano—successfully challenged the pro-APRA labor organization, the Confederación de Trabajadores del Perú (Confederation of Peruvian Workers—CTP).

The political impact of the emergence of a strong leftist union bloc combined with the opportunity presented by the Velasco reforms to radicalize union organization. Reinforcing this radicalization was the emergence of groups and traditions farther to the Left that were highly critical of the Velasco model but took advantage of the opportunity it offered to build their own bases. Thus the 1970s saw the consolidation of left-wing revolutionary political groups and their union and community followings. The coherence of the CGTP provided the Left with a strong core around which to build.[3]

Economic crisis and opposition within the military to the radical nature of the first phase resulted in the usurpation of power by Morales Bermúdez in 1975, setting in train the second phase. In practice, the second phase had two important effects for the popular movement. First, it began to dismantle the reforms enacted during the first phase, particularly in the industrial and agricultural spheres. This inevitably produced a strong feeling of betrayal and anger that was readily expressed through the popular institutions created by the first phase and through the many political and social channels that had used the opportunity of the early 1970s to develop. In particular, the CGTP brought under its umbrella union groups that had in the 1970s been to the left of it and the PCP and that in the 1980s saw in it the focus of opposition to unpopular government policies. Simultaneously, however, the inclusion of these tendencies diluted the PCP control of the CGTP and created in the dominant union organization a more pluralist debate in tune with the political approach of the Izquierda Unida.[4] Secondly, the Morales Bermúdez government rapidly moved to a more orthodox economic model designed to stabilize the economy in the face of the post-1973 downturn.[5] The adoption in 1976 of a standard IMF package of reforms and the effects of this on the cost of living and the paychecks of working people compounded popular anger with the government for its betrayal of the first phase. Popular mobilization was unleashed from 1976 on and took myriad forms—workplace actions, community protests, student mobilizations, and the publication of popular manifestos.[6]

Crucially, it is argued by many commentators that two general strikes fatally wounded the Morales Bermúdez government.[7] The July 1977 strike—the first general strike in Peruvian history—was followed within nine days by the announcement by Morales Bermúdez of the democratic transition program, with details of the elections proposed for 1978 and 1980. The May 1978 strike forced the military to confirm its intention to relinquish political power.

Popular Mobilization: Crucial or Incidental?

An issue of some importance for an understanding of the Left is whether the fall of the Morales Bermúdez government was the consequence of popular mobilization or of institutional factors to which that mobilization played a supporting role. Julio Cotler, for example, argues that the significance of popular mobilization should be measured against its inability to defeat the policies against which it railed.[8] He gives greater primacy to the debate within the military between the supporters of a return to democracy—who were, he suggests, motivated primarily by the damage being done to the prestige of the armed forces by their continuing involvement in government—and those who favored a Pinochet-style "third phase." The pressure brought to bear by the Carter administration in the United States resolved the internal debate in favor of the former line, and this explains the mode of return to democracy adopted.

Other analysts place popular mobilization center stage,[9] arguing that the scope and intensity of popular anger was such that it stripped the military government of legitimacy and forced it to seek a democratic solution. Implicit in this argument is the belief that the "third phase" model was made impractical by the quality of popular mobilization. Eduardo Ballón makes the important point that popular mobilization was not simply beyond the power of the state to control; it was also beyond the power of the Left to order.[10] His implicit rejection of the "institutionalist" explanation of democratization suggests that popular action sought nothing less than the overthrow of the Morales Bermúdez government and that the failure to win particular or sectional demands (a central thesis of Cotler's case) was secondary to the achievement of this fundamental goal. As Morales Bermúdez was forced to retreat to the barracks, so, he argues, may the success of the mobilization be measured.

Ballón's argument, amply supported by many other accounts of this period, places the popular mobilization beyond the organizational scope of the Left and in advance of the Left's strategic perspectives.[11] It follows, therefore, that a Left resurgence under the newly established democratic order—even composed of leftist organizations and traditions that had been part of the mobilization—would face a critical appraisal from the diverse sectors that constituted the popular mobilization, politically empowered by their recent success.

The Left and the Constituent Assembly Elections

The sections of the Left that decided to stand in the 1978 Assembly elections did remarkably well. The PCP gained 5.9 percent; the *velasquista* Partido Socialista Revolucionario (Revolutionary Socialist party—PSR) polled 6.6 percent; the Unidad Democrática Popular (Popular Democratic

Unity—UDP)—an alliance of the Vanguardia Revolucionaria (the Revolutionary Vanguard—VR), the Movimiento de Izquierda Revolucionaria (the Movement of the Revolutionary Left—MIR), and others—polled 4.5 percent; and the Frente Obrero Campesino Estudiantil y Popular (the Worker, Peasant, Student, and Popular Front—FOCEP) —a mainly Trotskyist grouping—gained a singular 12.34 percent, with ex-guerrilla Hugo Blanco at its head. Some key groups, the Maoist Patria Roja (Red Fatherland—PR) in particular, boycotted the elections.

The decision to participate in the 1978 elections involved a watershed debate within the Peruvian Left, the ramifications of which continue. Until the announcement of a democratization process by Morales Bermúdez, the Left was uniformly opposed to the "fraud" of liberal democratic electoral politics.[12] This opposition took a number of forms. One universal argument uniting the Left was its association of the call for the rebirth of electoral politics with the parties of the Center and the Right— the APRA, AP, and Democracia Cristiana (Christian Democracy—DC), parties deemed to represent the interests of the oligarchy and its supporters. It followed from this that the Left could not be associated either with these demands or with the possibility that the Center or Right might regain power. Within the Left, however, there were other reasons for adopting a "rejectionist" stance.

One tradition, linked to the first phase model—notably the PSR and the PCP—sought a deepening of the Velasco reforms and, in particular, a full social democracy in which direct participation of diverse interests would transcend the "limited" democracy of the electoral process. In many ways supporting a Left-corporatist perspective, this tradition saw the democratization process as a betrayal of the Velasco "revolution." During the 1980s, this tendency shared many views with the moderate wing of the IU and also contributed to the "participationist" tradition represented by the now venerable and stately journal *Socialismo y Participación*.

A second tradition simply argued that liberal democratic politics were a fraud or a trick played upon the masses and that participation in electoral politics would lead to demobilization of popular action and its incorporation into "reformism." Both Maoist and Trotskyist organizations associated themselves with this interpretation, variously seeing the situation as "prerevolutionary" or as requiring "an indefinite general strike" and asserting the need for vanguard elements to seize the opportunities offered by the conjuncture. The organizations of popular mobilization thrown up in the late 1970s—popular assemblies and defense fronts— seemed to bear out their revolutionary assessment, although in fact, they were mistaken.[13]

Fertile ground for internecine warfare existed between the two analytical traditions and within the second. For much of the 1970s, the Peruvian

Left was a highly fragmented, highly formalistic tradition, arguing about the esoterica of theory and applying the "lessons" of Lenin and José Carlos Mariátegui (Peru's leading Marxist theoretician and icon and key founder of the Peruvian Communist party) to the conjuncture in a cabalistic manner. With the APRA appropriating the terrain of social democracy and, significantly, the possibility of political power through its pragmatic willingness to enter the electoral lists, it was left primarily to independent socialists, grouped in research institutes and universities, to recognize the strategic possibility of a break with this formalistic past as democratization took place. Their actions and the transformation of the rejectionist Left were an attempt to respond to the insistent demands of popular mobilization for an effective leftist option.[14]

What brought the Left into the Constituent Assembly elections? A number of answers may be suggested.[15] Once Morales Bermúdez announced the democratization process, the parties of the Center and Right (with the exception of AP) moved quickly to participate in the elections, seeking to dominate the writing of the new constitution and organize for the 1980 general election.[16] They were active in the barrios, and their campaigning presence, combined with the Left's absence from that terrain, reflected badly on the Left. With the extension of the franchise anticipated for the 1980 election to persons over eighteen and others previously excluded from the voting procedure, the Left's rejectionist perspective seemed even more illogical. The feeling grew that nonparticipation might not be understood by many people and that this would threaten the Left–popular mobilization relationship.

It is also argued that the leadership of the Left was and is primarily Lima-based and has a strong desire to be heard in national councils. This desire was frustrated by the oligarchic system before 1968 and was only slightly reduced under the post-1968 military government. The opening of a new liberal democratic period offered to this leadership a role in national life that had long been denied it, and it may have been motivated to take this opportunity.

At another level altogether, the Left was generally unable to offer an alternative to participation in the electoral process. With the obvious exception of Sendero Luminoso, which consistently maintained its opposition to electoral involvement, and a few minor groups, none of the rejectionist parties were able or willing to begin an armed struggle for revolutionary overthrow of the state. Caught between the inability to wage armed struggle and the insistence of the masses that they do something, such organizations found themselves drawn into the electoral process.

However, the overwhelming argument for electoral participation confronted the question of the nature of democracy and, implicitly, the relationship between liberal democracy and socialism. This debate, conducted formally through the pages of tracts, journals, and newspapers, also became a discourse in the popular organizations in which the Left sought to base itself, although often it was translated into the practical language of expectation fulfillment.

The structure of the debate followed a universal pattern of analysis in leftist thinking.[17] Liberal democracy was considered a constrained form of democracy emerging from a particular historical juxtaposition of class forces. Two key conclusions followed. First, one could counterpose other forms of democracy to liberal democracy, and even while participating in the latter one could be developing other democratic forms more appropriate to socialism. Thus, participation in the liberal democratic process was seen not as an end in itself but as one aspect of a wider struggle for popular power.[18]

Secondly, it was argued that neither the power of capitalism as a system nor that of the capitalist state could be eroded in any fundamental way by success in the electoral forum; rather, such success offered an environment in which tactical gains might be made in preparation for a future rupture with the capitalist system. Thus, rhetorically at least, social democracy was written out of the debate and replaced by a strategic-tactical assessment of participation in liberal democratic processes.

Complementing this view of democracy were two other veterans of the revolutionary discourse. The MIR and the Partido Revolucionario de los Trabajadores (Revolutionary Workers' Party—PRT), for example, chose to participate in the 1978 elections on the basis of exposing their fraudulence, thereby making revolutionary circumstances more likely to arise. In addition, the VR and some Trotskyists participated in the firm belief that a revolutionary conjuncture lay ahead and that the electoral process was merely useful agitation.

The tension between these responses and the process of participation in the elections is clear. A campaign arguing that liberal democracy is simply a context for future change or a fraud risked confusing and alienating potential voters. Moreover, it raised the question how "realist" the Left would be if it won a majority and came to control the "bourgeois" state. This question was a constant source of concern in the 1980s.

The Popular Movement

The nature of the mobilizations of the later 1970s and 1980s has been a constant source of debate on the Left. Five elements of popular mobilization stand out—youth, women, the urban community in general, the unions, and the rural sector. The young—unemployed, casually employed, unstably employed, manifesting unfulfilled expectations, atomized, excluded—are generally considered to have been radicalized outside the institutions controlled by the Left, especially beyond the limits of trade unionism. Consequently, their radicalization is complex and unstable. Young people may choose violence and accept the logic of Sendero Luminoso; they may be moved by populist rhetoric of the Center-Right, as was the case in the 1985 APRA electoral success; they may provide the organized Left with a constituency in which radical alternatives may be built. It cannot, however, be assumed automatically to provide a popular electoral or organizational constituency.

The same has been argued for the other notable sectors. Women's mobilizations have often occurred around particular issues and organizations—welfare, health, education, and nutrition, for example, which not only separate women from other elements of popular mobilization but also may induce different responses to change from those engendered elsewhere. Women's mobilizations do not automatically conform to the expectations and understandings held about popular mobilization by traditional leftist thinking. Indeed, Susan Stokes, in a detailed empirical survey of popular organizations, indicates that there may be an inverse relationship between women's participation in popular mobilizations and their commitment to the Left. Her explanation of this paradox suggests that women become active in a range of organizations only some of which are linked to the Left and some of which, implicitly, are critical of it. A diffused popular involvement thus weakens the Left's hold on women's organizations.[19]

Community mobilizations such as those promoted during the first phase involve complex political and ideological oppositions that may not always coincide with the strategies of the Left. The Left has never been able to incorporate community organizations into its ranks; at best it has been able to converge with aspects of community struggle.[20] There are a number of reasons for this weakness. Perhaps the primary factor is the narrow, localized focus of popular community campaigns, which do not lend themselves to the programmatic approach of the Left. The schisms within the Left and the trade union movement exacerbate this difficulty. Autonomous organizations set up by communities interpose themselves between the Left and the community and are often not easily won over to the Left's line. The state, through agencies such as the Sistema Nacional de Apoyo a la Movilización Social (National System for the Support of Social Mobilization—SINAMOS), has played its part in separating the Left from community organization, although without managing to create a state-community political axis. Similar arguments may be made for the rural sector.[21]

The unions, perhaps the most powerful of the popular movements of the late 1970s, are also a contradictory environment for the Left.

The CGTP may be allied with the PCP, but, as noted above, its membership encompasses a much more pluralist political spectrum. In particular, economistic mobilization at the plant level may have little to do with national CGTP political perspectives. Since the late 1970s unions have also been subjected to both repression and erosion of employment and incomes. It is argued that this has fragmented union unity, demobilized sections of the union movement, and promoted asymmetry between the economic and the political in union members' consciousness. Consequently, the relationship between the union movement's members, as opposed to union leaderships, and the Left is complex and ambiguous. Of course, the PCP has played an important role in union mobilizations since the late 1970s, but because of the increasing pluralism of the CGTP and the burgeoning of a "reformist" electoral tradition, its powers must not be overestimated. The difficulties created for the PCP and the Left in general by the events in the Eastern bloc have reinforced this movement toward a more pluralist union tradition.[22]

The Question of Unity

The Left's disappointing vote in the 1980 general election stimulated moves toward greater operative unity. The Izquierda Unida, created in September 1980 under the leadership of the independent socialist Alfonso Barrantes, included the FOCEP, the UDP, the Unión Nacional de la Izquierda Revolucionaria (National Union of the Revolutionary Left— UNIR), of which Patria Roja was the key component, the PCP, and the PSR. Only the Trotskyist groups remained outside the unity, incanting nostrums against popular-frontism. Since the municipal elections of 1980, the IU has participated in all elections, with varying degrees of success.

However, there is a continuing and fundamental debate within the ranks of the IU about its functions and the broader politics of participation in the democratic process. Much effort has been expended to keep the unity afloat between the cathartic periods of electoral activity, and it is generally felt that the time and effort spent on internal appraisal have resulted in a continuing distance between the IU and its constituency. This has been translated into a particular debate within the IU in which, with almost ritualistic frequency, it is pointed out that the popular masses are still alienated from the party-based debates and that the popular mobilizations that reemerged under the Fernando Belaúnde and post-1985 APRA governments have lacked significant political input from the IU. The nonaligned IU membership, particularly the intellectual wing, has been quick to formulate and repeat this criticism.

This concern is justified. After a brief honeymoon under Belaúnde, the application by Prime Minister Manuel Ulloa of supply-side policies brought about a remobilization of popular sentiment in the face of economic restructuring and a dramatic worsening of living conditions for the mass of Peruvians.[23] In principle, a unified and mobilized IU should have been able to capitalize on this mobilization; yet, although election results continued to be reasonably good and there were outstanding victories, particularly in the 1983 municipal elections, still the IU failed to attract the electoral support anticipated by many. Perhaps most obvious, the resurgence of the APRA in both municipal and general elections and the 1985 victory putting Alan García in office as the first APRA president were in large part based on the APRA's electoral success in areas in which the IU might have expected greater support. Notwithstanding the APRA tradition of organization, the inability of the IU to marginalize it in the barrios stands as an indictment of the internal divisions within the IU. It produced a classic debate around the issue of whether the IU message was too "watered down" and therefore had lost popular support, was not coherent enough, or had not been delivered satisfactorily.[24] The performance of the Left in the 1990 general elections against a background of mounting economic and social distress confirms this analysis. The unforeseen success of the Cambio 90 candidate, Alberto Fujimori, standing on a platform of rejection of the old political traditions and drawing on substantial popular support, is a worrying phenomenon for the democratic Left.

Organizational Angst in the 1980s

The unimpressive performance of the Left in the 1990 elections has to be seen against the background of the splits within the IU that led to two candidacies—one of Henry Pease for the IU, the other of Alfonso Barrantes and the newly created breakaway from the IU, the Izquierda Socialista (Socialist Left—IS).

Barrantes was seen by many in 1980 to be the only person on the Left capable of welding together the disparate elements of the IU. A labor lawyer of notably independent views, he was the first truly national leftist personality in Peru.[25] His status was enhanced by a period as mayor of Lima after a major success in the 1983 municipal elections. In office, he proceeded to stimulate a range of policies designed to promote the welfare of the popular masses, stressing the need for democratic institutions that accurately reflected people's requirements. His pragmatism and his increasing personal stature gave him the power to attempt a "democratization" of the IU, including the building-up of a nonaligned IU membership. The parties in the IU saw this as an attempt to create an independent bloc tied to Barrantes's "realism" or "reformism."[26] After 1985, Barrantes was widely criticized for his willingness to consort with the APRA government and his unwillingness to take the lead in criticizing it.[27] In the event, he was forced to resign from the leadership of the IU in May 1987 and eventually took a section of the IU with him into the explicitly reformist IS. This split did not resolve the debate within the IU about revolution or reform, as numbers of supporters of Barrantes remained within the IU, hoping to effect a reconciliation and promote his approach to social change.

The paralysis within the IU continued. In many ways it was worsened by the decline of the APRA government into what is often described as *caudillismo* (strong-man rule) under García. His increasing use of decrees rather than legislation, his compromises with the military (particularly after the horrific prison massacres of 1986 and generally in relation to the security situation), and his dealings with the national and the international financial community were but the most important of the reasons that some elements within the IU questioned their involvement in the democratic process.[28] The challenge from Sendero Luminoso also placed strains on the alliance.

The IU in Power

Despite its uncertain future, the IU has presented Peru with an alternative vision of government when given the chance of municipal power.[29] The Barrantes team in Lima implemented a practical version of IU policy with some success. This experience showed both the need for and the acceptance by the IU of a pragmatic approach when in power. The most significant policy tackled the issue of nutrition through an emergency health and nutrition program based on popular participation. Attached to this was a campaign to distribute one million glasses of milk daily to children in need of dietary supplementation. Seventy-five hundred milk committees involving a hundred thousand mothers were established and linked to basic health education, vaccination, and health care programs. Two hundred soup kitchens were also established. Programs in the housing area were based on the creation of community housing units bringing together sixty families on a quasi-cooperative basis to carry out housing improvements. Further programs were established to deal with the problem of infrastructural provision in barrios lacking basic services.

In the area of local democracy, more than 350 neighborhood committees were established, each covering a specific geographical area and each assuming responsibility for rubbish disposal, public works, consumer rights, and a range of other functions as it thought fit. Within the development of local democratic procedures also fell the creation of democratic planning structures, the most important of which were the district planning committees. These efforts were a response to a number of imperatives. First, the overwhelming support given to Barrantes and the IU by barrio voters required a serious response from elected representatives, and popular participation was a vital and exciting feature of the local programs. Secondly, local democracy complemented the decentralization model at the heart of the IU's national economic and political strategy. The IU proposed to decentralize decision making to regional bodies, which were in turn expected to respond to popular demands at the regional level. Thirdly, the IU was reflecting an international democratic Left model of decentralization seen in the proliferation of "alternative economic strategies" in the Organization for Economic Cooperation and Development economies in the late 1970s and early 1980s. As in the international experience generally, the Left found the funding of these local initiatives a major problem, particularly in the face of central government obstruction. In the case of Lima, much of the funding for the programs discussed above came from Europe. A World Bank loan for U.S. $150 million was used to improve transport and garbage collection in Lima and contribute to effective city planning.

In the Lima experience of local democratic government may be found all the contradictions of leftist access to power under capitalism. Nothing captures this as much as the approach to the World Bank for local government funding. Those faced with the problem of governing Lima were convinced that under the circumstances there was little choice but to use the channels of funding available, whatever they might be.[30] For them such measures were not inappropriate because access to power in no way constituted a move toward socialist local government; it was, rather, a move within a particular limited space to prepare for a future transition. Henry Pease argued that municipal politics serves as a school for democracy, a particular space in which the political process may be captured. Alfonso Barrantes also saw such activity as illustrating the Left's commitment to democracy and consequently helping to eliminate the threat of antidemocratic coups.[31]

A second context in which the Left became involved in the "bourgeois" manipulation of power occurred in Parliament. Once elected, IU deputies and senators were forced to decide what was an appropriate attitude to the institutions of liberal democracy. Their response was mixed: some chose to take a serious view of the proceedings;[32] some were described as behaving in a childish, callow way in order to satisfy personal sentiments of rejection and also to establish their credentials as "noncollaborationist";[33] and still others felt that the Left was confused and therefore poorly organized in Parliament.[34] The motivation of the "responsible" Left in Parliament was to support the new democracy and in no way contribute to its erosion. It was felt that the popular masses would not forgive a Left that allowed democracy to decay after the struggle waged to achieve it.

The result was to create a close parliamentary relationship with the APRA during the AP government, especially once the effects of Ulloa's economic policies had begun to be felt.[35] In time, the parliamentary wing of the IU came to be seen by many as a moderating force, influenced by the Barrantes perspective.[36] Such moderation continued under the APRA government until the prison massacre trauma of 1986, which forced the parliamentary Left to reassess its behavior. Sections of the IU outside Parliament had been demanding such an appraisal since 1985.

Parliamentary involvement illustrates further contradictions for the IU. Once in the process, it was forced to take it seriously because it was felt that the IU's constituency expected responsible representative behavior. Parliamentary involvement carried with it the possibility of becoming an end in itself rather than one of a number of means to other ends. The jockeying for positions on election slates, although couched in the terms of political debate, was viewed by the cynical as a tacit recognition by many party leaders of the privileges accruing to parliamentary status.[37] Once García's caudillismo became the dominant feature of the APRA government, the criticism of the parliamentary wing of the IU increased, particularly when it was compounded by the challenge posed by the growth and relative success of Sendero Luminoso.

A third aspect of the IU and its approach to power is its development of an economic policy to deal with Peru's economic crisis. It advanced a very explicit economic strategy at two levels: a rhetorical account of worker and popular input into decision making related to economic performance and a detailed set of proposals.[38] The essential feature of the economic program was that it could be pragmatically implemented in the absence of democratic participatory structures, a reality vigorously denied by IU commentators but true all the same and specifically required if the IU was to arrive in government still distanced to any extent from popular organizations. In other words, the IU economic program elaborated in 1985 was orthodox enough to be implemented even if popular participation was disavowed.[39] It was to focus on increasing production and employment, establishing external equilibrium, resolving the problem of inflation, creating investment, and promoting income distribution. The means by which these ends would be achieved were primarily interventionist, directive, and participatory, with elements of both increased centralization and decentralization.

Perhaps not an orthodox Left-Keynesian policy in its details, it was in all essentials a Left social democratic package adapted to Peru's particular situation. It could be little else, because its basic tenets were determined by the possibility that it might become the economic strategy of government—a strategy with which IU politicians and technical staffs might have to confront both national and international economic assessment.

Such "realism," however understandable and necessary, could not sit easily with groups in the "revolutionary bloc" calling for workers' control of the means of production as an essential component of a truly left-wing strategy. Thus, the economic policy of the IU was presented to its constituency simultaneously as a practical way forward for popularly elected government and, implicitly, as at best a smokescreen behind which "real" socialism might be gestating and at worst a betrayal by reformists. This context raises the interesting hypothetical question what would have happened in 1985 had the IU been elected. Accession to power would surely have caused a major disruption of its unity.

The Challenge from the Left

The decision of the Sendero Luminoso, an offshoot of the pro-Albanian Bandera Roja, itself an originally Maoist grouping from the same stable as Patria Roja, to resort to armed struggle in 1980 has made the pursuit of unity on the Left substantially more difficult. Sendero is a peculiarly Peruvian political movement not only in its often perverse analyses of Peruvian society but also in its jesuitical purism. Abimael Guzmán, its main ideologue, is an exceptionally talented philosopher, schooled in the high abstractions of Peruvian revolutionary thought in the 1960s and 1970s—precisely that period in which the revolutionary Left came to the view that the parliamentary road was ineffective in Peru.

Arguably, it is less surprising that the SL took the path it did than that more parties did not do the same. Assessing the Left's publications of the late 1970s, the constant preoccupation of many groups with the prerevolutionary conjuncture offered by the second phase is striking. Similarly, their rejection of the liberal democratic path was unyielding. Despite the plethora of analyses of the SL on offer, the choice of armed struggle seems to have hinged on the existence of a degree of preparation by the SL in a conducive environment, in line with the abstract analysis offered by most groups to the left of the PCP.[40] Faced with the choice between the dangers of reformism and the true way, the SL kept the faith, only to be betrayed by its fellow revolutionaries; hence the vituperation heaped upon the erstwhile revolutionary groups for their backsliding and the consequent discomfort felt by many participants in the IU. Inevitably, this created ambivalence with regard to the SL's actions in some sectors of the IU; equally inevitably, its "responsible" sectors have condemned the SL, if only to ward off attacks from the Right and the threat of repression from a hard-pressed police and army.[41] In turn, there has been some erosion of the IU under the influence of the SL's "backsliding" critique.[42]

The intra-IU effects of the SL's militant critique of the electoral path were to be expected. Its rapid defeat would have removed a dilemma for the Left in general and the IU in particular; its survival and growth opens up another more pressing issue for the IU and the democratic model. We have seen that the popular movements in both town and city are not "hegemonized" (to use a popular term) by the Left. There is evidence of volatility in social forces, especially among young people. Few assume from this volatility an inevitable or even likely bond between the SL and the popular movement, but the potential is there for direct action to usurp the complex strategies for change embedded in the formation and activity of the IU.

The position of the legal Left toward the SL has come under the microscope of the army and the Right, now eager to associate any leftist activity with the SL. This has become a central issue for the Left and an important feature of the post-1980 period. Early wishes to preserve the stability of democratization were displaced by the authoritarianism of Belaúnde and the caudillismo of García. Underpinning the criticisms of both governments were three features: the conduct of government, the handling of the economy, and—at times looming largest—the question of human rights. Since the eruption of armed struggle in the sierra and, later, the cities, the government has perceptibly increased the powers of the armed forces to deal with the emergency. As a consequence, there have been well-documented and often terrible abuses of human rights, frequently by state forces. To question the armed forces' activities is for many politicians on the Right to support the SL (a view shared by the military). One extreme consequence of this situation is that many now think that the Left, if ever elected to national power, would be swept away by the army. This is a valuable weapon for the Right to use against the IU. It matters little what the IU may say in response; its association with the SL and other groups waging armed struggle is a constant theme of commentaries and analysis. The polarizing effect of this propaganda in a situation fraught with political, social, and economic tension threatens to undermine the stability of the democratic process assiduously fostered by sections of the IU.

Conclusions

A number of themes emerge from this account of the Left since the mid-1970s. First, the status of the Left as a mainstream political tradition both in and out of Parliament is a great achievement. The creation of the IU as an umbrella organization uniting previously warring factions is a further success, although by no means total. The contribution of the Left to the maintenance of a decade of liberal democratic politics is also positive. The development of new ideological and political perspectives on the Left—local democracy, the popular movement, the approach to democratic power, and interpretations of socialism, for example—stand out. Equally significant is the incorporation of new layers of people—the urban poor, previously marginalized women, peasants remembering Velasco's promises, and newly unionized urban workers.

Of course, the other side of this coin includes the continuing fragmentation of the Left, the inability to overcome problems within the IU, leading to a degree of paralysis in its activities, the challenge from the extra-Parliamentary Left, the threat from the Right and the army, the erosion of the democratic model by authoritarianism and caudillismo, the country's difficult economic circumstances, the growth of a dangerously destabilizing drug industry, and the distance between the organized Left and its potential constituency, to name but the most obvious problems.

Elsewhere, the situation of the Peruvian Left has been described as "brilliant and precarious," and this phrase captures the complex circumstances of political life in Peru.[43] The future is uncertain. The divided Left did poorly in the 1990 general elections; a common view is that all established parties suffered from skepticism of political parties, thus explaining the precipitous rise to prominence of Cambio 90. If the combination of economic uncertainty, social unrest, and political violence continues, it is difficult to see a situation emerging in which a government of the democratic Left would be permitted to take office even if it could win an election.

A more likely scenario is the continuation of an IU–IS-type division, reflecting a clash between pragmatic and revolutionary perspectives, with further realignments across this divide. In the recent elections, the continuing pragmatism of Barrantes was clear, as was the more radical "ideological" position of Pease, although rhetorically there was little to distinguish between the IU and the IS campaign. The poor showing of the APRA in government and in the 1990 elections adds another element to the equation. In the past, the issue of IU-APRA cooperation was raised; it may surface again. There may also be a movement of disillusioned *apristas* to the Left, particularly toward more social-democratic traditions.

On balance, the Left's relationship with the popular movement during the 1980s has been close. The successes of the IU, the development of a radical pluralism in popular political debates, and the organizational achievements in the parties and the unions testify to this. However, there is an intractable tension in the democratic Left as it looks simultaneously to formal political power and its attendant compromises and to the demands of a mobilized and often angry popular movement. The adoption of the electoral road has inevitably led to a sense of betrayal within the groups that helped propel the military back to barracks and give electoral and popular support to the IU, primarily because the Left has been unable to deliver economic improvement, political stability, and a restructured power distribution in Peruvian society. Despite this, the Left has entered the national political scene after fifty years in the wilderness and in the process has radically altered the nation's political landscape.

Notes

1. There is a substantial literature on the Velasco reforms. Among the more recent works is David Booth and Bernardo Sorj, eds., *Military Reformism and Social Classes: The Peruvian Experience* (London: Macmillan, 1983).

2. For more detailed discussion of the trade union movement, see Nigel Haworth, "The Peruvian Working Class: 1968–1979," in Booth and Sorj, *Military Reformism*, and "Political Transition and the Peruvian Labor Movement 1968–1985," in E. Epstein, ed., *Labor Autonomy and the State in Latin America* (Boston: Unwin Hyman, 1989); Jorge Parodi, "La desmovilización del sindicalismo industrial peruano en el segundo belaundismo," in Eduardo Ballón, ed., *Movimientos sociales y crisis: El caso peruano* (Lima: Desco, 1986); Isabel Yepez and Jorge Bernedo, *La sindicalización en el Perú* (Lima: Fundación F. Ebert, 1984); Carmen Rosa Balbi, *Identidad clasista en el sindicalismo: Su impacto en las fábricas* (Lima: Desco, 1989); and Pedro Galin et al., *Asalariados y clases populares en Lima* (Lima: IEP, 1986).

3. Fernando Rospigliosi, "Izquierda y clases populares: Democracia y subversión en el Perú," in Julio Cotler, ed., *Clases populares, crisis y democracia en América Latina* (Lima: IEP, 1989).

4. Rospigliosi, "Izquierda y clases populares."

5. The issue of economic policy during the second phase is dealt with in, for example, Oscar Dancourt, "Deuda o crecimiento: Un dilema político," in Luis Pasara and Jorge Parodi, eds., *Democracia, sociedad y gobierno en el Perú* (Lima: Centro de Estudios de Democracia y Sociedad, 1988).

6. On popular mobilization generally, the best starting points for its study are Ballón, *Movimientos sociales y crisis*, and *Movimientos sociales y democracia: La fundación de un nuevo orden* (Lima: Desco, 1986); Teresa Tovar, *Movimientos populares y paros nacionales* (Lima: Desco, 1982); idem, "Movimiento popular: Otra historia prohibida," *Quehacer*, 16 (April 1982):68–75, idem, *Velasquismo y movimiento popular* (Lima: Desco, 1985); Steve Stein and Carlos Monge, *La crisis del estado patrimonial en el Perú* (Lima: IEP, 1988).

7. For example, Jorge Nieto, *Izquierda y democracia en el Perú: 1975–1980* (Lima: Desco, 1983); Rolando Ames, "Gran burguesía y movimientos populares," *Quehacer*, 5 (August 1980): 14–24.

8. Julio Cotler, "Los partidos políticos en la democracia peruana," in Pasara and Parodi, *Democracia, sociedad y gobierno en el Perú*.

9. For example, Nieto, *Izquierda y democracia*, and Rospigliosi, "Izquierda y clases populares."

10. Eduardo Ballón, "El movimiento popular: De la derrota de enero a la victoria de julio," *Quehacer*, 1 (October 1979).

11. Rolando Ames, "Gran burguesía y movimientos populares," *Quehacer*, 5 (August 1980):14–24; J. Calderón, "La batalla de los pueblos jovenes," *Quehacer*, 2 (November–December 1979).

12. Luis Pasara, "La 'libanización' en democracia," in Pasara and Parodi, *Democracia, sociedad y gobierno en el Perú*; Henry Pease, "Los partidos de izquierda en la transición democrática," in Henry Pease, *Democracia y precariedad bajo el populismo aprista* (Lima: Desco, 1988).

13. Ballón, "El movimiento popular."

14. Eduardo Ballón, Fernando Eguren, and Diego García Sayan, "El partido en el Perú: A propósito de un estilo y una manera de construir la organización," *Quehacer*, 10 (March–April 1981):6–15.

15. Rospigliosi, "Izquierda y clases populares."

16. The decision of AP not to participate had as much to do with personal pique on the part of Belaúnde as with tactics, but it did allow AP to enter the 1980 elections as the unsullied renewer of democracy.

17. Pease, *Democracia y precariedad*.

18. Henry Pease, "Triunfo popular: La alternativa que se aleja," *Quehacer*, 7 (October 1980):4–19.

19. Susan Stokes, "Política y conciencia popular en Lima: El caso de Independencia," Working Paper 31 (Lima: IEP, 1989). See also Cecilia Blondet, "Muchas vidas construyendo una identidad: Mujeres pobladoras de un barrio limeño," Working Paper 9 (Lima: IEP, 1987), and Maruja Barrig, "Crisis y empleo feminino," *Actualidad Económica Especial*, no. 8 (January 1986) and *Las obreras* (Lima: ADEC, 1986).

20. Stokes, "Política y conciencia popular en Lima"; Ballón, *Movimientos sociales y crisis*; Stein and Carlos, *La crisis del estado patrimonial*.

21. See, for example, Fernando Eguren, "Democracia y sociedad rural," in Pasara and Parodi, *Democracia, sociedad y gobierno*; Carlos Franco, "Movimiento agrario y restructuración del estado," in Hector Béjar and Carlos Franco, *Organización campesina y restructuración del estado* (Lima: CEDEP, 1985); Efraín Gonzales de Olarte, *Economía de una comunidad campesina* (Lima: IEP, 1984).

22. On the trade union movement see, for example, Jorge Parodi, "La desmovilización," in Ballón, *"Movimientos sociales y crisis*, and *Ser obrero es algo relativo: Obreros, clasismo y política* (Lima: IEP, 1986); Julio Carrion, "Los jovenes en el Perú: Un examen de sus condiciones económicas y sociales," Ms, IEP, Lima, 1987.

23. See Rosemary Thorp, "Políticas de ajuste en el Perú, 1978–1985," *Economía*, 7, 14 (1986)," and Parodi, "La desmovilización del sindicalismo," for a discussion of the consequences of the Ulloa approach. Mike Reid, *Peru: Paths to Poverty* (London: Latin America Bureau, 1985), also offers a useful summary of events in the period.

24. "Pueblos jóvenes: ¿Que pasó con la IU?," *Quehacer*, 35 (June 1985):41–46.

25. *Latin American Weekly Report* [henceforth *LAWR*], 84–04.

26. *LAWR*, 84–09, 84–23.

27. *LAWR*, 85–15, 85–17, 85–49.

28. *LAWR*, 86–26.

29. Henry Pease, *Democracia local: Reflexiones y experiencias* (Lima: Desco, 1989).

30. Pease, *Democracia local*.

31. Alfonso Barrantes, "Trabajar con la comunidad democráticamente organizada en la solución de sus problemas," *Quehacer*, 7 (October 1980):14–21.

32. Enrique Bernales, "La izquierda ejerce la iniciativa parlamentaria," *Quehacer*, 8 (December 1980):18–23.

33. Pasara, "La 'libanización.' "

34. Henry Pease, "Izquierda Unida, primer año: Balance y perspectivas," *Quehacer*, 13 (November 1981):4–12.

35. *LAWR*, 80–32, 82–01, 82–05.

36. See, for example, Eduardo Ballón, "IU y el APRA en la encrucijada de la oposición," *Quehacer*, 19 (October 1982):28–34.

37. *LAWR*, 84–17.

38. The proposals can be found in Izquierda Unida, "Programa Económico 1985–1990," *Actualidad Económica Especial*, no. 6 (March 1985).

39. "La ruptura de la herencia colonial: Entrevista con Javier Iguiniz," *Actualidad Económica Especial*, no. 6 (March 1985).

40. Among the offerings are Gustavo Gorriti, "Democracia, narcotráfico y la insurrección de Sendero Luminoso," in Pasara and Parodi, *Democracia, sociedad y gobierno*; Carlos Ivan

Degregori, *Sendero Luminoso: 1. Los hondos y mortales desencuentros. 2. Lucha armada y utopia autoritaria*, Anthropological Series nos. 2 and 3 (Lima: IEP, 1987), and *El surgimiento de Sendero Luminoso* (Lima: IEP, 1990); David Palmer, "The Sendero Luminoso Rebellion in Peru," in *Latin American Insurgencies* (Washington, DC: Georgetown University Center for Strategic and International Studies, 1985); Cynthia McClintock, "Peru's Sendero Luminoso Rebellion: Origins and Trajectory," in Susan Eckstein, ed., *Power and Popular Protest: Latin American Social Movements* (Berkeley: University of California Press, 1989), 61–101. Gorriti suggests that a crucial, if virtually unobtainable, source is the thesis of Manuel Granados Aponte, submitted to the University of Huamanga in 1980. Its importance lies in the current status of Granados as a leading thinker in Sendero's ranks.

41. *LAWR*, 87–24; José María Salcedo, "Sendero: ¿Conciencia de la izquierda?" *Quehacer*, 16 (April 1982):14–20.

42. *LAWR*, 87–18.

43. Haworth, "Between a Rock, a Hard Place, and Divine Wrath."

4

Popular Liberalism, Radical Democracy, and Marxism: Leftist Politics in Contemporary Colombia, 1974–1991

Marc W. Chernick and Michael F. Jiménez

The formal end of the sixteen-year joint rule of Colombia's two tradi-tional parties in 1974 was followed by more than a decade and a half of social protest, leftist electoral initiatives, and revolutionary armed insur-gencies. Through the 1970s, revitalized working-class organizations with strong links to leftist groups complemented a rising tide of rural protest throughout the country, from various pockets of indigenous populations to new zones of settlement such as the banana districts in the country's northeastern corner. Simultaneously, widespread demands in the princi-pal cities and in the provinces for basic state services evolved into formi-dable civic protests. Such mobilizations nurtured embryonic human-rights, feminist, ecological, civic, and Christian-based social movements among the middle and lower classes. Many of these suffered harsh repres-sion at the hands of the state and paramilitary groups, although some did survive and continue to play a major role locally. Several short-lived leftist electoral coalitions failed repeatedly throughout this period to break the hold of the traditional parties at the ballot box. Ultimately, however, electoral challenges and popular organizations on the Left were over-shadowed by the dramatic expansion of revolutionary guerrilla move-ments. These leftist insurgencies, inspired and supported by the Soviet Union, China, Cuba, and later Nicaragua, grew markedly after 1980. By decade's end, a handful of guerrilla organizations with diverse programs, varying degrees of military capacity, and uneven support from the populace played crucial roles in Colombian politics.

The dramatic upsurge in protests against oligarchically rooted bipartisan rule after 1974 has been understood primarily in three ways. The principal interpretation, cogently advanced by Francisco Leal Buitrago, is that Colombia's traditional bipartisan system and the evolution of the state and its sponsorship of a narrowly cast pattern of capitalist development have prevented the "emergence of civil society and the forging of citizenship," thereby providing few vehicles for the channeling of "conflicts generated by the process of permanent change" of the past half-century.[1] Jonathan Hartlyn and others present a more Huntingtonian version of this view, arguing that the elite bipartisan coalition established in 1958 could not respond to the new social and political challenges of the 1970s and 1980s.[2]

A second major argument for the marked rise of violence and social protest during the past two decades asserts that the survival of a vanguardist model rooted in the national-liberation enthusiasm of the 1960s privileged revolutionary insurgency over a leftist electoral strategy; this, more than the restricted nature of its political regime, prevented the emergence of a broad-based leftist politics in Colombia.[3] In effect, the guerrillas are regarded as captive to a Marxist-Leninist illusion that became more and more irrelevant in the face of the increasingly complex problems of developing societies and the crisis in the Soviet Union and other communist regimes.

Finally, a structuralist analysis suggests that the redesign of Colombian capitalism in the 1970s and 1980s contributed to the growing social protest, violence, and reduced space for democratic options in that period.[4] The unevenness of the world coffee trade, the volatility of nontraditional exports such as flowers and textiles, and, most important, the explosive growth of the illegal commerce in marijuana and cocaine led to rising social conflict in the cities and the countryside. A beleaguered and increasingly divided upper class responded savagely to these demands from below even as it sought accommodation with a powerful emergent drug elite.

This essay ultimately diverges from these interpretations. We argue that the recent history of the Colombian Left is not principally the result of the failure of modernizing elite coalitions or of the survival of atavistic revolutionary ideologies ill-suited to a new era or merely the outcome of a crisis in dependent capitalism exacerbated by the drug trade. Rather, leftist politics after 1974 are best understood as the working out of long-standing forms of opposition to elite rule within a major redesign of Colombian capitalism and the state.

During the course of the twentieth century, neither a viable liberal democratic challenge by middle-class reformers nor a social democratic alternative under the aegis of a coherent working class with independent political organizations emerged in Colombia. Rather, opposition to oligarchical rule was channeled primarily through widely dispersed social movements or armed guerrilla organizations. The social movements, both in the cities and more extensively in the countryside, sought *radical democratic* transformations in social relations and politics at the local level but had limited national projection. The armed insurgents, for their part, possessed a revolutionary vision that combined in various ways national political dissident traditions, Marxism-Leninism, and national liberation doctrines.

Colombia's guerrilla movements fall into two broad categories. First, the Communist-affiliated Fuerzas Armadas Revolucionarias de Colombia originated in the midcentury agrarian struggles. Linked with radical democratic movements in the countryside, particularly in areas of recent colonization, this movement became the pillar of a nationwide insurgency in the 1980s but seemed stymied in its efforts to evolve into a broad-based, nonviolent popular movement of urban and rural poor. Second, three insurgencies—the Ejército de Liberación Nacional (Army of National Liberation—ELN), the Ejército Popular de Liberación (Popular Liberation Army—EPL), and the Movimiento 19 de Abril were born in the 1960s and early 1970s among the middle class. Guided by an ideal of major social and political change initiated from above and identified here as popular liberalism, these groups generally lacked enduring popular support in their principal areas of military action but proved successful in projecting themselves as a national political force either by spectacular armed initiatives or, by the 1990s, through reincorporation into public life as novel political actors challenging the traditional elites.

The National Front Period

With the initiation of the power-sharing agreement known as the National Front in 1958, Colombia's elites sought to establish the foundations for stable oligarchical rule and capitalist development. The country was exhausted after more than a decade of partisan civil war, having suffered between two hundred thousand and three hundred thousand deaths and massive destruction during the previous decade. After 1958, the leadership of the elite-dominated Liberal and Conservative parties ensured partisan peace by guaranteeing parity at all levels of government and, until 1974, presidential alternation between the two parties. This arrangement formally excluded other movements and organizations from participation in the nation's public life.

While some middle-class elements attempted without success to bring about democratic reform in the 1970s, others had no such optimism about peacefully transforming Colombia's variant of oligarchical capitalism. From its outset, the National Front faced various middle-class revolutionary movements. In the first place, the Movimiento Revolucionario Liberal (Liberal Revolutionary Movement—MRL), headed by Alfonso López Michelsen (the son of a former president), won over intellectual dissidents, Communists, and veterans of the midcentury Liberal guerrillas who were attracted to armed struggle against the elites, especially following the victory of the 26th of July Movement in Cuba. With the disbanding of the MRL in 1964, several middle-class armed insurrectionary initiatives arose in its wake. The ELN was founded in 1965 by Colombian students in Havana, including some elements of the MRL's youth wing and radical petroleum workers from Santander; the group quickly earned notoriety for its kidnappings and assaults on police stations and widespread sympathy after the radical priest Camilo Torres joined its ranks and perished in an encounter with the Colombian army. Inspired by the Cuban Revolution and Che Guevara's foco model of revolutionary warfare, the ELN expanded from its initial area of operations in the northeastern department of Santander to other regions only to be virtually annihilated by the Colombian military in 1973.

In 1968 the EPL, another predominantly middle-class guerrilla group, made its appearance. Formed as the military wing of the pro-Chinese Partido Comunista de Colombia, Marxista–Leninista (Colombian Communist party, Marxist-Leninist—PCCM-L), which had split from the orthodox Communists in 1965, it too followed a foco strategy and was also nearly destroyed by a successful counterinsurgency offensive in the early 1970s. Finally, in 1974, on the eve of the formal end of the National Front, another major guerrilla insurgency began with the theft of Simón Bolívar's sword from the National Museum. The M-19 was composed of middle-class activists from the Alianza Nacional Popular (Popular National Alliance—ANAPO), a movement that had supported the former dictator Gustavo Rojas Pinilla in the 1970 presidential elections, and dissidents from the Communist guerrillas. Determined to shift guerrilla activity from the countryside to the city, these radical nationalists concurred with the other groups in seeking to overthrow the regime by force of arms in order to establish a more democratic and egalitarian society.

The middle-class guerrilla insurgencies of the National Front years had complex origins. The middle class had grown frustrated by the limits placed on its social mobility and exercise of political power. The guerrillas also represented a generational protest—nurtured in the rapidly expanding Colombian universities and inspired by the Cuban Revolution and national revolutionary movements elsewhere in the Third World—against orthodox Communists, reformers, and oligarchs alike. Marxism-Leninism certainly resonated among these young men and women hopeful of overthrowing the *ancien régime* through a carefully planned and organized insurgency and creating a new, egalitarian order from above. But, in the Colombian context at least, this vanguardist project must also be understood as continuing a long tradition of insurrectionism rooted in the nation's highly sectarian political culture and its particular manifestations within Colombian liberalism.

Popular liberalism originated in antioligarchical and anticlerical sentiments during the middle decades of the nineteenth century. It was characterized by powerful antagonism toward the upper classes, a deep suspicion of political pluralism, and an affinity for armed struggle. As in many traditional agrarian societies on the European periphery penetrated by liberal ideals during the nineteenth and early twentieth centuries, politics became an extension of war. This jacobinist sensibility persisted among large sectors of the Liberal party through the first half of the twentieth century. In the three decades before the Great Depression, constant political agitation and occasional conspiracies, including a failed uprising in July 1929, marked the persistent popular liberal resistance by provincial elites, urban middle-class groups, and elements of the rural poor against Conservative rule. With the victory of the Liberals in the 1930 presidential elections, popular liberalism found a channel for a reformist program from above through the succeeding decade and a half of party rule. But insurrectionism within the ranks of liberalism erupted once again at midcentury in the face of Conservative repression.

The Liberal guerrillas of the late 1940s and 1950s saw armed struggle as the means of reasserting Liberal control over the state. Several of these Liberal insurgents joined the ranks of the MRL in the late 1950s, and the MRL in turn spawned the *foquista* ELN in 1964. The middle-class guerrillas of the 1960s did not simply respond to the enthusiasms and paradigms of global revolution, especially its particular incarnation in Cuba after 1959. Rather, their notions of politics, whether national liberationist or more explicitly Marxist-Leninist, stood squarely in the militarized, vanguardist, and exclusionary Colombian tradition. Their struggle was directed against political and social inequalities, but they distrusted the rule of law and rejected a pluralist, representative government as the basis of Colombian democracy.[5]

An alternative oppositional politics also with deep roots in Colombian history existed alongside popular liberalism. A radical democratic tradition was present in small, regional lower-class movements against local notables and the state, especially in rural areas. The oldest, most sustained radical democratic protests were to be found among southeastern Colombia's indigenous communities. During the Great Depression, peasant organizations in the Upper Magdalena Valley undertook programs of local transformation with the assistance of the newly founded

Communist party. By the late 1960s, the National Front government itself had spawned considerable local claims making. Community organizations and particularly a national agrarian union, the Asociación Nacional de Usuarios Campesinos (National Association of Peasant Users—ANUC) promoted by Liberal President Carlos Lleras Restrepo, soon escaped their developmentalist tutelage to become increasingly defiant in the provinces.[6]

Radical democracy had highly diverse local origins and histories. In these various contexts, it meant the freeing of the rural poor from dependent social relations, guarantees for small proprietorship, community control over the market, widespread participation in local organizations, and the achievement of the full benefits of national citizenship. At the same time, as did the popular liberals, participants in such movements expressed ambivalence about electoral competition and constitutionalism given shape by oligarchical rule.

The Communist party, founded in 1930, was the principal legatee of radical democracy and the latter's historically ambiguous relation with popular liberalism.[7] Despite their middle-class, artisan, and to a lesser degree trade-union origins, the Communists' principal arena of action became the large-estate districts southwest of the nation's capital. During the Great Depression and its aftermath, they fashioned a successful strategy of agrarian opposition based on electoral challenges, mass organizations, and armed self-defense. The Communist orientation toward a local, peasant agenda in the decade after 1935 generated a revolutionary agrarianism focusing on the formation and protection of autonomous smallholder communities as opposed to a nationwide insurgency. Under these circumstances, Marxism-Leninism became less a strategy for taking control of the central government than a guide for local struggles against *hacendados* (estate owners) and government officials and a sensibility linking a small segment of Colombia's rural poor to international revolutionary movements.

Early in the National Front period, political elites seemed most intent on eliminating these pockets of radical agrarianism linked to the Communist party. In 1964, the government launched a massive military operation against them that propelled these marginal, geographically remote communes onto center stage. The military action transformed a colonizing peasantry organized into armed self-defense units into a mobile peasant guerrilla movement armed against the state. The Colombian Communist party backed the transformation even as its counterparts throughout the continent opted for the popular-front strategies of coalitions and elections. It hoped to gain a competitor in the field with the middle-class insurgencies inspired by Cuba and China that were then taking root in Colombian soil.

The FARC, the outgrowth of these peasant communities, was formally established in 1966; this new guerrilla army deepened its base in central and southern Colombia during the succeeding decade and a half. In contrast to the middle-class guerrillas, with their foquista strategy, these agrarian revolutionaries guided local social transformations and earned the support of the rural poor. While they did not aspire to national power, their presence in the mountains and plains of Colombia nonetheless signaled the government's failed agrarian policies and uneven hold over the countryside.

Political Struggle in the 1970s

The end of the National Front in 1974 did not lead to the democratiza-tion of Colombia's oligarchical republic. On the contrary, the 1970s and 1980s witnessed greater concentration of political and economic power in the hands of old as well as emergent elites. They also saw the expanded influence of the armed forces in the nation's public life and a dramatic increase in official violence against both guerrillas and the generally peaceful movements of peasants, workers, and varied civic groups. These circumstances reinforced the character of the Colombian Left as predom-inantly nonelectoral and tending toward armed insurgency. In effect, in the sixteen years after the end of formal bipartisan rule, leftist opposition, unable to find a base of support among either middle-class liberal democrats or organized labor, oscillated between radical democracy and popular liberalism, both strongly rooted in traditional forms of political resistance and influenced by contemporary revolutionary ideology and strategic doctrine.

There was hope that the presidency of Alfonso López Michelsen (1974–1978) would break decisively from the National Front; López had been the leader of the MRL, its principal Liberal dissidency. However, this hope proved illusory. Although López had come to power with broad popular support for a reformist program, both he and his fellow Liberal successor, Julio César Turbay (1978–1982), helped midwife major transformations in the nation's political economy that resulted in a further consolidation of elite rule and the strengthening of state power. Their two administrations assisted in the fundamental restructuring of the Colombian economy begun in the latter years of the National Front. This entailed a shift from import substitution toward more capital-intensive manufacturing and the encouragement of agricultural and mineral exports. Large-scale invest-ments in metallurgy, automobile assembly, and chemicals coincided with the expansion of petroleum, coal, nickel, and banana enclaves. Foreign capital played a major role in this reconfiguration of the Colombian econ-omy. At the same time, accelerated capitalist development in agriculture reduced the peasant share of foodstuff production from two-thirds in the 1960s to one-third in 1980. Finally, the drug trade became important, beginning with marijuana in the early 1970s and culminating with the boom in cocaine production and export a decade later.

The redesign of Colombian capitalism in the 1970s was accompanied by the affirmation of the most authoritarian features of the National Front. On the one hand, a resurgent regional bossism, previously held in abeyance by the centralizing technocratic elites of the 1960s, smothered free electoral competition and popular organizations in the provinces. Local elites and national politicians created a latticework of influence extending from Congress to the lowest levels of public administration. The majority Liberal party, in particular, benefited from this process even though it still shared high bureaucratic posts with the Conservative minority. At the same time, the military assumed an ever-greater political role. In the face of popular resistance in the countryside and the cities and emboldened guerrilla movements, the elites ceded virtually unqualified control over public order to the armed forces.

The labor movement during this period found itself increasingly debilitated. Proletarians endured high unemployment, reduced salaries, the dismantling of social security provisions, and restrictions on trade union activity. More Colombians found jobs in the informal sector, where they were unprotected either by the state or by the labor movement. In the mid-1970s, feuding trade unionists temporarily resolved their differences to form a national labor committee, the Consejo Nacional Sindical (National Union Council—CNS), which staged a massive national shutdown on September 14, 1977. Yet the national strike proved to be a turning point for the regime, as López showed no hesitation in responding with force and converting popular protest into a bloody confrontation with the state. Following the national strike, the fortunes of the Colombian labor movement declined in the face of sectarian struggles, government cooptation, and harsh official repression. In the early 1980s, efforts to mobilize the population once again in large-scale protests failed repeatedly. As López and then Turbay pursued neoliberal economic and social policies, Colombia's working-class organizations offered little resistance.

Radical democratic movements among the urban and rural poor suffered much the same fate as the working-class organizations through the 1970s. With the onset of the López administration, the nationwide peasant mobilization spawned by Lleras Restrepo in 1968 lay prostrate. ANUC was divided from within by disputing leftist factions and battered by official repression in areas where land invasions and strikes gave affront to provincial landowning elites. Similarly, the indigenous movements, particularly the Consejo Regional Indígena del Cauca (Cauca Regional

Indigenous Council—CRIC), which had emerged under ANUC sponsorship, suffered intense repression in Colombia's southwestern corner.[8]

The other principal agrarian challenger, the FARC, began to move from its traditional zone of influence in the Upper Magdalena into new frontier zones in the eastern plains, the mid–Magdalena Valley, and the banana districts of western Antioquia. Although projecting a national liberation program and linked to the Communist party, at this stage the FARC, in William Ramírez Tobón's words, remained "little more than the advance guard of a colonizing peasantry . . . whose objective [was] the establishment of a democratic statute concerning the agrarian question."[9]

The cities became the principal foci of radical democratic politics in the second half of the 1970s. Community organizations created by National Front technocrats went beyond their developmentalist and integrationist charge to become far more radical, especially with regard to public services. The mid-decade mobilizations instigated by the labor movement, including the national shutdown of September 1977, could not have had their powerful impact without the participation of neighborhood associations, cooperatives, and a host of other popular organizations.[10] By the early 1980s, these dispersed movements felt the harsh hand of the Turbay government, whose increasingly autonomous military apparatus could not or would not distinguish guerrilla subversion from other forms of social protest. Significantly, the Catholic church in Colombia provided neither the resources nor the legitimation of radical democratic movements as it did in other parts of Latin America, notably Brazil and Chile, in the 1970s and 1980s.[11]

After 1974, these repeated outbreaks of radical democratic claims making could not be channeled by the Left. The Communists and other leftist groups had forged a tenuous electoral alliance, the Unión Nacional de Oposición (National Opposition Union—UNO), in the 1974 election. However, the UNO was unable to overcome factional differences or effectively challenge the remnants of ANAPO for support among the urban poor. Toward the end of the decade, radical intellectuals formed Firmes (Stalwarts) in the hope of reducing the bitter sectarian disputes that persistently crippled leftist electoral politics. Despite its radical-democratic credentials, Firmes too was unable to serve as a standard bearer for diverse local and regional organizations, being systematically destroyed by official repression. It had even less success with guerrilla organizations as yet unprepared to conceive of an electoral challenge to elite rule.[12]

With liberals, proletarians, and radical democrats silenced and the FARC still a relatively marginal, regional guerrilla movement, armed popular liberalism emerged as the principal opposition to the Colombian oligarchy in the years immediately after the formal end of the National

Front in 1974. Whereas the major popular-liberal initiatives of the 1960s, the ELN and the EPL, suffered serious military defeats in the late 1960s and early 1970s, the M-19 quickly emerged as a formidable challenger to the elites.

The M-19 consciously embraced both populism and nationalism. It also asserted a revolutionary stance through its determination to bring guerrilla war to the cities in the manner of the Tupamaros and Montoneros of the Southern Cone. Both its nationalist and urban emphases set it apart from the earlier Maoist and Castroite initiatives in the countryside. Its kidnappings and other spectacular actions provoked and even embarrassed the elites and drew the applause of the lower classes. It was not, however, a revolutionary politics with strong organizational roots either among trade unionists or the urban poor. Intent on "nationalizing the revolution," in the words of its principal leader, Jaime Bateman, the M-19 proved to be ideologically flexible and capable of incorporating lower-class languages of protest.[13] Nonetheless, it remained committed to a revolution from above, fusing Colombia's jacobinist tradition with national liberation doctrines of the late 1970s and early 1980s.

By the 1980s, the M-19 had transformed leftist politics in Colombia and raised the ante for revolutionary action for all the nation's guerrilla movements. The M-19's spectacular public presence, combined with the example of the Sandinistas in Nicaragua and the Frente Farabundo Martí para la Liberación Nacional (Farabundo Martí National Liberation Front—FMLN) in El Salvador, reignited armed popular liberalism. After the military defeats of the 1970s the foquista groups found more fertile soil for their actions. The ELN was able to rebuild itself, emphasizing its Christian revolutionary legacy, in the petroleum zones of Santander and Arauca. The EPL also reemerged with renewed force in the 1980s in the banana districts in western Antioquia and the cattle lands of Córdoba. Most important in this regard, the FARC too reconceptualized its revolutionary strategy and made a strategic decision in the early 1980s to expand its regional bases and project itself nationally. In effect, the rural Communists who had historically maintained themselves essentially as an armed social movement based in peasant communities in the old self-defense zones and the newer areas of colonization along the agriculture frontier shifted toward a more insurrectionist position. In so doing, they effectively joined and began to compete with the M-19 and the other guerrilla organizations.

The resurrection of armed popular liberalism and the concurrent militarization of the regime transformed Colombia's guerrillas from a marginal position, defined largely in military terms, into central protagonists in national politics. Throughout the 1980s, their proposals for peace and critique of the government undermined the legitimacy of the traditional political class on its own terrain and forced the traditional parties to respond to the growing legitimacy crisis of the regime.[14]

The Legal Opposition in the 1980s

The economic changes of the late 1960s and 1970s crystallized during the administrations of the popular Conservative Belisario Betancur (1982–1986) and the Liberal Virgilio Barco Vargas (1986–1990) and accelerated after the election of César Gaviria in 1990. The neoliberal program of free trade, privatization, foreign investment, and responsiveness to international financiers achieved more concrete expression in this period, resulting in the expansion of extractive industries, metallurgical and chemical manufacturing, and other capital-intensive enterprises. In the countryside, large-scale commercial agriculture acquired greater territory, state resources, and share of production. At the same time, the burgeoning drug trade had a powerful impact. Marijuana in the late 1970s and cocaine in the 1980s displaced coffee as the nation's principal export. The illegal but highly profitable trade cushioned the economy against international recession but also produced a new agro-exporting elite among traffickers investing in agriculture, finance, construction, and communications. The reshaping of Colombian capitalism in this period resulted not only in expansion at the national level but also in the further growth and consolidation of regional economies with their correspondingly powerful regional upper classes.

Barco took office in 1986 in the wake of the breakdown of the first round of peace negotiations with the country's major guerrilla movements. The erosion and collapse of the peace process sponsored by his predecessor Belisario Betancur, together with the newer forms of conflict associated with the drug trade, resulted in a dramatic escalation of political violence, returning the country to levels of bloodshed not seen since the 1950s. Yet Barco, too, ultimately returned to a politics of political opening toward the armed Left as the centerpiece of a program to restore political legitimacy and political order. In his final year of office, his government signed a peace accord with a militarily debilitated M-19. Within months of ceremoniously laying down its arms, the M-19 was transformed from a small band of armed insurgents into an electoral movement seeking to recover the loose populist coalition that had not coalesced since the fateful presidential elections of April 19, 1970.

The efforts at political change of the previous decade finally seemed to bear fruit after Gaviria became president in 1990. The new administration in its first year of office made substantial advances toward peace accords with other guerrilla movements, negotiations with the drug traffickers, and the convening of a constitutional assembly based on the unofficial plebiscite that had been orchestrated by Barco during his last year of office.

Yet there were major obstacles to political reform. In the first place, neoliberal economic policies would limit the scope of these changes after 1982. Budgetary constraints undermined government efforts to rehabilitate former guerrillas and finance critical welfare target areas such as rural integrated-development programs. Second, regional clientelist networks restrained the reach and impact of political reforms. Third, the drug elites penetrated local and departmental bureaucracies and increased the militarization of politics in their alliance with regional upper classes and local military officials against peasants, trade unionists, and guerrillas.[15] Finally, the military, with its corrupt ties to drug traffickers and death squads against the armed Left, asserted ever greater autonomy vis-à-vis civilian authorities and undermined efforts to reach a settlement with the insurrectionists.[16]

For its part, the labor movement, severely battered during the López and Turbay years, was unable to generate any substantial social democratic initiatives.[17] The economy undercut the ability of labor organizations to assert their influence; as the informal sector grew rapidly, the unionization rate declined from 15 percent to 9 percent of the work force, with only one-third covered by social security and minimum salary decrees. The emergence of a coherent labor movement was made the less likely by the continuing political disarray in the trade unions.

The mid-1980s did witness a realignment of the labor movement with the formation of the Central Unitaria de Trabajadores (Unitary Workers' Central—CUT). Founded in 1986, the CUT presented a formidable challenge to the traditional confederations. Moreover, it envisioned itself as the social democratic core for a renovated Colombian Left in the manner of the highly successful Partido dos Trabalhadores in Brazil; it rejected a narrowly trade unionist strategy, beckoning popular movements to its side. But, in contrast to the situation in Brazil, the divided, weak, and demoralized working class failed to become the fulcrum for a new leftist politics. The CUT became the target of death squads; by 1991 hundreds of its leaders and followers had been assassinated.

Radical democrats throughout the country faced a similar quandary in these years. The political opening of the post-Turbay era stimulated widespread mobilization at a local level, but Colombia's variants of the new social movements found themselves in complex relation to the country's still principal leftist protagonists in arms. This grass-roots politics attended to local demands and circumstances, bridged ideological and political divisions to forge new alliances, and stimulated multiple forms of nonviolent struggle, including marches, civic strikes, trade union organizing, neighborhood associations, and diverse cultural activities.[18] Such movements emerged with surprising force and vigor in the larger urban areas, which had suffered harsh repression in the wake of the 1977 national strike. However, the countryside was the scene of the most formidable popular protests, with organizations of small-town artisans and merchants, the rural poor, and, in the southwest, indigenous groups pressing the state for improved services, greater accountability of bureaucrats, and protection from local elites and the military.[19]

This ground swell of mobilization acquired greater coherence and national projection when several guerrilla groups in the mid-1980s decided to test the government's policy of widening political participation and negotiated settlement to armed struggle. In 1985, the FARC sponsored the Unión Patriótica, and a year later the ELN established A Luchar (To Struggle).[20] Although intended by the guerrillas to be political fronts, they captured the imagination of the demoralized and divided radical democrats. The FARC, with its links to local movements (particularly strong in zones of colonization), played some role in more than two-thirds of the popular mobilizations of the mid- and late 1980s. The UP, in particular, provided a focus for popular organizations and challenges to local elites; electorally the new party's gains were more modest but nevertheless did garner support at the polls in the 1986 congressional races that translated into fourteen congressional seats. In the 1988 balloting for mayors, the nation's first direct election of municipal executives, the UP again demonstrated its electoral presence.

However, economic interests and political bosses in the provinces attacked the UP, particularly for its ties to an armed guerrilla movement. The assassination in October 1987 of the UP's presidential candidate, Jaime Pardo Leal, marked a new phase in the "dirty war." More than fifteen hundred UP members, including dozens of elected officials— senators, mayors, councilmen, and two presidential candidates—have been assassinated. Drug traffickers played a major supporting role for right-wing reaction, but the ties of the death squads reached well into the military, parts of the state, local elites, and party bosses.

The dirty war of the 1980s, directed principally at new political parties and social movements, constricted the emergence of an unarmed Left, and one result of this was to strengthen the hand of elements intent on pursuing an insurrectionist strategy. In effect, a fragile popular mobilization and the dirty war prevented these new social movements from turning the Betancur-Barco political reforms into a springboard for a broad-based radical democratic politics.

The Guerrilla Movement Since 1980

The crucial actors on the Left in the 1980s thus continued to be the armed guerrilla organizations. Throughout this period, the guerrillas attempted both to expand the scope of their military challenges to Colombia's ruling elites and to augment their influence as political actors, particularly within the framework of negotiations with successive administrations representing both traditional parties.

By the decade's end, one-third of the country's municipalities had been the scene of guerrilla activity.[21] On the one hand, an unambiguous vanguardism persisted among a substantial portion of the armed Left. The EPL and the ELN revived dramatically in this period, and new groups, such as the proindigenous revolutionary movement Quintin Lame (named for an Indian leader of the 1914–1918 period) and the Partido Revolucionario de Trabajadores (Revolutionary Workers' Party—PRT) were founded. The M-19 and the FARC, however, continued to represent the different forms of armed and popular struggle during this period. Moreover, these two movements became the key protagonists for political change, and one or the other became the principal interlocutor for a succession of government initiatives to open up the political system, reflecting the weakness of the social movements and the legal Left.

The M-19 was seriously weakened during the peace processes of the 1980s as they exposed its leadership to public view. From 1982 to 1990, almost all of the M-19's founding leaders were assassinated or killed in combat. Major military reversals in the cities in the early 1980s led the M-19 to search, unsuccessfully, for a rural base of operations in the eastern llanos and then in the Cauca. Failing to establish any strong base of popular support, these radical nationalist, middle-class rebels persisted in a vanguard strategy consistent with their popular liberal origins. In August 1984, the M-19 signed a cease-fire agreement with the Betancur government; it withdrew ten months later, claiming that the government and the military had violated the agreement's terms.

Five months after breaking the cease-fire, on November 6, 1985, the M-19 seized the Palace of Justice in the center of Bogotá and held the Supreme Court hostage. It intended to use the judicial building as a symbolic backdrop against which to charge Betancur with violating the cease-fire agreement, but the strategy backfired. The guerrilla takeover provoked a brutal military response that left twelve Supreme Court justices, scores of civilian employees, and all but one of the estimated thirty-five guerrillas dead in an orgy of counterinsurgency violence. Although many questioned the military's response, almost no one rallied to the M-19's defense. This time its spectacular armed propaganda actions had failed to create a degree of public sympathy. Moreover, some of its ablest political leaders, such as former ANAPO senator Andrés Almirales, died inside the palace.

The Supreme Court takeover and subsequent massacre proved to be a crucial turning point for the popular liberals, causing them to shift from a predominantly military strategy to electoral politics and intraelite competition for power. Weakened militarily, lacking any substantial base of regional support, and unable to contest the FARC's influence within the guerrilla movement, the M-19, the EPL, Quintin Lame, and PRT entered into negotiations with the Barco administration in 1989. Four years in the wilderness after the Palace of Justice tragedy persuaded the surviving leadership to change.

The M-19 was the first to lay down its arms and enter directly into electoral politics, even though it was evident that the government was unable to provide political guarantees or protect the lives of its leaders. The M-19 reincorporated at a moment when the dirty war and the armed challenge of the drug traffickers to the Colombian government had engulfed the nation in unparalleled violence.[22] That violence quickly claimed the life of the M-19's leader and presidential candidate, Carlos Pizarro. Yet the M-19 persisted and won support and sympathy for its political courage. Pizarro's funeral was a national catharsis; the M-19 and multitudes of mourners in the streets of Bogotá reaffirmed their commitment to peace with chants of "The votes for Pizarro will now be given to Navarro" (Antonio Navarro Wolff, then the number-two leader of the M-19). Navarro received 12 percent of the vote, a margin with no precedent for the Left or for any third party not affiliated with the two traditional ones.

Led by the M-19, the popular liberal guerrillas' extraordinarily swift reincorporation reflected their affinity with the prevailing hierarchical and clientelist configuration of Colombian politics; deftly using their charismatic history and populist rhetoric, the M-19 framed politics as a choice between peace and war, with itself as the nation's principal conciliator.

This strategy redefined the elements of Colombian politics and dovetailed with the Barco-Gaviria strategy to reform the constitution. The M-19, under the same banner of peace and political reform as Gaviria, won 27 percent of the vote in a special election for the constitutional assembly. Navarro, who briefly served as Gaviria's minister of health before resigning to run for the assembly, became a central player—perhaps the central player—in the writing of a new constitution for Colombia.

The new constitution, a potpourri of liberal reform instruments to encourage pluralism and a welfare state wish list, appeared to provide the highly popular former guerrillas with a vehicle for reform from above. But without a major social base of support and a coherent political organization, the triumph of disarmed popular liberals was imperiled from the outset. These former guerrillas now faced the prospect of the domestication by the elites that had occurred with the MRL a generation before. At the same time, their own deep-seated vanguardist and exclusionary sensibilities presented serious obstacles to the development of a strategy combining electoral coalitions with popular nonviolent mobilization in order to implement the historic leftist program of dismantling elite economic and political power. In the absence of a political party with an organizational base of support and participation, the ground swell of enthusiasm for the M-19 leading up to the constitutional assembly could thus prove as ephemeral as the vote for ANAPO in the presidential elections of April 19, 1970.

The politics of the country's largest guerrilla group, the FARC, and, to a lesser extent, its principal ally, the ELN, differed from that of the M-19 and the other fragments of armed popular liberalism during the 1980s and early 1990s.[23] The FARC aligned the idea of peaceful resolution of armed conflict with a program of economic and social transformation along generally socialist lines, in contrast to the popular liberals' emphasis on a political opening. This programmatic gap was mirrored in the difference between the two groups in social bases of support. Whereas the popular liberals had only a transitory presence among the lower classes in most of their zones of military operation, the FARC, in particular, commanded considerable support at the local level, especially in its pre-1980 areas of influence. With the advent of the first peace process under the Betancur government, it sought to convert popular mobilization and the limited electoral strength of the Communist party into a national movement. The ELN's A Luchar represented a largely instrumental effort to form a political front, but it did have some foundation among local organizations working on behalf of lower-class claims in various zones in northeastern Colombia.

The FARC had far greater range and influence in this regard. Under the leadership of Manuel Marulanda Vélez, the agrarian revolutionaries recreated peasant communism elsewhere in the country, particularly in the new colonizing zones. From such communities the FARC was able to launch itself into the national political arena through the UP in 1985. Certainly, this focus on the ballot box and popular mobilization by the FARC, the armed wing of the Colombian Communist party, well served the latter's view of the necessity to combine armed and nonviolent forms of struggle against the elites. But it also demonstrated the persistence of the radical-democratic strain that had originally spawned these peasant rebels long before the Cuban Revolution.

The political coherence and efficacy of such a politics was demonstrated in the early and mid-1980s in Caquetá, in the northern reaches of the Amazonian basin. There the FARC built an autonomous rebel territory that, during the cease-fire period, achieved rapprochement with the state in order to preserve gains for the rural poor under its influence.[24]

However, the FARC and the ELN also demonstrated a certain ideological kinship with the M-19 and the other popular liberals in these years as Colombia slid into a period of general violence and war with multiple protagonists. The ELN, especially, had much shallower support than the FARC in areas under its influence and never entirely jettisoned its vanguardist vision of revolutionary action. In the late 1980s the FARC assumed a much more insurrectionist position, thereby losing some of its earlier will and capacity to focus on local concerns. This was partly because the M-19 had raised the stakes for the Communist guerrillas early in the decade, forcing the FARC to abandon its discrete cultivation of regional agrarian communism. At the same time, the flow of resources into the FARC's coffers from taxes on the cocaine trade in areas under its control gave an added impetus to a national insurrectionist strategy. The combination of a more unified guerrilla movement, greater access to arms, and widespread popular protest suggested a critical revolutionary conjuncture. Under these circumstances, the local politics of revolutionary agrarianism was necessarily subordinated to the broad strategy of strengthening the FARC militarily. In effect, radical democracy, in a tense relation since the 1930s with the Marxist-Leninist variant of popular liberalism, seemed nearly overwhelmed by the latter as the country descended into multipolar civil war.

This dilemma persisted with the political opening of the early 1990s. The FARC and the ELN, now allied through the Coordinadora Guerrillera Simón Bolívar (Simón Bolívar Guerrilla Coordinator), failed to reach agreement with the government on terms that would have permitted them to participate in the constitutional assembly. Consequently, they did not participate in the restructuring of Colombia's political institutions.

The dramatic collapse of the Soviet Union, the FARC's principal external supporter, together with the new constitutional regime, could provide it both the incentive and the opportunity to transform the continent's oldest guerrilla movement into a legally constituted political force. However, the FARC may find it difficult to make the transition from an agrarian revolutionary movement into a national contender on the Left within the new constitutional arrangements. The Communist guerrillas have traditionally made devolution of elite wealth and power the centerpiece of any political agreement leading to a cessation of hostilities and their incorporation into the nation's public life. But such preconditions would likely be unacceptable to government authorities resistant to any linkage of peace with a full-scale reformism under the aegis of leftist mobilization.

Beyond the wide gap between the elites and the agrarian revolutionaries, the latter faced other difficulties in transforming themselves into a nonmilitary popular movement of national dimensions. The FARC's influence was largely limited to the newly colonized zones in the country. The insurgency had created geographical bases of support in zones far from the major concentrations of rural poor in the Andean corridor. It did not appear, however, that the FARC's long experience among the peasantry would be easily translated into the bases for a radical agrarian party, particularly in areas where commercial agriculture had dramatically altered the social landscape in the last quarter-century. Moreover, the FARC's three decades of rural insurgency and deep roots in areas of peasant colonization had left them unprepared for the social complexity and the political challenges of a rapidly industrialized and urbanized Colombia as the century drew to a close.

Most important, however, the traditional tensions within the FARC between radical-democratic and popular-liberal elements would likely be heightened during an expected lengthy process of peace making and political integration of the armed agrarian revolutionaries. On the one hand, the M-19's example might prove attractive to many middle-class cadres hoping to compete for political power within the new constitutional regime. The strains on the radical-democratic aspirations and practices of the FARC during the period of escalated military action in the 1980s could thus be exacerbated by efforts to project power nationally; popular mobilization and electoral politics at that level threatened to drain local claims making of resources and leadership. Peasant communism, which had pushed the country toward major social and political reforms during more than three decades of armed struggle, seemed incapable of becoming the centerpiece of a renewed Left. The radical-democratic elements within the FARC thus faced the prospect of being overwhelmed by the popular-liberal model of politics rooted in Colombian political culture and reinforced by the continuing, if much diminished, influence of Marxist-Leninism on the left.

Simultaneously, the participation in Colombia's civic life by a disarmed FARC would likely encounter major obstacles in the provinces, where the dirty war has continued. Persistent social conflicts in the countryside have the potential to reaffirm the older forms of self-defense within which radical democracy flourished in the middle decades of the century in the Upper Magdalena and elsewhere. However, revolutionary agrarianism may have reached so high a level of militarization during the 1980s as to erode the fragile bases of radical democratic practice within the FARC. In effect, continuing social warfare in vast areas of rural Colombia has seemingly led the Communist guerrillas into a critical deadlock: unable to raise the level of rural mobilization in support of a widened insurgency and yet constrained from transforming themselves into a nationwide movement for radical change within the new constitutional regime.

Concluding Remarks

In conclusion, as the last decade of the century opened, the patterns of leftist opposition to oligarchical rule of the early 1970s remained largely unaltered, despite surface appearances to the contrary. Exhausted by guerrilla war and escalated drug violence in the late 1980s, Colombians of all classes favored peaceful resolution of conflicts and political renovation. The enthusiasm for the Constituent Assembly and the breathtaking pace of charter revision presented new opportunities for the historically marginal democrats, whether liberal or leftist. However, major obstacles appeared to contain the prospect of a remaking of Colombian civil society and the emergence of a renovated, parliamentary Left. The will and capacity of traditional political elites, especially within the Liberal party, to obstruct a more inclusionary politics within the new constitutional framework could very well constrict the political space for either a multiclass liberal democratic politics or a social democratic project emanating from the trade union movement, as in Brazil. In short, the infrastructure of oligarchical politics remained in place despite charter reform and widespread public debate, including the beginnings of a policy of increased civilian control over the armed forces.

Moreover, the quickened pace of neoliberal policy initiatives and the continued restructuring of Colombian capitalism in favor of a narrow economic elite and foreign interests appeared likely to continue to extact major sacrifices from the mass of the Colombian population; downward pressures on the middle class and increased impoverishment of the rural and urban poor would soon place considerable pressures on the largely untested new political framework. More broadly, the permeation of the nation's institutions and everyday life by violence imperiled the long journey toward creating a new civil society. Under such circumstances, opposition to oligarchical rule would likely continue to find its customary expression. On the one hand, popular liberalism—either in populist guise or through Colombia's native reworking of Marxism-Leninism— would reassert itself. On the other, efforts to make claims and defend rights would persist at the local level and struggle, probably with little success, to coalesce into national movements wherein social reform and democratic politics would be conjoined.

Notes

1. Francisco Leal Buitrago, *Estado y política en Colombia* (Bogotá: Siglo XXI, 1984), and "Los movimientos políticos y sociales: Un producto de la relación entre estado y sociedad civil," *Análisis Político*, no. 13 (May–August 1991):7–21.

2. Jonathan Hartlyn, *The Politics of Coalition Rule in Colombia* (New York: Cambridge University Press, 1988). Huntington's analysis of political change overwhelming the capacity

of political institutions to maintain authority can be found in Samuel F. Huntington, *Political Order and Changing Societies* (New Haven and London: Yale University Press, 1968).

3. Eduardo Pizarro Leóngomez, "Elementos para una sociología de la guerrilla colombiana," *Análisis Político*, no. 12 (January–April 1991):7–22, and, with a different theoretical accent, Daniel Pecaut, "Colombia: Violencia y democracia," *Análisis Político*, no. 13 (May–August 1991):35–50.

4. Jenny Pearce, *Colombia: Inside the Labyrinth* (London: Latin America Bureau, 1990).

5. For an argument that mirrors this view of the guerrillas but differs in emphasizing foreign influences, see León Zamosc, "The Political Crisis and the Prospects for Rural Democracy in Colombia," *Journal of Development Studies*, 26, 4 (July 1990):44–78. Zamosc, referring to the ELN and the EPL, writes that "their subjective orientations reflected a mechanistic brand of revolutionism. They were revolutionaries because they wanted to achieve radical change through violent means. At the same time, their mechanistic bent was revealed in the transplantation of foreign models, and in the sway of an extreme vanguardism that took for granted that the masses would automatically join their armed project" (57).

6. León Zamosc, *The Agrarian Question and the Peasant Movement in Colombia: Struggles of the National Peasant Association, 1967–1981* (Cambridge: Cambridge University Press, 1986).

7. Medófilo Medina, *Historia del partido comunista de Colombia* (Bogotá: CEIS, 1980).

8. Cristina Escobar, *Experiencias de organización campesina en el Valle de Cauca, 1960–1980* (Bogotá: Taller PRODESAL, 1987); Equipo de capacitación del CRIC, "El movimiento indígena," in Gustavo Gallón, comp., *Entre movimientos y caudillos: 50 años de bipartidismo, izquierda y alternativas populares en Colombia* (Bogotá: CINEP/CEREC, 1989).

9. W. Ramírez Gustavo Tobón, "La guerrilla rural: Una vía hacia la colonización armada," *Estudios Rurales Latinoamericanos*, 4, 2 (May–August 1981), my translation.

10. Oscar Delgado, comp., *Los paros cívicos en Colombia* (Bogotá: Editorial Latina, 1978); Jaime Carrillo Borda, *Los paros cívicos en Colombia* (Bogotá: Editorial La Oveja Negra, 1981); Luís Alberto Restrepo, "Movimientos cívicos en la década de los ochentas," in Francisco Leal Buitrago and León Zamosc, eds., *Al filo del caos: Crisis política en Colombia de los años 80* (Bogotá: Tercer Mundo Editores/Universidad Nacional, Instituto de Estudios Políticos y Relaciones Internacionales, 1990), 381–409.

11. Daniel H. Levine, "Colombia: The Institutional Church and the Popular," in Daniel H. Levine, ed., *Religion and Political Conflict in Latin America* (Chapel Hill: University of North Carolina Press, 1986), 187–218; Fernán González, "La iglesia jerárquica: Un actor ausente," in Leal Buitrago and Zamosc, *Al filo del caos*, 229–273.

12. Diego Montana Cuellar, "Núcleos para el análisis de experiencias organizativas: Izquierda legal, *Firmes*, Frente Democrático," in Gallón, *Entre movimientos y caudillos*, 172–180.

13. Jaime Bateman, interview, in Patricia Lara, *Siembra vientos y recogerás tempestades* (Bogotá: Planeta, 1982), 110–112.

14. Eduardo Pizarro Leóngomez, "La insurgencia armada: Raíces y perspectivas," in Leal Buitrago and Zamosc, *Al filo del caos*, 341; also Marc Chernick, "Insurgency and Negotiations: Defining the Boundaries of the Political Regime in Colombia," unpublished Ph.D. dissertation, Columbia University, 1990, especially Chapters 3 and 4.

15. Bruce M. Bagley, "Narcotráfico: Colombia asediada," in Leal Buitrago and Zamosc, *Al filo del caos*, 445–474; Alejandro Reyes Posada, "Paramilitares en Colombia: Contexto, aliados y consecuencias," *Análisis Político*, no. 12 (January–April 1991):35–42.

16. See Chernick, "Insurgency and Negotiations," 4.

17. Rocío Londoño Botero, "Problemas laborales y reestucturación del sindicalismo," in Leal Buitrago and Zamosc, *Al filo del caos*, 275–308.

18. Luis Alberto Restrepo, "Movimientos cívicos en la década de los ochentas," in Leal Buitrago and Zamosc, *Al filo del caos*, 381–408; Jairo Chaparro, "Los movimientos políticos regionales: Un aporte para la unidad nacional," in Gallón, *Entre movimientos y caudillos*,

208–226; J. Giraldo and Sergio Camargo, *Paros y movimientos cívicos en Colombia* (Bogotá: Centro de Investigación y Educación Popular/Controversia 128, 1985); William J. Cartier, "Civic Movements and Politics in Colombia," *Canadian Journal of Latin American and Caribbean Studies* 12, 24 (1989):103–120.

19. León Zamosc, "El campesinado y las perspectivas para la democracia rural," in Leal Buitrago and Zamosc, *Al filo del caos*, 311–380.

20. Nicolás Buenaventura, *Unión Patriótica y poder popular* (Bogotá: CEIS, 1987); José Arizala, "Unión Patriótica," in Gallón, *Entre movimientos y caudillos*, 159–165; Comité Ejecutivo Nacional, Organización 'A Luchar,'" in Gallón, *Entre movimientos y caudillos*, 181–186.

21. Alejandro Reyes Posada and Ana María Bejarano, "Conflictos agrarios y luchas armadas en la Colombia contemporánea: Una visión geográfica," *Análisis Político*, no. 5 (September–December 1988):6–27.

22. W. Ramírez Tobón, "La liebre mecánica y el galgo corredor: La paz actual con el M-19," *Análisis Político*, no. 7 (1989):46–59.

23. This echoes Zamosc, who writes in "The Political Crisis and the Prospects for Rural Democracy" that the "mechanistic variant is that of the M-19, whose demobilization follows the long-standing Colombian model of re-incorporation of armed counter-elites. The variant that tries to be organic is that of the FARC and the EPL, whose incorporation project includes an effort to represent the peasants and lead their struggles" (60).

24. A rich portrait of the FARC's role in the colonizing zone of Caquetá is Jaime Eduardo Jaramillo, Leonidas Mora, and Fernando Cubides, *Colonización, coca y guerrilla* (Bogotá: Alianza Editorial Colombiana, 1989).

5

Mexico: The Perils of Unity and the Challenge of Modernization

Barry Carr

In October 1968 the army's bloody suppression of the student-popular movement led most sectors of the fragmented and weak Mexican Left to campaign for electoral abstention in protest against presidential despotism and the antidemocracy of the ruling Partido Revolucionario Institucional (Institutional Revolutionary party—PRI). Small sections of the Communist Youth and groups of radicalized Christians embraced a futile campaign of armed struggle. Twenty years later, however, in the July 1988 presidential elections, a Center-Left coalition led by Cuauhtémoc Cárdenas (son of Mexico's nationalist president of the 1930s) came close to defeating the PRI. A Center-Left coalition incorporating dissidents from the ruling PRI now emerged as the second largest political force in the country, displacing the conservative Partido de Acción Nacional (National Action party—PAN), traditionally the PRI's most important opposition. However, in the period since the election the Left, and in particular its major organizational focus, the Partido de la Revolución Democrática (Party of the Democratic Revolution—PRD), has been unable to consolidate the gains of 1988 and confront the many challenges posed by the neoliberal project of the government of Carlos Salinas de Gortari (1988–).

Portions of this chapter draw heavily on my chapter "The Left and Its Potential Role in Political Change" in Wayne A. Cornelius, Judith Gentleman, and Peter H. Smith, eds., *Mexico's Alternative Political Futures* (La Jolla: Center for U.S.-Mexican Studies, University of California, San Diego 1989).

The transactional environment within which the Left operates is partly to blame. Whereas a degree of democratization (more accurately civilianization) has occurred elsewhere in Latin America, political change has been blocked in Mexico. The neoliberal economic policies of the Salinas government reject the corporatist and statist traditions of post-1940s Mexico while at the same time modernizing and preserving the authoritarian character of the political system that sustains the PRI's monopoly of power. A new electoral code has recently strengthened the PRI's position and has done little to minimize electoral fraud—the "political alchemy" of Mexican folklore.

The biggest long-term challenge to the Left is posed by the deepening integration of the Mexican and U.S. economies signaled by the proposal that Mexico join the North American Free Trade Agreement. The enthusiastic embrace of the concept by the Salinas government suggests that the technocratic managers of the official party (as well as their strong supporters in the Bush administration) see the NAFTA as the key to stabilizing the PRI-dominated regime. Building closer political alliances with the United States will necessarily erode what remains of the economic and political nationalism bequeathed by the revolutionary nationalist tradition that has shaped much of the Left's strategic orientation.

The Transformation of the Left

The changes in the map of the Left need to be considered against the background of the political and economic shocks delivered to the postwar Mexican model of development during the past twenty years. The 1970s and 1980s witnessed the exhaustion of Mexico's model of "stabilizing development." The student-popular movement of 1968 and its bloody repression by the government of Gustavo Díaz Ordaz (1964–1970) delivered a massive shock to the Mexican political system, a shock that was followed in the mid- and late 1970s by a rising curve of worker militancy linked to a resurgent independent trade unionism. Moreover, the official party of the Mexican Revolution, the PRI, showed growing signs of sclerosis, and a disturbing trend toward electoral abstentionism began to accelerate.

The 1970s and 1980s also produced growing inflation, a burgeoning foreign debt, high interest rates, and balance-of-payments deficits. The crisis of 1976–1977 introduced a series of economic stabilization programs that mounted a sharp attack on the real wages and living standards of working Mexicans. The massive development of Mexico's petroleum reserves softened the blows for a while, but by the beginning of 1982 petroleum prices had begun to decline. This event, combined with an international liquidity crisis and Mexico's huge foreign debt, produced an economic debacle of formidable proportions.

These economic and political difficulties opened up new options for the Mexican Left and created important breaches in the corporatist system of domination. The Mexican state responded with initiatives designed to relegitimate the ruling party and weaken radical opposition by channeling it in an electoral direction. The *apertura democrática* (democratic opening) of President Luis Echeverría (1970–1976) involved the selective release of political prisoners, the incorporation of political dissidents into the state administration, and attempts to accentuate the Third Worldist features of Mexico's foreign policy.

The most important of the state's responses, however, was the political reform of 1976–1977, initiated by the Echeverría administration but implemented during the first year of the presidency of José López Portillo (1976–1982). Under the political reform legislation, the Partido Comunista Mexicano (Mexican Communist party—PCM) obtained its official registration as a political party, and in 1979 it legally participated in elections for the first time since 1948.

The political "earthquake" of 1988, therefore, was the culmination of more than fifteen years of major developments in which the map of the Mexican Left underwent a drastic transformation. Moves to unify the Left, initially driven by electoral concerns, led to the formation of a series of multiparty electoral coalitions, forced the dissolution in 1981 of the Mexican Communist party, Mexico's oldest leftist organization, and gave birth to a number of broad Left "successor" parties—the Partido Socialista Unificado de México (Unified Socialist party of Mexico—PSUM) in 1981, the Partido Mexicano Socialista (Mexican Socialist party—PMS) in March 1987, and the Partido de la Revolución Democrática in 1989.

But the transformation of the Left involved more than changes to the political "alphabet soup." Even more important was the appearance of new sensibilities and ways of expressing political awareness through art, literature, and popular culture. Parallel with these developments was the emergence of new associational forms linked to a variety of projects that were critical of postwar capitalism. The working class and the peasantry, traditionally viewed as the natural subjects of the Left, were joined in the 1970s and 1980s by new urban social movements and coalitions. Class was now just one of many constructs around which the Left and the popular movements coalesced. Community, place of residence, religiosity, and gender also become powerful mobilizing forces.

New grass-roots social movements emerged, especially in urban areas, and a series of networking organizations or *coordinadoras*—the earliest and best-known being the Coordinadora Nacional del Movimiento Urbano

Popular (Coordinating Committee of the Urban Popular Movement—CONAMUP), founded in 1981—sprang up. What became known as the urban popular movement received a further boost in the aftermath of the September 1985 earthquake, when the impotence and corruption exhibited by the state in the face of the disaster gave birth to a second wave of popular organizations. The activities of the Coordinadora Unica de Damnificados (Coordinating Body of Earthquake Victims—CUD), for example, and later the Neighborhoods Assembly—founded in 1987 and linked to the spectacularly effective work of the hooded and masked "Superbarrio Gómez," a Superman with class consciousness—have become symbols of the rebirth of civil society.[1]

Challenges to the corporatist style and practice of the PRI and its affiliated mass organizations also produced new peasant groups such as the Coordinadora Nacional "Plan de Ayala" (National Plan of Ayala Coordinating Body—CNPA), launched in 1979 with the encouragement of Mateo Zapata (the son of the peasant revolutionary). In the urban labor sector the best-known of the new coordinadoras was the Coordinadora Nacional de Trabajadores de la Educación (National Coordinating Body of Educational Workers—CNTE), which became a powerful site of mass resistance to the corrupt leadership of Mexico's largest (750,000 strong) trade union, the Sindicato Nacional de Trabajadores de la Educación (National Union of Educational Workers—SNTE). The latest wave of coordinadoras (prominent examples are the National Coordinating Body of Indian Peoples and the Emiliano Zapata Union of Comuneros) has developed among indigenous peoples, an area in which the political, union, and social-movement Left has been notoriously absent.

While the new social movement protagonists (impoverished urban dwellers or *colonos*, students, university workers, poor peasants) clearly form part of the Left, ideologically they are very diverse, drawing on anarchist and syndicalist traditions, prophetic-revolutionary Christianity, and Maoist-tinged populism ("learn from the people"). During the early 1980s, from these last two tendencies sprang such organizations as the Organización de Izquierda Revolucionaria–Línea de Masas (Revolutionary Left Organization–Mass Line—OIR-LM), the Movimiento Revolucionario del Pueblo (People's Revolutionary Movement—MRP), and the Línea Proletaria (Proletarian Line—LP), all three of which were active on such fronts as the mine-workers' and teachers' unions, struggles for the democratization of municipalities, and collectivist and cooperative experiments among the urban poor in several areas (including Colonia "Tierra y Libertad" in Monterrey, Colonia "Rubén Jaramillo" in Morelos, and Campamento "2 de Octubre" in the Federal District).

The coordinadoras and the urban popular movement, concerned more with the politics of reproduction and consumption than with the more traditional "classist" issues of production, certainly opened up fertile terrain for struggle, but they also posed major challenges to the forces of the more traditional Left. Although some of the organizations incorporated activists from socialist parties (the dissident teachers in the CNTE, for example, attracted a number of cadres schooled in Maoism and Maoist populism), many of the newer groups were suspicious of and sometimes hostile to the involvement of the traditional parties of the Left. Their suspicions were fueled by bitter memories of the way in which the Left had sometimes subordinated the concerns and needs of specific movements to the interests and goals of its own organizations.

This newer Left also argued that some of the new spaces (municipalities, for example) were more promising terrain for its activities because they had not been so heavily colonized by bureaucratized union structures and organs of the state. This municipal orientation occasionally facilitated the development of broad coalitions (*frentes de masas*) of Left parties and local and regional grass-roots organizations that have helped smooth some of the tensions between the older "party Left" and the newer tendencies, with their ultraradical political style and discourse. The best-known example of a frente de masas in action was the alliance between the Coalición Obrera-Campesina-Estudiantil del Istmo (Worker-Peasant-Student Coalition of the Isthmus—COCEI) and the PSUM, which in 1981 won a short-lived municipal victory in Juchitán, the second city of Oaxaca state.[2]

Alongside these organizational changes has come a major alteration in the strategic orientation and style of the Left. The past weighs heavily on all the participants in the Mexican political game. Over the years the major Left currents have not only uncritically assimilated a series of imported and often deformed socialist models but also, more than they are prepared to admit, replicated many of the antidemocratic traditions of the official party. Nevertheless, slowly and unevenly but with growing self-confidence, the Mexican Left has begun to discard the most backward aspects of its heritage. It has embraced the logic of unity, moved away from sectarian positions and, to a much lesser extent, personalist rivalries, and tried to forge a distinctively Mexican socialist agenda. The Left has also begun to accept that socialism requires not only a change in property relations but also the transformation of social relations in a democratic direction.

Central to the overall revision of the Left's strategy (at least until the late 1980s) was the contention that the Mexican Revolution had finally exhausted its progressive potential. As a result the Left, led by the now-dissolved Mexican Communist party, finally abandoned its illusions about the possibility of transforming the PRI and pushing it to the left. The rejection of the conception of "vanguard party" was another significant development that led to moves to unify the fragmented collection of Left parties. The new opening took a number of forms. In 1976, for example, the PCM forged a tactical electoral alliance with the major Trotskyist party, the Partido Revolucionario de los Trabajadores (Workers' Revolutionary party—PRT). Later, the PCM formed a programmatic alliance with a number of other small left-wing parties and groupings sympathetic to the Mexican Communists' style. This initiative resulted in the creation of the Coalition of the Left in 1979. Led by the PCM, the Coalition received three quarters of a million votes in the congressional elections and won eighteen seats in the Chamber of Deputies.

The demand for Left unity eventually embraced calls for the formation of a single party of the socialist Left. The attempt to forge such a party began in the 1980s, when the Communist party dissolved itself and, together with some former satellite parties, established the PSUM in 1981 and later the PMS in 1987.[3] On the eve of the 1988 presidential elections the map of the Left looked like this:

The independent Left consisted of parties or movements that did not depend on state subsidies and political largesse. They supported the independence of mass organizations of workers, peasants, and agricultural laborers and embraced political and economic policies that challenged both neoliberal economic programs and the populist and corporatist heritage that formed part of the Left's ideological baggage from the 1930s until the Cuban Revolution. This independent Left was represented by the PMS, various Trotskyist organizations of which the largest was the PRT, and the rapidly proliferating regional and local frentes and social movements such as the Comité de Defensa Popular (Popular Defense Committee—CDP) in Chihuahua, the COCEI in Juchitán, and the Colonia "Tierra y Libertad" in Monterrey.

The largest grouping within the independent Left was the PMS. Its style and the policies it articulated maintained and deepened the principal characteristics with which the independent Left (the PCM and the PSUM, for example) had come to be associated since the mid-1970s—greater openness to the notion of Left unity, a commitment to seeking indigenous solutions to problems, and a preparedness to dialogue with progressive sectors of the PRI. On the negative side, the formation of the PMS resembled the creation of earlier umbrella parties (such as the PSUM) in several other ways. For example, negotiations about the merger process tended to take place at the level of national leaderships, with limited grass-roots participation.

The PMS announced its intention to adjust its brand of socialism to Mexican traditions and to underline the indissoluble ties between democracy and pluralism, on the one hand, and its socialist goals, on the other. This meant an abandonment of some elements of the Left's traditional baggage—for example, a final rejection of democratic centralism and a strong critique of statism. It also involved the acceptance of a mixed economy and regulated foreign investment, the development of good relations with the United States, and the now-obligatory rejection of "foreign socialist models."

The PMS reaffirmed some positions that had been rejected by certain sectors of the Left during the 1980s—the commitment to political rights for the clergy being one example. It now began to conform to the vision of a "Mexicanized" and pragmatic party of the kind that left-wing nationalists such as Heberto Castillo, an influential engineer and activist, had long demanded.

The PMS and later its successor, the PRD, also made substantial if somewhat uneven progress toward democratizing its own structure and processes. In September 1987, for example, it had organized primaries to select the party's presidential candidate in an attempt to show up the authoritarian methods that the PRI used to "uncork" its chosen candidate and to deepen grass-roots participation. In order to underline its claim to represent a broad swath of progressive opinion, the PMS even allowed nonmembers to vote in the primary.

The "loyal Left" or "satellite Left" comprised parties that, in spite of the dogmatic Marxist and Marxist-Leninist rhetoric on certain issues exhibited by some of its constituents, such as the Partido Popular Socialista (Popular Socialist party—PPS), have subordinated their action and electoral politics to the PRI. Ideologically, this segment of the Left combines an ossified Marxism (and even Stalinism) with a continuing belief in the progressive and socialist potential of the Mexican Revolution.

The "loyal Left" has limited tactical independence in the political arena and has normally supported the PRI's presidential candidate in national elections in return for financial support and, sometimes, an officially engineered inflation of its vote in elections.[4] The best-known representatives of this current are the PPS and the Partido Frente Cardenista para la Reconstrucción Nacional (Party of the Cárdenas Front for National Reconstruction—PFCRN), surely one of the most opportunistic examples of party naming in Mexican history.

The Political Earthquake of 1988

Although the drive for unification, internal democratization, and a serious engagement with electoral politics were positive developments, other parts of the Left's heritage took longer to jettison. There were continuing problems with caudillismo—a tendency to see parties as an extension of the personality of particular individuals. Moreover, within the new umbrella or "successor" parties to the old PCM "party patriotism" was slow to disappear. At the same time, the Mexican state had lost none of its skills in dividing and co-opting sections of the Left. The PRI continued covertly to sponsor, reward, and electorally register new parties of the Left, so that by the late 1980s there were more self-styled socialist parties represented in the Mexican Congress than in any other Latin American legislature. Also, some of the Left's hopes with regard to urban popular movements were dashed in the 1980s. Some analysts and activists concluded that movements that are concerned with quotidian struggles cannot articulate theory and practice capable of democratizing the broader national political culture. Many urban social movements were still trapped in webs of clientelism and patrimonialism and easily fell prey to the government's strategy of signing agreements and entering into dialogues.[5]

But it was the 1988 elections and the preelection mobilizations that most radically modified the new composition of the Left and forced a reevaluation of some of the changes introduced during the preceding decade. The appearance of a Left critical current within the PRI and its subsequent split from the ruling party introduced a radically new element into the calculus. The neo-cardenistas who abandoned ship in 1987–1988 posed several challenges to the independent Left. In particular, their mobilizing capacity seemed to demonstrate the continuing vitality of a discourse that appealed to elements of the ideology of the Mexican Revolution and thereby challenged one of the Left's major gains of the 1968–1988 period—its declaration of independence from the populism and nationalism of that tradition.

The Neo-Cardenistas

Revolutionary nationalism has for a long time been part of the intellectual and political baggage of progressive members of the PRI and of large sections of the Mexican Left, especially parties in the satellite group discussed above. In mid-1986 a number of leading figures within the revolutionary nationalist current of the PRI formed a pressure group to press for a democratic modernization of the official party. The Corriente Democrática (Democratic Current—CD), as it was called, was the nucleus around which the Center-Left challenge to the PRI was mounted in 1988.[6]

The CD is very difficult to locate politically. For some of its adherents it was simply the "the Left of the PRI," and its members saw themselves as convinced priistas as far as the ideological program of the official party was concerned.[7] Porfirio Muñoz Ledo, a major CD figure, characterized the coalition built around Cuauhtémoc Cárdenas as a "populist-nationalist current of the Mexican Revolution—but we do not stand for socialism."[8] The CD and its leading propagandists did not indeed define themselves as socialist. Time and time again Cuauhtémoc Cárdenas insisted that he was simply calling for the effective implementation of the precepts of the 1917 constitution.

However, the platform of the CD and of its electoral coalition, the Frente Democrático Nacional, involved more than just a restatement of the classic slogans of economic and political sovereignty and support for self-determination and nonintervention in foreign policy outlined in the 1917 constitution. It included calls for an end to presidentialism (echoing the positions of socialist Left parties such as the PMS) and the abandonment of electoral corruption and manipulation.[9] The directing authority of the state in economic matters was reaffirmed, and there was an explicit rejection of many of the features of the neoliberal economic model. The neo-cardenistas all saw the internal market as the engine of economic activity. Finally, they strongly supported calls for the independence of worker and peasant organizations and a break with the authoritarianism, *caciquismo* (bossism), and vertical power relations that have disempowered working people.[10]

The campaign appeal of neo-cardenismo was very striking. Almost overnight, an independent mass movement of impressive size and national character had arisen in Mexico. In its long history, the independent Left had never been able to mobilize the population to this degree.[11] Even more remarkable was the extent to which neo-cardenismo attracted the support of sectors of the socialist Left that were normally suspicious of, if not openly hostile to, the cardenista legacy of revolutionary nationalism because of its reputation for crude populism and political opportunism. There is no more striking example of this phenomenon than the embrace of the cardenista drive by a number of leading Trotskyists who considered the mass mobilizations around the Cárdenas campaign a springboard for socialist politics and a sign of the disintegration of the corporatist structures in place since the late 1930s. In another indication of the hold that neo-cardenismo has on the Left the FDN also won the support of several former guerrilla organizations, including the Guerrero-based Revolutionary National Civic Association founded by Genaro Vásquez in the late 1960s.

The official results of the July 1988 elections gave Cárdenas 31.29 percent of the presidential vote (with a bare majority of 50.03 percent to the PRI), but there was evidence of massive fraud. The Center-Left emerged as the second-largest political force in Mexico, with acknowledged majorities in such key areas as the Federal District. A closer examination of the election results, however, reveals a more complex picture. The big losers in the 1988 elections were the parties of the independent Left (the PMS and the PRT). The percentage of the total vote cast for the PMS (3.57 percent) actually fell slightly in comparison with the 1982 presidential elections (3.84 percent). The satellite or loyal Left, however, was massively rewarded. The PPS saw its vote increase from 1.53 percent in 1982 to 10.53 percent, while that of the PFCRN rose equally dramatically from 1.43 percent to 10.51 percent.

The impressive performance of the FDN coalition and the size of the satellite Left's vote could be seen as proof that revolutionary nationalism was the only consistent and vital current within the Mexican socialist tradition and certainly the only current capable of mobilizing successive generations of students, professionals, and skilled workers. If this is the case, in the short run at least, the rise of neo-cardenismo involves a repudiation of attempts to establish a clear separation between the socialist agenda and the ideology of the Mexican Revolution.

One must also ask whether the large vote for the FDN was in any sense a vote for the Left. The nearly six million votes cast for Cuauhtémoc Cárdenas certainly represented a protest against the neoliberal strategy of modernization. It would be wrong, however, to label the neo-cardenista phenomenon merely a negative vote. The growing involvement of the independent Left in the cardenista mobilizations provided excellent opportunities for advancing debate beyond the narrow limits of revolutionary nationalism.

Into the 1990s

In the past three years the unification process that created the FDN electoral coalition and the PRD (founded the year after the 1988 elections) has faltered. Of the parties that formed the FDN, only the old PMS and the cardenistas joined the PRD. The satellite PPS remained outside, and the PFCRN also quickly dropped out.

This rapid disintegration has many causes. The PRD does not seem to have been able to make the jump from being a conjunctural coalition of anti-PRI forces to creating an organically new political force. Its leaders, and in particular the figures around Cuauhtémoc Cárdenas, have been accused of caudillismo. Although this is probably an unfair characterization of the leadership style, there is no doubt that the enormous personal popularity, appeal, and prestige of Cárdenas have encouraged an uneasy centralization of authority in the party.

The new party's fragility is also partly a function of the character of the PRD itself, an amalgam of different tendencies hegemonized by the neo-cardenistas, most of whom are imprisoned in a discourse of uncompromising anti-*priismo* that has at times been prepared to envisage a violent break with the system. Cárdenas himself after July 1988 denounced the elections as a "technical coup d'état."[12] Some sectors of the Left have even accused the PRD of encouraging or not restraining popular mobilizations of party rank and file that threatened violence. The ongoing debates between different tendencies within the PRD was brought to the surface in December 1990 with the resignation of Jorge Alcocer, who represents a group of former Communists and social democrats open to the possibility of dialogue proposed by President Salinas. Alcocer accused Cárdenas of excessive confrontationalism designed to further his electoral ambitions, antidemocracy, intolerance, and authoritarianism.[13]

There is also a problem with the party's definition of its relationship to Left projects. It is certainly not a socialist party. According to its secretary of organization Saúl Escobar Toledo, the PRD identifies with social democracy and has applied for membership of the Socialist International.[14] Finally, repression continues to weaken the Left; fifty of the party's members have been killed and more than five hundred injured in the short period since the PRD was formed.

The PRD's Electoral Performance

Superficially, the PRD's organic development has been impressive. At the PRD's first national congress (November 1990), Cárdenas claimed that the party had 1,730,000 members, of whom 900,000 had joined during the period November 1989–November 1990. The PRD claimed control of 118 municipalities (with the exception of Morelia, most of them were very small) and minority representation in another 680. The party had 63 deputies in local congresses, 4 senators, and 54 federal deputies (out of 500) in the national congress.[15] These figures should be compared with the 140 deputies that the parties of the pro-Cárdenas coalition won in the July 1988 elections, when it still included several parties of the satellite Left.

Given that the PRD has placed so much importance on electoral mobilizations, its poor performance on the hustings has been a shock. To some extent this outcome can be explained by the PRI's ever more sophisticated use of fraud. A recognition that the struggle for democracy and against fraud required the forging of broad tactical alliances with all antiregime forces had led the PRD to sign a national agreement for democracy with a number of groups, including the rightist PAN, in early 1991. Thus far, however, the results have been poor. The national leadership of the PAN has made deals with the Salinas administration, and it is only at the state level that antiregime pacts have worked—as in the state of San Luis Potosí, where the PRD, the PAN, and even the far-right PDM (Mexican Democratic Party) came together to support a long-established political crusader, Salvador Nava, in the August 1991 gubernatorial elections.

The Left's electoral decline culminated in the PRD's disappointing performance in the mid-term congressional elections of August 1991, but those results had already been anticipated in a series of local elections for state governors and the renewal of state legislatures. In the northwestern state of Baja California, for example, where Cárdenas won 37 percent of the total vote in the 1988 presidential elections (Baja California being one of five states and territories in which the anti-PRI opposition came first even in the official figures), the PRD vote had fallen to 6 percent by the time gubernatorial elections were held the following year. It was clear that in the absence of an effective and relevant Left option, a large part of the pro-Cárdenas vote moved swiftly over to the rightist PAN. Two years later the internal elections (open also to the general public) that chose the PRD's candidate for the senate seat of Baja California for the midterm 1991 elections attracted only thirteen hundred voters, a mere 1 percent of the votes captured by the Center-Left in 1988.[16]

In the ardently cardenista state of Michoacán, another even more important center of the Left with the largest number of PRD state legislature deputies, town councilmen, and federal deputies in the country, the municipal and state legislative elections of 1989 substantially reduced the PRD's representation. In this case the impact of fraud was amplified by the party's difficulties in delivering promised benefits to its supporters, a familiar problem facing the strategists of municipal socialism in a country where the penury of local government is so marked.

In the Federal District, where the FDN did best of all in 1988 (winning 72.4 percent of all votes cast), the situation seemed unlikely to be repeated. In 1988 the Left had gained votes from disaffected *priistas* (21 percent), *panistas* (19 percent), and former abstentionists or new voters (44 percent)—in other words, a very unstable blend of support.[17] A return to abstentionism was predicted for the 1991 elections in the Federal District as had already happened in the Mexico State elections a few months before. The early signs were certainly not good. The PRD's internal "primary" to select a senate candidate attracted only twenty-five thousand voters.[18]

Against the background of these disappointing events, the poor performance of the Left in the congressional elections of August 1991 is not so surprising. The PRD gained only forty-one seats (down from fifty-four) and the satellite Left thirty-five. The Trotskyist PRT once again lost its electoral registration, as did the newly formed Green party and the Labor party, the latest in a long line of leftist parties with close ties to the PRI. The PRI, meanwhile, seems to have recovered its nerve (and some of its support). Its two-thirds majority in the Chamber of Deputies will enable it to push through the constitutional amendments (modification of the status of the *ejido* [collective property], reforms to the labor code, etc.) that Mexico's impending incorporation into the NAFTA will require.

Clearly, the electoral gamble of the independent Left has not yet paid off. The PRD has been unable to break down widespread public cynicism and the long-standing tendency to see all political action (including that of the Left) as tainted by corruption, demagoguery, and struggles among rival *camarillas* (clans). But perhaps the greatest failure of the Left has been its inability to incorporate into its strategy and practice the concerns that spring from the massively changed conditions of the lives (in workplaces, homes, and urban environments) of ordinary Mexicans. Thus a particularly disturbing omission in the Left's performance so far has been its failure to move beyond mere protest and translate anti-PRI sentiment into actions in the labor and peasant arena that challenge the traditional power relations of corporatism. The great popular mobilizations that accompanied the 1988 presidential campaign certainly aroused the enthusiasm of millions of workers, peasants, and middle-sector activists—what one author has recently labeled "a civic-electoral insurrection."[19] But the energy they unleashed was channeled largely into the electoral fight and into protests against the "antipopular" consequences of government economic policy rather than into the creation of *new* organizational forms that could promote empowerment and deepen the newly won self-confidence of the disenfranchised.

If the Left is to maintain the momentum it exhibited in 1987–1988, it must, therefore, intensify its efforts to intersect labor and peasant organizations as well as the new social movements. Here the Left, as we have already seen, faces a number of problems. It will have to overcome deeply rooted suspicion concerning political parties' involvement in the affairs of unions and popular organizations. The Left has a long way to go to dispel fears that political parties view their union and mass-movement cadres as conveyor belts for party directives. It also faces the dilemma of how to gain a presence in the unions and social movements without provoking a violent response by the state. Mexican governments have always blocked moves by the Left to gain a foothold in the organizations that form the base of the corporatist structure.

The big challenge for the independent Left is to come up with a definition of modernization that defies the conservative agenda of the PRI and its conservative opponents without returning uncritically to the shibboleths of an unreconstructed cardenismo—crude statism, populism, and the restoration of the authority and prestige of the increasingly displaced *oficialista* (state-supported) mass organizations such as the Confederación de Trabajadores de México (Confederation of Mexican Workers—CTM) and the Confederación Nacional Campesina (National Confederation of Peasants—CNC).

This is a major challenge because the revolutionary nationalist and populist Left that is so strongly represented in the PRD (especially among the neo-cardenistas) has not confronted its own traditions with the same reforming zeal as have some of the Marxists who joined with them to form the new party. As we have seen, certain features of the old corporatist system were clearly rejected in the discourse of the cardenistas. But the men and women of the CD are, when all is said and done, authentic children of the PRI and they will have to struggle hard to break out of the straitjacket represented by the dream of a revived corporatism that some of them, especially those with strong ties to the labor sector, still harbor.

The extent of the neo-cardenistas' ties to the corporatist labor system and its most regressive features was eloquently revealed during the first month of the new presidential term. When the Salinas government mounted a violent assault on the labor czar of the Sindicato de Trabajadores Petroleros Mexicanos (Oil Workers Union—STPRM), Joaquín (La Quina) Hernández Galicia, arresting him on weapons charges in mid-January 1989, it was clear that for the first time in the labor history of modern Mexico a *charro* had fallen victim to a *charrazo*![20] Cárdenas and his supporters criticized the move, branding it a blatant intervention in the internal affairs of a major union, which was certainly the case, and an assault on an authentically nationalist labor figure, a much more dubious claim. The government's move against the STPRM leadership not only exposed the cardenistas' debt to a union that had reputedly helped finance the FDN's election campaign but also produced a damaging split within the independent Left. Part of the leadership of the PMS condemned the government's moves against Hernández, while an influential group of socialist intellectuals and labor movement figures publicly disassociated itself from any action that defended one of the most arbitrary and antidemocratic labor fiefdoms in Mexico.[21]

Challenges and Opportunities

In spite of the generally disappointing electoral results of the past few years, the events of the late 1980s and early 1990s demonstrated that the Mexican Left is learning from its mistakes. A significant development has been the decision by a number of urban social movements to modify and in some cases abandon their previous policy of electoral abstention and shunning of parties and national organizations of the Left. The major breakthrough here occurred in the mobilizations that preceded the 1988 elections, when thousands of social movements moved from isolated civic protests to a national civic insurrection in support of the Cárdenas candidacy. In Mexico City, for example, the powerful Neighborhoods Assembly entered the fray in support of the FDN. This trend was continued in the 1991 congressional elections, when, as one campaigner in the sprawling "lost city" of Nezahualcóyotl north of Mexico City explained to a North American researcher, "people's desire to exercise and defend their vote is as strong as their desire for water, housing, or services."[22]

The 1991 elections also saw the establishment of much more significant ties between the women's movement and the independent Left. The formation of the Women's Convention for Democracy in early 1991, for example, was accompanied by a decision to develop a cross-party strategy in which the Convention selected thirty candidates whose sponsorship was then to be negotiated with the various opposition forces.[23]

It is on the economic front, however, that the independent Left has experienced most difficulties.[24] Often, the Left has limited its intervention to oppositional rhetoric or nostalgic repetition of slogans from the statist and populist repertoire and has been unable to offer a coherent response to the economic project of the Salinas government. The state's obsession with deregulation and sell-offs of public enterprises has been fiercely and in most cases correctly contested, but neither the Center-Left (such as the PRD) nor the older Marxist Left (such as the PRT) has devoted much effort to thinking through how socialists might exploit issues such as privatization and antistatism to promote democratic and noncorrupt forms of social and economic organization in production.

The disorientation of the Left on economic issues grew as certain indicators began to show signs of improvement during the first two years of the new decade; the 1991 inflation rate, for example, was about 20 percent compared with the heady 170 percent registered in 1987, and government revenues have boomed with the massive drive toward privatization. The problem has been compounded by the appearance of divisions within the grass-roots Left and some national Left parties over whether to accept dialogue (*concertación*) with the state and the material resources offered under the National Solidarity Program or preserve at all costs the popular movements' autonomy from the state.

The Left is also divided over whether to reject the integrationist project of the Salinas government or work within current NAFTA proposals. There have been demands for an alternative model of economic integration that rejects Mexico's assigned role under NAFTA as a permanent supplier of cheap labor power as well as calls for an expansion of the project to embrace the entire Latin American region.[25] But so far these are rhetorical wish lists and yearnings for a renewed model of economic nationalism. They do not demonstrate a serious commitment to grappling with the painful fact that an ever-more-dominant and unitary international financial system makes the notion of independent capitalist (let alone socialist) development very problematic.[26]

However, while the Left has been unable to specify concretely how its economic vision can be translated into a viable program of action under current conditions, the actual *practice* of old and new Lefts is already showing signs of creative responses to the challenge posed by projects of regional economic integration. There is now greater continental consultation between left-wing parties; in June 1991, for example, representatives from sixty-eight Left parties in Latin America met in Mexico City under the sponsorship of the PRD.[27]

At a more grass-roots level, the NAFTA concept has spawned a series of developments that could greatly accelerate the creation of horizontal relations between labor, community, ecological, and political activists and their organizations across national borders. This can already be seen in the automotive industry (where Mexican, U.S., and Canadian automobile unions in the Ford empire have intensified exchanges during 1990 and 1991), in the dramatic emergence of cross-border discussion and organization by progressive groups concerned with the impact of the NAFTA, and in the deepening of the PRD's lobbying and organizational efforts in the United States among the Anglo and Latino populations.[28]

It may very well be that the development of these binational and even trinational links will partly compensate for the erosion of the Left's "socialist identity" over the last three years. But with most of the Marxist Left in dissolution and the PRD's relationship to socialist objectives barely discernible, it is increasingly difficult to give a clear answer to the question "What is left of the Mexican Left?"

Notes

1. "Superbarrio: Bane of the Landlords, Defender of Poor Tenants," *The Other Side of Mexico*, 3 (October–December 1987):3–4; "Superbarrio: We Didn't Make the Border, We Don't Want the Border," *The Other Side of Mexico*, 9 (March–April 1989):1–2.

2. On Juchitán, see Jeffrey W. Rubin, "State Policies, Leftist Oppositions, and Municipal Elections: The Case of the COCEI in Juchitán," in Arturo Alvarado, ed., *Electoral Patterns and Perspectives in Mexico* (La Jolla: Center for U.S.-Mexican Studies, 1987), 127–160.

3. For developments on the Mexican Left during the 1970s and 1980s see Barry Carr and Ricardo Anzaldúa Montoya, eds., *The Mexican Left, the Popular Movements, and the Politics of Austerity* (La Jolla: Center for US-Mexican Studies, University of California, San Diego, 1986); Barry Carr, "The PSUM: The Unification Process on the Mexican Left, 1981–1985," in Judith Gentleman, ed., *Mexican Politics in Transition* (Boulder: Westview Press, 1987), 281–304.

4. For example, Rafael Aguilar Talamantes, a leader of the PFCRN, has admitted that his party received funds from the PRI before 1987.

5. Judith Adler Hellman, "Mexican Popular Movements and the Process of Democratization: Is There a Link?," paper presented to the Latin American Studies Association conference, Washington, DC, April 4–6, 1991.

6. The formation of the Corriente Democrática can be traced back to a series of discussions in mid-1986 held by some twenty-five PRI figures in Mexico and overseas, where some of the *priistas* were serving as ambassadors (among them Porfirio Muñoz Ledo, who was ambassador to the UN, and Rodolfo González Guevara, who was ambassador to Spain). "The Democratic Current: A New Era in Mexican Politics: Interviews by Andrew Reding," *World Policy Journal*, 5, 2 (Spring 1988):323–366.

7. Martínez proudly noted in May 1988 that the members of the Democratic Current left the PRI only because the party had shifted so much to the right. José Luis Gaona Vega, "Somos priistas convencidos de ideología y programa," *Punto*, May 9, 1988, 11.

8. Reding, "The Democratic Current," 35.

9. The first item on the PMS electoral program deals with "presidentialism—obstacle for democracy." *PMS: Plataforma Electoral*, 5. On the peculiarity of Mexican presidentialism, see Luis Javier Garrido, "The Crisis of Presidencialismo," in Wayne A. Cornelius, Judith Gentleman, and Peter H. Smith, eds., *Mexico's Alternative Political Futures* (La Jolla: Center for U.S.-Mexican Studies, University of California, San Diego, 1989), 417–434.

10. Trejo, *Punto*, May 2, 1988, 8; *La Jornada*, April 6, 1988, 32; May 2, 1988, 11; *Excelsior*, May 12, 1989, 4, 14.

11. The enthusiastic analyses of the neo-cardenista phenomenon written by the Trotskyist Adolfo Gilly reflect the awe felt by much of the socialist Left. See, for example, "Cartucho quemado," *La Jornada*, May 23, 1988, 1.

12. Adolfo Gilly, "El perfil del PRD," *Nexos*, 152 (August 1990):63.

13. *Latin America Regional Report, Mexico-Central America*, February 21, 1991:6.

14. Osvaldo León, "PRD: Democracy, Country for Every One," *The Other Side of Mexico*, 18 (September–December 1990):8–9.

15. "Cuauhtémoc Cárdenas' Political Message in the Opening Session of the First Congress of the PRD," *The Other Side of Mexico*, 18 (September–December 1990):9.

16. Gustavo Hirales M., "Baja California: El siguiente experimento," *Cuadernos de Nexos*, 36 (June 1991):xix–xx.

17. Guadalupe Pacheco Méndez, "La batalla por el Distrito Federal," *Cuadernos de Nexos*, 36 (June 1991):viii.

18. Luis Salazar C., "PRI y PRD: El show del enfrentamiento," *Cuadernos de Nexos*, 36 (June 1991):v–vi.

19. Alberto Aziz Nassif, "Regional Dimensions of Democratization," in Cornelius, Gentleman, and Smith, *Mexico's Alternative Political Futures*.

20. The term *charro* (cowboy) has been used to designate the corrupt and antidemocratic trade unionism practiced by much of the "official" trade union leadership ever since the more militant national industrial unions were "tamed" by the state in the late 1940s and early 1950s (during the so-called *charrazos* against the oil, railroad, and mining unions).

21. The veteran railway workers' leader Valentín Campa was particularly outspoken in his criticism of the arrest of the oil union leaders. For a characteristically sharp criticism of the Left's failure to disassociate itself from the authoritarianism of the union bureaucracy, see Roger Bartra, "Nacionalismo, democracia y socialismo: Invitación a la polémica," *La Jornada Semanal*, 84 (January 20, 1991):35–37.

22. Elaine Burns, "Mexico's PRI Wins Bid to Ensure that Change Continues," Peacenet: Carnet Mexnews.

23. *Mexico Insight*, October 28, 1991.

24. A representative sample of the PRD's thinking on economic issues can be seen in the party's fortnightly magazine *Coyuntura*. See, for example, the special issue entitled *1990: Situación nacional (balance y propuestas)*.

25. Cuauhtémoc Cárdenas, "TLC: Una propuesta alternativa," *Nexos*, 162 (June 1991): 51–55.

26. Bartra, "Nacionalismo, democracia y socialismo," 41–43.

27. The first such meeting was held in 1990 under the auspices of the Brazilian PT. *Latin America Weekly Report*, WR 91-24 (June 17, 1991):12; Victor Quintana, "The Popular Summit of the Americas," *The Other Side of Mexico*, 17 (July–August 1990):6–8.

28. Apart from Cárdenas himself, the most active international lobbyists of the PRD have been Jorge Castañeda and Adolfo Aguilar Zinser. Luis Javier Garrido, interview, Mexico City, February 19, 1991. There have been meetings between Canadian and Mexican unions as in the First Mexico-Canada Encounter: "Social Organizations and Free Trade," in October 1990. See "Mexico-Canada: Common Borders," *The Other Side of Mexico*, 18 (September–December 1990):1–2.

6

Armed Struggle and Popular Resistance in El Salvador: The Struggle for Peace

Tommie Sue Montgomery

On December 31, 1991, the Frente Farabundo Martí para la Liberación Nacional and the government of El Salvador reached agreement to end a civil war that had raged for eleven years. The war itself, however, was only the longest and most violent chapter in a struggle that began with the conquest, with the first efforts of the Spaniards in the early 1520s to establish a permanent settlement in what was then called Cuscatlán. The colonists soon found that El Salvador's only wealth lay in the land, and they proceeded, throughout the colonial period, to usurp the indigenes' communal lands and plant them in a succession of export crops. As land was increasingly concentrated in fewer hands, the Indians periodically revolted but were put down with ruthless efficiency. In an 1882 decree the government of El Salvador eliminated the last of the communal lands on the ground that such lands were "contrary to the political and social principles on which the Republic was established"—in other words, the Lockean principle of private property. This was accompanied by another Hobbesean-Lockean principle: that the purpose of government is to maintain order. These two principles undergirded Salvadorian state and society until 1979; they were also the root, if not the proximate cause, of a series of peasant revolts that occurred in the last quarter of the nineteenth century, the 1932 uprising, and the contemporary revolutionary movement that began in 1970.

The Course of Revolution

Four themes shape this chapter. The first is that, since 1970, El Salvador's revolutionary movement has evolved through a series of five phases into a sixth that began with the signing of the peace treaty.

The second theme is that the Left in El Salvador encompasses more than the constituent organizations of the FMLN. It also includes labor unions, political parties, church-related institutions, and grass-roots organizations that are not affiliated with the FMLN but that do share with it important components of a common vision of a just society and political democracy.

The third theme is that the FMLN as a coalition and its constituent organizations have gone through a slow and sometimes painful process in the past two decades of political maturation, becoming progressively less ideological and more pragmatic along the way without sacrificing their fundamental principles of social and economic justice for all Salvadorians. While becoming militarily the most successful leftist movement in Latin America, they have also become politicians capable of compromising with each other and meeting and talking rationally with heads of state and, more significant, with Salvadorian military and political opponents.

The fourth theme is reflected in a comment that Commander Roberto Cañas made in early 1980: "The armed struggle is necessarily a part of the struggle not because we would have chosen that path but because there is no other way to wrest political and economic power from the dominant forces and change the structures to a more just and humane system."[1] I will argue, by way of conclusion, that while the FMLN has not "wrested political and economic power from the dominant forces," Cañas was correct on the fundamentals: without the armed struggle, despite its extremely high cost, none of the FMLN's socioeconomic and political goals would have been achieved. The armed struggle forced the dominant forces, especially the economic elite, to change their attitudes and behavior.[2]

The history of the Left in El Salvador over the past two decades breaks down into six periods:

- *Mass Struggle, 1970–March 1980.* During this decade the emphasis was on building broad, mass-based organizations and on political education. Some attention was given to training a military arm, but the accent was on political work. Many young people, in particular, gave up on traditional politics after the army refused to honor presidential election results in 1972 that would have brought a civilian, José Napoleón Duarte, to office.
- *Transition, March 1980–January 1981.* This period begins with the assassination of Archbishop Oscar Romero on March 24 and ends

with the FMLN's first offensive, initiated on January 11. During these months, as repression increased, the mass organizations were dismantled and resources were shifted to building a revolutionary army.

- *Armed Struggle, January 1981–1984.* During these three years the emphasis was on military expansion and training. The FMLN, which was concentrated in five departments, organized its forces in units of as many as a thousand combatants and kept the government army off balance and on the run.[3] In zones under the FMLN's political control campesinos were organized politically and provided the food, clothing, medicine, information, and other forms of support necessary to sustain a guerrilla army.
- *Armed and Political Struggle, 1984–1988.* In 1983 the United States supplied enough air power and armaments to carry out an unrelenting air war against the FMLN and the zones in which its civilian supporters lived. This led to a change in strategy, in which the FMLN broke down its large units into small, self-sufficient platoons of about fifteen combatants even as it expanded operations into all fourteen departments.

Meanwhile, a series of U.S.-sponsored elections, beginning with the election of a Constituent Assembly in 1982 and followed by presidential contests in 1984, had the unanticipated effect of opening political space that had been closed by the massive repression of the early 1980s. Although repression did not end, it diminished significantly, and unions, cooperatives, and new grass-roots organizations waded, then plunged into the new political waters, much to the chagrin of the government, the military, and the U.S. embassy, which hastened to paint them as FMLN "fronts" and to create parallel organizations to siphon off their support. In addition, Center-Left political parties, which had formed a political alliance with the FMLN in 1980, began sending members back to El Salvador in 1985 and all of their leaders by late 1987.

- *Negotiating Struggle, 1989–1991.* The FMLN opened this phase in January 1989 with an audacious offer to participate in the presidential election, scheduled for March, if it were postponed until September. The offer was rejected, and the candidate of the Alianza Republicana Nacionalista (Nationalist Republican Alliance—ARENA), Alfredo Cristiani, was elected to succeed the Christian Democrat Duarte. In the spring FMLN Commander Joaquín Villalobos published a thoughtful and largely nonideological analysis of the Salvadorian situation in *Foreign Policy*[4] that was widely interpreted as a message to the new Bush administration that the FMLN was reasonable and seriously interested in a negotiated settlement. The FMLN sent Cristiani a message proposing talks, and the new president, in his inaugural address, pledged to seek negotiations with the rebels. This was the beginning of a difficult process that took place in the context of a civil war that ended only with the formal cease-fire and that was punctuated by the entry of the United Nations, the largest FMLN military offensive of the war, and growing international pressure for a negotiated settlement.

- *Political Struggle by Other Means, 1992–.* The formal cease-fire and all the agreements leading up to it did not spell the end of the revolutionary movement in El Salvador. It did signify standing Clausewitz on his head; if war is the continuation of politics by other means, which was certainly the case in El Salvador for a decade, the peace agreement signified the formal declaration of intent by the FMLN to pursue its struggle to transform Salvadorian society by other, political means, including electoral politics. It would be an irony of history if some of the FMLN's leaders, whose disillusionment with traditional politics following the stolen 1972 election caused them to take up arms, became candidates for public office in 1994. They would, however, be competing in a vastly different electoral setting, with the army in its barracks and a radically different set of electoral rules—both political victories for the FMLN in the peace negotiations.

Antecedents to War

Until 1932, peasant revolts in El Salvador had a nonideological character: they were generally spontaneous uprisings against perceived injustices. The only organized revolt, in 1831, lasted a year, until its leader, Anastacio Aquino, was captured and beheaded and his head displayed as a warning to other would-be rebels. In the 1980s the FMLN would name one of its four war zones, the Central Front, for Aquino. The January 1932 uprising, however, had a decidedly ideological cast. The Left formally emerged with the founding of the Partido Comunista de El Salvador (Communist Party of El Salvador—PCS) during a period of political liberalization in the late 1920s. Founded by Augustín Farabundo Martí, the educated son of a mestizo landowner, the party focused its early organizing in urban areas and in the southwest, where there was still a sizable indigenous population. Miguel Sáenz, a physician who joined the PCS as a teenager, has related how, when José Feliciano Ama, an indigenous *cacique* or leader, joined the party he held up his card and said, "This card represents membership for all my people." The party leaders were appalled and tried to disabuse Ama of the idea of collective membership, but Ama was adamant; his card would represent membership for everyone—or no one.[5] Ama kept his card and became the most prominent indigenous leader of the 1932 revolt, for which he was subsequently hanged in the plaza of Izalco, Sonsonate, the center of the failed rebellion. The FMLN's Western Front would be named for him. After the brutal suppression of the revolt the party was proscribed and went underground for the next forty years, its members being subjected to severe repression.[6] Nonetheless, every significant popular protest against the military governments from 1944 on included PCS militants.

In the 1960s a debate arose over whether the time had once again come for armed struggle. Those who followed Moscow's recommended policy of entering mainstream politics created the Unión Democrática Nacionalista (Nationalist Democratic Union—UDN) in 1967, a legal political party. Salvador Cayetano Carpio, the PCS secretary-general, argued, however, that traditional political parties and organizations "denied the possibility and necessity of the Salvadorean people undertaking the process of revolutionary armed struggle. . . . By the end of 1969 it was very clear that El Salvador, its people, needed an overall strategy in which all methods of struggle could be used and combined in dialectical fashion."[7] The party itself acknowledged in a January 1982 declaration that "tendencies appeared that, evaluating the [1932] insurrection only on the basis of its results, renounced the armed struggle thereby giving birth to and perpetuating reformist positions."[8] In 1986 Secretary-General Schafik Handal explained that elections were not "to achieve power" but "an instrument for placing our program at the center of political debate, and . . . for raising the political consciousness of the masses of workers arriving from the countryside to work in the factories.[9] Not until 1977, following a massacre in a downtown plaza in the wake of yet another stolen presidential election, did the PCS adopt a policy of armed struggle and begin training militia in the Salvadorian countryside. By 1979 these guerrillas had become the Fuerzas Armadas de Liberación (Armed Forces of Liberation—FAL).

The Rise of the Contemporary Revolutionary Organizations

As a result of this position, the Communist party split; Carpio and his faction went underground and began organizing the first contemporary revolutionary organization, the Fuerzas Populares de Liberación (Popular Forces of Liberation—FPL). Meanwhile, the PCS, behind its legal front, the UDN, participated in elections between 1968 and 1977. In 1972 it joined a three-party coalition that ran Christian Democrat Duarte for president—an election denied him by the army, which refused to give up power. Three other revolutionary organizations appeared in the 1970s, each with some previous link to the PCS: the Ejército Revolucionario del Pueblo (Revolutionary Army of the People—ERP) in 1972, the Resistencia Nacional (National Resistance—RN) in 1975, and the Partido Revolucionario de Trabajadores Centroamericanos (Revolutionary Party of Central American Workers—PRTC) in 1976.

The ERP drew its membership from Young Communists, youth from the Christian Democratic party (PDC), and the radicalized sector of the Salvadorian bourgeoisie—even, in a few instances, the oligarchy. In contrast to Carpio, who was fifty when he resigned from the PCS, most members of the ERP were teenagers or in their early twenties. The two organizations shared, however, a militaristic conception of the revolutionary struggle. The ERP adhered to that line, consistently placing less emphasis on political organization of the grass roots, while the FPL soon came to recognize the importance of an organized mass base.

Within the ERP, two tendencies struggled for supremacy. One was the militaristic tendency just described. The other, the RN, believed that political as well as military action was required. By 1975 ERP hardliners had decided that the RN's principal theoretician, the poet Roque Dalton, was not only politically incorrect but a traitor. A kangaroo court tried and convicted him in absentia, condemned him to death, and subsequently assassinated him. The RN split from the ERP, which became an outcast among the other revolutionary groups for the next five years.

The founders of the PRTC came out of the ERP as well as unions under PCS influence. In contrast to the other four organizations, whose focus was national, the PRTC had a regional conception of revolutionary struggle and, at the time of its founding in January 1976, was part of a pan–Central American party. In late 1980, however, after the FMLN was formed, the party broke up into its national units while retaining intraregional ties.

The Development and Demise of the Mass Movement

About 1970, members of the RN faction began working around Suchitoto, forty-five kilometers northeast of the capital, among peasants who had been dispossessed of their lands by construction of the Cerrón Grande hydroelectric dam. This work coincided with the pastoral work of two young Salvadorian priests, José and Higinio Alas, who had been sent to Suchitoto in 1968. Both Alas brothers had been strongly influenced by the Second Vatican Council and, more immediately, the Catholic Bishops' Conference at Medellín, Colombia, in 1968. They set out to organize Christian base communities among their parishioners, to conduct bible study classes, and to encourage people to reflect on the biblical message in the context of their own lives. One former parishioner told Charles Clements in the early 1980s that when, one day, Father José asked his opinion about some issue, it was the first time anyone other than another peasant had ever done so.[10] The pastoral work, in short, gave people experience in organizing; selecting leadership from among themselves, receiving training in catechism, leadership, health care, and agricultural techniques—in sum, beginning to take responsibility for their lives both collectively and individually.

The pastoral work of the Alas brothers and others awakened thousands of Salvadorian peasants and urban poor from the slumber of fatalism into which the traditional, sacramental church had lulled them; a process of "consciousness raising" occurred, and that process coincided with the founding of the modern revolutionary organizations. It became clear to the people of Suchitoto that their church organizations were both inadequate and inappropriate to press eminently political demands concerning land and agrarian reform. Therefore, in April 1974, a group of people from the parish of Suchitoto, accompanied by José Alas and joined by members of teacher and student organizations, labor unions, and people allied with the RN and the FPL, met in the Basilica of the Sacred Heart in San Salvador and formally organized the first of five "popular organizations" to emerge in the 1970s—the Frente de Acción Popular Unificado (United Popular Action Front—FAPU). While the FAPU was the only popular organization to emerge directly from the nexus between radical Christianity and revolutionary politics, one cannot explain the rapid expansion of the popular organizations during the 1970s without acknowledging the evangelizing role of the church after 1968.

The modern Left in El Salvador is heir not only to a tradition of revolt against economic oppression and political repression dating back to the colonial period and to an organizational tradition represented in the Communist party but also to a tradition of urban public demonstrations against authoritarianism and dictatorship dating back to 1944, when a series of massive, public demonstrations led to the resignation and exile of Maximiliano Hernández Martínez.[11] Periodically throughout the next three decades, the political frustration level of students, teachers, and unionists boiled over and into the streets. (Peasants were notably absent, any organization thereof having been proscribed after the abortive 1932 uprising.) Predictably, demonstrations were met with the full, repressive apparatus of the state. Miguel Sáenz, who as a high school and university student in the 1950s and 1960s participated in many demonstrations, has described how they learned, experience by experience, how to confront the security forces.[12]

By 1979 each of the five "political-military organizations," as they described themselves, had an affiliated popular organization. The first of these organizations, the FAPU, grew rapidly, but political, strategic, and tactical squabbles grew as well. The main political debate was over how to view the struggle: Should it be in terms of a "prolonged war," as Carpio insisted, or in terms of short-, medium-, and long-term stages? The most significant difference was over who should be the primary focus of their organizing efforts. The RN faction favored an emphasis on trade unions; the FPL believed the focus should be on the peasantry. By July 1975 the latter had split off and created the second popular organization, the Bloque Popular Revolucionario (Popular Revolutionary Bloc—BPR). By 1979 the BPR was the largest mass organization in El Salvador, with sixty thousand members and nine affiliated organizations. The FAPU's membership was estimated at half that, with much of its leadership more middle-class and union-based. The FAPU, meanwhile, had acquired a reputation for incisive political analysis and for its theoretical publications. It had great influence on the development of a unified program in 1980. Most significant, its insistence on revolution *and* democracy and on forming alliances with progressive sectors of the churches, political parties, labor unions, and private sector became the official policy of the FMLN.

The same tactics that had been honed through three decades were increasingly employed in the 1970s—and met by increasingly virulent repression. The Catholic church, which had become more and more identified with the Left in the eyes of the extreme Right, was not spared; José Alas was kidnapped and left for dead in 1970; a priest was killed in 1972 and two more in 1977; by 1990 sixteen priests, an archbishop, and at least four nuns had been murdered by security forces or death squads.[13] Hundreds of catechists (lay teachers) had also died or disappeared. It was the popular organizations, however, that bore the brunt of the repression. In May 1979 the national police opened fire on unarmed BPR members who had occupied the San Salvador cathedral and three embassies to demand the release of five political prisoners. Twenty-three died. In late October, less than two weeks after a coup d'état by progressive young officers overthrew General Carlos Humberto Romero, the national guard fired on another demonstration, killing twenty-one.

The Left also employed tactics that were clear violations of human rights; apart from the occupation of embassies and public buildings in which people were held hostage, most notorious was the kidnapping of ten Salvadorian oligarchs and several foreign businessmen for at least sixty-five million dollars in ransom. Roberto Cañas explained that the kidnappings were viewed as a means of "recouping some of this wealth for the people, to shape and develop the political struggle for their liberation." He denied that all the money was used to buy arms; "much of it," he said, "has been used to build the popular organizations."[14] Given the size of the organizations (at least two hundred thousand by late 1979), the quantity of flyers and pamphlets they produced, and the number of people working full-time in the movement with no visible source of income, this is not difficult to believe.[15]

Women were incorporated into both political-military and popular organizations very early and had become significant by the late 1970s.[16] They assumed the same responsibilities as the men in political and military activities, including combat, diplomacy, communications, public relations, education, cooking, health, and, for women at home, caring for the children of combatants. At the military level women commonly composed 20–30 percent of military units; both the FPL and the FAL had units composed entirely of women; over a dozen rose to the rank of commander and, by 1988, composed 20 percent of the FMLN's national leadership. In 1991 Commander Ana Guadalupe Martínez was one of the FMLN's three top negotiators in the peace talks.

Despite El Salvador's being an extremely sexist society, most guerrilla women say that they encountered little machismo among their *compañeros*. While some women suffered the breakup of a relationship or marriage because their mates or spouses did not share their political commitments, many others found enduring relationships within the movement or saw their husbands evolved along with them, remaining supportive of their political activities and often learning to do nontraditional (for men) tasks such as cooking and taking care of the children.[17] By the early 1980s, the male leaders recognized that many women were mired in support roles and not working to their full potential. They began pushing for women to take on more responsibilities, and it became formal policy for the FMLN to enroll, train, and change the responsibilities of women and men. In the field, for example, men were forced to work in the kitchens. By the late 1980s perhaps half of all the radio operators with FMLN units were women, whereas in the early 1980s very few were.

Attitudes toward women among the Salvadorian Left are radically different from those of the larger society. Charles Clements has said that, in his year on the Guazapa Front, north of San Salvador, he never observed a case of wife or child abuse. Rape was virtually unknown in zones under FMLN control—except when the army moved through; it was a crime punishable by death, a punishment that was meted out once or twice in the early 1980s. A different attitude toward women also extends to the democratic Left; an employee in the Legislative Assembly confided that sexual harassment is rampant among the deputies—except for the proleftist ones who won a total of nine seats in the Assembly in the March 1991 elections.[18]

By late 1979 there were demonstrations in the streets of San Salvador at least once a week; occupations of various sites occurred on an almost weekly basis; the cathedral was occupied more often than not, forcing Archbishop Romero to hold Sunday mass in the Basilica of the Sacred Heart. In this period the five organizations, which had been characterized by nothing so much as their sectarianism, began serious talks about unity.

One lesson they had learned from the triumph of the Sandinista Revolution in Nicaragua the previous July was the need to unify. In late December the FPL, RN, and the PCS quietly formed the Dirección Revolucionaria Unificada (Unified Revolutionary Directorate—DRU); two weeks later all five popular organizations called a press conference and announced the creation of the Coordinadora Revolucionaria de las Masas (Revolutionary Coordination of the Masses—CRM). On January 22, 1980, the forty-eighth anniversary of the 1932 insurrection, the CRM put the largest demonstration in Salvadorian history on the streets of San Salvador; at least two hundred thousand people joined in a march characterized by extraordinary order, discipline, and patience—until security forces and paramilitary groups began firing, simultaneously, on the marchers from fourteen public and private buildings in the city center.

The march, in historical perspective, was the culmination of the mass struggle. Repression increased almost weekly thereafter, and the number killed would reach almost twelve thousand in 1980 and over sixteen thousand in 1981. The assassination of Archbishop Romero brought the era of mass struggle to a close. During the summer the organizations shifted to a strategy of general strikes, with diminishing success. Again repression was part of the problem; poor planning was another factor.

In March the Christian Democratic party split, following the assassination of Attorney General Mario Zamora. Led by his brother, Rubén, former Christian Democrats soon organized the Movimiento Popular Social Cristiano (Popular Social Christian Movement—MPSC) and helped found the Frente Democrático Revolucionario (Democratic Revolutionary Front—FDR), an alliance of popular organizations, parties, unions, professionals, and small business people. In May the DRU voted to include the PRTC and the ERP. In October the five political-military organizations founded the FMLN and began to prepare for their first military offensive. The FMLN's strategic alliance with the FDR was a concrete recognition of the need to reach out to broader sectors of Salvadorian society and not remain a narrowly based Marxist-Leninist revolutionary movement.

The Long Road to Peace

On January 11, 1980, after the five popular organizations announced the formation of the CRM, they issued a document that described the "profound economic and political crisis" in El Salvador and argued that "the revolutionary alternative is the only solution to the crisis."[19] The "revolutionary alternative," however, as published in late February by the CRM, included a series of proposals all of which would be acted on in the 1980s or directly addressed in the final peace agreements in 1991. It was the first in a series of documents that would appear over the next eleven years, each of which demonstrated increasing flexibility and pragmatism.

In an effort to steal the Left's thunder, the United States pushed the Salvadorian government to implement most of the structural changes for which the CRM had called just a week earlier, in particular bank and external commerce nationalization and agrarian reform. After the ARENA gained control of the Constituent Assembly in 1982, it sought to reimpose the Lockean principles of private property with which cooperatives are inconsistent and succeeded to a great extent in gutting the agrarian reform by denying technical assistance and credits to the co-ops and holding up paperwork for titling the farms. Nonetheless, in late 1991 there were four hundred cooperatives, though many were deeply in debt; land reform covered 13 percent of the national territory; and 23 percent of agrarian land was in the reform sector. Furthermore, the FMLN had extracted a commitment at the peace table to allow all tenants of land in conflict zones to remain on their land. This was critical because in many areas government supporters had abandoned their lands in the late 1970s or early 1980s, never to return. The FMLN was concerned that they would return after a peace accord, reclaim their lands, and force the people who had been working it to leave or once again become virtual serfs.

On no issue was the FMLN's policy evolution greater than with regard to the future of the armed forces. The February document called for a "*Popular Army,* incorporating those elements of the troops, noncommissioned officers, officers, and commanders of the present Army who maintain 'clean conduct,' reject foreign intervention, . . . and support the liberating struggle of our people." In August 1981, the FMLN's General Command spoke of "*the integration* of the Popular Revolutionary Army and the patriotic and democratic sector of the army . . . in an army of a new type." Two months later, in a document read by Nicaraguan President Daniel Ortega before the UN General Assembly, the FMLN said, "The . . . Armed Forces [will be restructured], based on the officers and troops of the present Army who are not responsible for crimes and genocide against the people, *and . . . the commanders and troops of the FMLN.*"[20]

The FMLN's growing flexibility was attributable to three factors: increasing military capability and confidence, recognition by France and Mexico in August 1981 of the FDR/FMLN as a "representative political force," and a growing unwillingness to prolong the war unnecessarily by holding out for an absolute military victory. By 1991, the FMLN position regarding the armed forces bore little resemblance to that of a decade earlier. For most of the 1980s, however, the Left's calls for negotiations were dismissed or ignored, the result of a U.S.-imposed policy of seeking the FMLN's military defeat and civilian governments incapable of defying the Reagan administration.

U.S. policy and an ARENA-controlled Constituent Assembly ensured that no negotiations would take place between 1982 and 1984. Meanwhile, the FMLN passed through its worst internal crisis since the murder of Roque Dalton. In April Carpio, who had become increasingly dogmatic and intransigent on two critical issues—unity and negotiations—and whose position against both had lost in an FPL congress earlier in the year, ordered the murder of the FPL's second-in-command, Mélida Anaya Montes, who had led the winning faction at the congress. When the Nicaraguan government confronted Carpio with the evidence of his own perfidy, he committed suicide. His demise removed the single greatest obstacle to further unity of the FMLN, and within a month greater coordination between the FPL and the other four organizations was evident.

For most of the 1980s the FMLN did not learn how to respond in a politically appropriate manner to the elections that the United States had engineered as a means of giving El Salvador a "legitimate, moderate and reformist" government.[21] Its various methods of disrupting and discrediting the elections included attacks on military targets in towns and villages on election day, cutting off the power to the capital, collecting the identity cards required to vote, destroying ballots and ballot boxes, and calling national transportation strikes. Meanwhile, in 1984 Christian Democrat presidential candidate José Napoleón Duarte ran on a platform of peace negotiations and economic reforms. Once Duarte had defeated the ARENA's extreme-Right candidate Roberto D'Aubuisson, the Left took a first step toward recognizing the new government as legitimate when in May 1984 the FDR acknowledged Duarte as a "valid speaker" in any negotiations and the FMLN put forth another proposal for a "provisional government of broad participation." At this point, however, the Left still did not accept the 1983 constitution as legitimate and argued that the 1984 elections were the result of a "dark, anti-democratic process" and did not have a "national character" because only two-thirds of the country had voted.[22]

The most significant development to come out of the early years of Duarte's rule was the permanent return to El Salvador of FDR leaders Rubén Zamora and Guillermo Manuel Ungo, secretary-general of the small, social democratic Movimiento Nacional Revolucionario (National Revolutionary Movement—MNR), after seven years in exile. On November 7, 1987, Ungo, Zamora, and Mario Reni Roldán, head of the new Partido Social Democrático (Social Democratic party—PSD) met in Guatemala and founded the Convergencia Democrática (Democratic Convergence—CD). They decided not to participate in the 1988 municipal elections, but in September 1988 the CD published a "Programmatic Platform" in which it defined "four great problems facing the country: civil war; loss of national sovereignty; absence of real democracy; and the extreme poverty of the Salvadorian people."[23] Some observers quickly interpreted the decision to return and the creation of the Convergencia as the result of a split with the FMLN. In fact, the FDR and FMLN had signed a pact in November 1986 in which they agreed that, although they would seek to strengthen their alliance, in certain areas each was autonomous. The decision to return, the creation of the CD, and, ultimately, its decision to participate in the 1989 and 1991 elections were all manifestations of this autonomy.

The decision of the Convergencia to participate in the 1989 presidential campaign drew considerable attention; it was, after all, the first time since 1977 that parties on the Left had participated in electoral politics. But the FMLN effectively derailed the campaign for a month with an audacious proposal, published on January 23, 1989, that the elections be postponed for six months, the military be kept in their barracks on election day, the CD be placed on the Central Election Council, and the possibility of voting in absentia be provided to Salvadorians living abroad, in return for which the rebels would agree to participate in the elections and to honor the outcome. According to Sáenz, the FMLN had gone through a long process of analysis of itself and the national reality during the previous fall and had concluded that it had broad support that would be converted into votes were it to participate in elections.[24]

In the end the FMLN's proposal was rejected; the elections went forward as originally planned, and the FMLN did its best to disrupt them with a blackout of the capital and a national transportation stoppage, and the ARENA candidate, the political neophyte Alfredo Cristiani, a relative moderate, won in the first round. The CD, with Guillermo Ungo as its presidential candidate and Mario Roldán for vice president, won 3.8 percent of the vote. But the FMLN had changed the political landscape of El Salvador, revived itself as a force with which other actors had to contend, and put peace back at the top of the national agenda.[25]

Two days after the March 19 election President-elect Cristiani called for immediate peace talks with the FMLN. The FMLN responded on April 6 in Washington with a new seven-point proposal:

- Negotiations with the participation of the three branches of government, the armed forces, and political parties.
- A cease-fire between the FMLN and the armed forces.
- General elections for president, mayors, and a Constituent Assembly.
- Discussions leading to measures that addressed the structural causes of the war—that is, socioeconomic reforms.
- FMLN participation in the elections under its own flag or with those who might wish to form coalitions with it.
- Reduction of the armed forces and judicial proceedings against those responsible for the repression.
- Cutting of military aid and withdrawal of U.S. advisors.[26]

In his inaugural speech on June 1, Cristiani unveiled a five-point plan for negotiations and, in contrast to Duarte, did not call for the FMLN's surrender. This was a popular position; on May 30 the Central American University published the results of a national poll showing that 76 percent of respondents believed that the new government "should open a dialogue and negotiate with the FMLN."[27]

The Central American presidents met in Tela, Honduras, in August, and soon thereafter the FMLN proposed "to initiate as soon as possible a definitive process of negotiation to put an end to the war and place all our forces at the service of constructing a true democracy."[28] These developments were the result of several factors: pressures on the FMLN and the government from Latin American leaders and others to negotiate; the escalating social and economic costs of the war; a U.S. administration no longer committed to military victory over the insurgents; a private sector that increasingly recognized the impossibility of economic recovery without an end to the war; and recognition that in the 1991 elections the ARENA could suffer the fate of the PDC in 1988 and lose its majority in the assembly and town halls.

A meeting between the two sides was scheduled for November 20, 1989, in Caracas, but, on October 31 a noontime bomb at the headquarters of the Federación National Sindical de Trabajadores Salvadoreños (National Union Federation of Salvadorian Workers—FENASTRAS), El Salvador's largest and most militant trade union federation, killed its secretary-general, Febe Elizabeth Velásquez, and nine others and wounded thirty. That assault had been preceded by several bombings, including bombings of Rubén Zamora's home and the Lutheran church offices, and a grenade attack on the National University. It was also preceded by increasingly frequent statements from the armed forces and the U.S. embassy indicating that they had come to believe their own propaganda: that the FMLN was militarily and politically finished. The FENASTRAS bombing, however, was the last straw; it convinced the FMLN that the government was not serious about negotiations. "We are faced with a new situation that forces us to defend the people's struggle," an FMLN communiqué said. "We had become more flexible in our positions in an effort to open real negotiations, but the current unacceptable situation reaffirms that we cannot abandon the armed struggle. We reaffirm before the nation that we will never lay down our guns in the face of state terrorism."[29] President Cristiani went on national radio, asked for calm, and promised a full investigation. Nothing happened. Two weeks later the FMLN opened a countrywide offensive, the largest of the war, and brought the war to San Salvador. When the army was unable to mount a counteroffensive in the streets of the capital the air force took over, bombing working-class and poor neighborhoods on the periphery of the city from which the offensive had been launched. (When, on two occasions, the rebels moved into the wealthy Escalón neighborhood, neither soldiers nor air force did anything, and the guerrillas had the run of the area as long as they chose to stay—much to the chagrin of its inhabitants.)

The FMLN shook the Salvadorian government, army, and oligarchy to its foundations. The army was confronted by insurgents who ran it in circles for days. Unable to respond in meaningful military form, a right-wing cabal of senior officers decided to cut off what they regarded as the head of the monster: the Jesuit scholars of the Central American University, who for twenty-three years had been calling for social and economic justice and an end to militarism in El Salvador. U.S.-trained units of the Atlacatl Batallion entered the Jesuits' residence on the campus at two in the morning and shot six of them, including the rector and vice-rector, as well as their housekeeper and her daughter. Not until the fall of 1991, under continual international pressure, including pressure from the U.S. Congress, were three officers and five soldiers tried for the crimes. Two officers were convicted; the rest were acquitted.[30]

Although some guerrillas in the streets told journalists that they were fighting to overthrow the government, the FMLN's official position, and the one expressed privately, was "unconditionally committed to a political-negotiated settlement."[31] In early 1990 the UN secretary-general's office, at the behest of both sides, initiated several months of shuttle diplomacy that led, on April 4, to an agreement between government and FMLN to begin UN-mediated negotiations. In May they met in Caracas and issued a joint statement on the schedule and agenda of future talks. They also agreed to address political issues prior to a cease-fire—a concession by the government—and aimed to achieve agreement on this by September. In June talks were held in Mexico and proposals regarding the future of the armed forces exchanged.

When they met in San José in July the government submitted a hardline proposal concerning the armed forces: they would regulate themselves and set the limits of their functions; abusive units would be transferred, intact, within the system. The fundamental difficulty was that the government viewed the problem within the military as a matter of criminal and corrupt individuals whereas the FMLN defined it as systemic.

A significant breakthrough came, however, with a partial human rights accord and an agreement to have the UN monitor human rights. This led, in July 1991, to the creation of the first—in history—UN human rights observer team to monitor the peace process at the end of a civil war; 150 observers from twenty-nine countries spread out across El Salvador to deal with human rights violations on both sides as they occurred.

In August 1990 the FMLN, seeking to drive home the point that the root of the problem was militarism, submitted a proposal for the total demilitarization of Salvadorian society, leading, through a series of preliminary steps, to the dismantling of both armies. The UN submitted a secret proposal that, when it became public in November, was widely seen as closer to the FMLN's position than to that of the government. The key elements included disbanding two of the three security forces and placing the third under civilian control, eliminating the armed forces intelligence branch, and establishing an independent commission to investigate and dismiss military officers guilty of human rights abuses. When the stalemate on this issue continued into September, the UN negotiator, Alvaro de Soto, convened a series of secret meetings separately and together as well as with other social forces in the country. One of the agreements that came out of these meetings was for the creation of a new, civilian police force, for which both honest, competent officers of the current national police and FMLN guerrillas who qualified would be retrained.[32]

By December 1990 the two sides were seen as close to signing a cease-fire agreement. In early January 1991 de Soto brought them together to discuss a confidential UN proposal on the future of the armed forces. Then the Bush administration, outraged over the cold-blooded murder of two U.S. servicemen by a guerrilla platoon in mid-January, restored 42.5 million dollars in military assistance that had been withheld by Congress and leaked its displeasure with de Soto to the press, accusing him of being too easy on the FMLN. When talks resumed the next day, February 2, they ended in a deadlock that continued through the March 10 assembly and mayoral elections. As had happened to the PDC in 1988, the ARENA lost its majority in the assembly and a significant number of mayoralties. Even more significant, however, was the performance of the Convergencia, which increased its vote total to almost 13 percent and won eight seats in the Legislative Assembly. Rubén Zamora was elected one of the assembly vice presidents.

Following the election, the FMLN submitted a new proposal that was introduced by Nicaraguan President Violeta Chamorro to foreign ministers of the European Community participating in a Central American summit meeting in Managua. The same day, Secretary of State James Baker and Soviet Foreign Minister Alexander Bessmertnykh expressed both countries' support for the negotiations and the UN role in them. April brought a marathon twenty-four-day negotiating session that produced the most significant military, political, electoral, and judicial agreements since the negotiations began. These agreements achieved in large measure what the Left had been fighting for:

- Under the 1983 constitution the armed forces were its "guarantor"; now they would be responsible for defending the territorial integrity of the country. They could be used to maintain domestic order by order of the president, with the possibility of veto by the assembly.

- The three security forces would be dissolved and a new national civil police created under civilian control.
- The armed forces intelligence directorate would be eliminated and replaced by a state intelligence agency under the president.
- The armed forces' ability to try civilians as well as military personnel and to determine what cases fell under its jurisdiction would be curtailed; it would have jurisdiction only over cases of a strictly military nature.
- The existing Central Election Council, with membership limited to the top three parties in the preceding election, would be replaced by a Supreme Electoral Tribunal whose membership was nonpartisan.
- Under judicial reform, the Supreme Court, attorney general, chief prosecutor, and head of a new national office of human rights would be elected by a two-thirds vote of the assembly.
- A three-member Truth Commission, appointed by the UN secretary-general, with wide authority to investigate the most serious crimes of the war years, would be created.

Talks continued through the summer in Mexico with some advances and a few setbacks. With awareness that a final cease-fire agreement was in sight, however, the extreme Right in El Salvador began to react in typical fashion: in July the Frente Anticomunista Salvadoreño (Salvadorian Anticommunist Front—FAS), issued a threat against supporters of the UN observers, the decade-old Crusade for Peace and Work published a thinly veiled threat against the observers in local papers, and death squad threats and murders slowly increased.

In late August UN Secretary-General Javier Pérez de Cuéllar invited President Cristiani and other top officials to New York for "consultations" on how to "unblock and breath new life" into the negotiations. When talks resumed in New York on September 16, things began to move, in large part because the Salvadorian government was under enormous pressure from Spain, the major Latin American countries, and the United States to reach an agreement. On September 26 the two sides signed an accord that went beyond Mexico. The FMLN, for its part, dropped its long insistence that it be incorporated into the army. At the same time, the agreement included incorporation of FMLN forces into the new civilian police—a much more significant victory, because the army, under the accords, will sit in its barracks while the police carry out the functions of a regular police force on a daily basis across the country.

After two more rounds of talks in Mexico in November, the negotiations returned to the United Nations on December 16. The remaining issues, according to Roberto Cañas, were important: details concerning the civil police, reduction of the army, socioeconomic issues, and the cease-fire itself were all on the agenda.[33] For two weeks the talks proceeded at a snail's pace. The government's delegation, with no authority to make decisions, had to consult on every detail by fax or phone. Then, under pressure from the UN and the United States, Cristiani flew to New York on December 28. On December 29 the Bush administration sent six senior State Department officials and diplomats to the UN to talk with Cristiani. The talks went into round-the-clock sessions, and the political will was found to reach agreement just minutes before New Year's Day, 1992, and the expiration of Pérez de Cuéllar's term. Discussions to iron out final details continued until January 11, 1992, and then both sides returned to Mexico to sign the accords on January 16.

Conclusions

The 1994 elections would be the first public test that the FMLN would face. In an election that happens only once every fifteen years, the presidency, Legislative Assembly, and mayors' positions are all open. Whereas the Convergencia had two electoral experiences under its belt and had learned how to conduct an electoral campaign, the FMLN not only had to reorganize itself as a political party but had to learn how to select candidates, make stump speeches, debate opponents, speak in "sound bites," and write and distribute campaign materials.

A frequent topic of conversation in San Salvador in the fall of 1991 was how the parties would line up in 1994. One principle was already widely held: "Everyone against ARENA." On the Left the most likely scenario was that the Convergencia and the FMLN would run their respective candidates and, at the local level, would probably not compete against each other. This would not be difficult, since the CD had been concentrating its organizing in urban areas and the FMLN's strength, in general, was in rural areas. At the national level, so the favorite scenario ran, each party would run its respective candidates for president and then unite behind the top vote-getter on the Left for the runoff against the ARENA.

Assessments of how well the FMLN would do were mixed. The FMLN itself had a favorable assessment of its chances to do well. A more critical view, however, pointed to public disenchantment with its long-standing policy of economic sabotage and suggested that it would take more than two years for the former guerrillas to overcome that negative image. The reality was that no one knew and only 1994, under new electoral rules and international observation, would tell.

Regardless of the outcome, the FMLN has already achieved extraordinary success, particularly given that the war ended in stalemate. Its victories include agreements on human rights, the creation of the UN observer team, constitutional reforms, the Truth Commission, elimination of the security forces, creation of a new national civil police with former

FMLN included, involvement in the education and training of the police, protection of land tenancy in former controlled zones, conversion of itself into a legal political party, purification and reduction of the armed forces, and the checkmating of the army.

The Salvadorian Left, in short, ended twenty-one years of struggle and eleven years of war with a political victory at the negotiating table. It remained to be seen if it could consolidate and expand that victory. If it did, it could legitimately claim that the Salvadorian revolution had triumphed.

Notes

1. Roberto Cañas, interview, San Salvador, January 1980, my translation. Cañas became the FMLN's chief spokesperson during the negotiating process.

2. A good example of pragmatism's winning out over ideology is the National Association of Private Enterprise, which in 1980 was controlled by men who, in the words of one, thought it necessary to kill a hundred thousand people in order to eliminate the Left and restore the status quo ante (privileged interview, March 1980). In January 1990, with new leadership, it advanced the idea of "concertación," which implies negotiating differences toward a common end. It met four times with the FMLN outside El Salvador between May 1990 and November 1991 (interview, November 19, 1991).

3. For a discussion of the military course of the war and the U.S. role, see Tommie Sue Montgomery, "Fighting Guerrillas: The United States and Low-Intensity Conflict in El Salvador," *New Political Science*, 17-18 (Fall/Winter 1990):21–53.

4. Joaquín Villalobos, "A Democratic Revolution for El Salvador," *Foreign Policy*, 74 (Spring 1989):103–122.

5. Sáenz recounted this anecdote in an interview in 1981. In the early 1980s he was an FMLN diplomat, primarily in Eastern Europe and the Soviet Union. By the end of the decade, however, he was a member of the Political-Diplomatic Commission, the FMLN's diplomatic arm, based in Mexico.

6. Salvador Cayetano Carpio, a baker by trade, recounts in detail the repression and methods of torture in the "reformist" regime of Colonel Oscar Osorio in the early 1950s. Carpio, *Secuestro y capucha en un país del "mundo libre"* (San José: EDUCA, 1979). The book was written in 1954.

7. Mario Menendez, "Salvador Cayetano Carpio: Top Leader of the Farabundo Martí FPL" (written for *Prensa Latina*), February 1980, mimeo.

8. "Declaración del CC del PCS en ocasión del 50 aniversario del levantamiento armado de 1932," El Salvador, January 1982, my translation.

9. Handal, interview. Handal was also a member of the FMLN's general command and, in 1990–1991, one of its top negotiators in the peace talks. Interestingly, he is from a wealthy Palestinian immigrant family that has a variety of investments in El Salvador.

10. Charles Clements, *Witness to War: An American Doctor in El Salvador* (New York: Bantam Books, 1984):101.

11. For an excellent study of the 1944 period, see Patricia Parkman, *Nonviolent Insurrection in El Salvador: The Fall of Maximiliano Hernández Martínez* (Tucson: University of Arizona Press, 1988).

12. Miguel Sáenz, interview, 1982.

13. There was not always a distinction between the two. Every security force had its death squads; there were also paramilitary units in the pay of extremist members of the oligarchy.

14. Roberto Cañas, interview, San Salvador, January 1980.

15. I was doing research in El Salvador from early November 1979 until mid-March 1980 and had ample opportunity to observe all of this firsthand.

16. The discussion in this section is based on interviews with over two dozen women in the FMLN, including nurses, combatants, and four of the top woman commanders, Ana Guadalupe Martínez, Mercedes del Carmen Letona, Sonia Aguiñada Carranza, and María Marta Valladares (Nidia Díaz). The interviews have been conducted since 1981; interviews with the commanders were conducted in Mexico in July 1989.

17. A wonderful example of a mutually supportive and understanding relationship is portrayed in "María's Story," a documentary that aired on public television's "P.O.V." in the summer of 1991. María and her husband, José, are campesinos; she is a political officer; he is in charge of supplies.

18. Conversation, September 1991.

19. Revolutionary Coordination of the Masses, "Nuestras organizaciones populares marchan hacia la unidad," January 11, 1980, mimeo.

20. "Avanza la guerra popular revolucionaria y se agrava la crisis de poder de la dictadura," Declaration of the FMLN General Command, *Boletín de Prensa*, 38 (August 12, 1981), my translation.

21. These were the terms most commonly used by U.S. officials in the early 1980s to explain and justify the elections.

22. "Declaración del Frente Democrático Revolucionario," reprinted in *Proceso*, 146 (May 14–27, 1984):12–13.

23. "Plataforma Programática de la Convergencia Democrática," September 1988, 1, my translation.

24. Miguel Sáenz, interview, January 13, 1989.

25. Contrary to conventional wisdom, the FMLN did not fear or worry about an ARENA victory; on the contrary, explained Miguel Sáenz in a January interview, the FMLN recognized that, were ARENA to win, the Left would for the first time be dealing not only with a government in control of the executive, legislative, and judicial branches but a government that enjoyed good relations with both the private sector and the military and was less under the thumb of the U.S. embassy. Thus, Sáenz argued, whatever position the Cristiani administration took, it would likely be clearer and more coherent than that of its predecessor, although it still had to deal with the extreme Right. In general, time proved Sáenz correct.

26. "Focus on El Salvador: Commentaries by the FDR-FMLN Political-Diplomatic Commission," April 18, 1989, mimeo.

27. "Poll Says Salvadoreans Want Talks With Rebels," UPI wire story, May 30, 1989; 1,303 people were polled in all fourteen departments between May 6 and May 20.

28. "Communiqué," FMLN General Command, September 7, 1989, mimeo, my translation.

29. Douglas Farah, "Salvador Rebels Vow Vengeance for Killings," *Washington Post*, November 2, 1989.

30. Reams have been written, in English and Spanish, about the Jesuits' case. The best, relatively short, overview is *The 'Jesuit Case': The Jury Trial* (New York: Lawyers' Committee for Human Rights, 1991).

31. "Radio Farabundo Martí Notices," November 11, 1989; privileged interviews.

32. The information in this section, unless otherwise cited, comes from "Highlights of El Salvador Negotiations—Chronology, April 1990–August 1991," San Francisco: U.S.-El Salvador Institute for Democratic Development, September 1991.

33. Telephone interview, Mexico City, December 13, 1991.

7

The Crisis of Bolivian Radicalism

James Dunkerley

At the end of the 1980s it was widely believed within the Bolivian Left that the country's radical movement was in crisis. Moreover, despite predictably varied views as to its precise depth, causes, and effects, this was broadly understood to result from the failure to exploit the considerable opportunities that had existed for socialists in the early years of the decade. It was, in effect, the consequence of a series of defeats at the center of national political life rather than—as had been the case during the 1970s—that of a failure to break out of a peripheral existence. The ramifications of this crisis were all the more acute because since the National Revolution of 1952 the Left had only been fully marginalized through coercion, and even in clandestinity it had enjoyed sufficient popular sympathy to hold justifiable expectations of consolidating socialist policies as a major feature of the political landscape. The fact that such expectations had been dashed in the mid-1980s under conditions of constitutional government was the cause of appreciable disorientation that delayed and complicated efforts at recovery.

In order to understand the special difficulties and challenges faced by the Bolivian Left, it is necessary to take into account the backward conditions of the country's economy. In particular, the industrial working class was very small—less than 10 percent of the labor force—and depended heavily upon the mine workers in the tin industry, which by the early 1980s was in sharp decline because of low ore content and weak international prices. At least one-third of urban workers did not receive a regular wage but were either self-employed or engaged on a daily basis in the informal economy. Similarly, very few rural laborers were hired, the overwhelming majority working on small subsistence farms distributed under the agrarian reform of 1953. Although large commercial farms predominated in the east of the country (Departments of Santa Cruz and Beni) and employed workers on a seasonal basis, the great bulk of the population was still concentrated in the Andean altiplano and valleys. This sector of the population was not fully integrated into the money economy, did not generally speak Spanish as its mother tongue, and remained closely preoccupied with local, community affairs as an essential means of survival. Although on occasion the peasantry could constitute a decisive force in national political life, it continued to be fragmented and prey to the overtures of local caciques, conservative populists, and military commanders.

The weakness of the Bolivian economy—the poorest in mainland America—was also reflected in the small size and cautious, highly conservative character of the national capitalist class. This elite had long lacked an independent economic project that might produce more than a few scattered enclaves of modernity and tended to concentrate its activity in speculative operations. As a rule, it was content to accept the vagaries of world mineral prices and to acquiesce in the stagnant rural economy. It also depended heavily upon the military, which had held political power almost continuously since 1964. This reliance had, in turn, provided the Left with a strong orientation toward antimilitarism as well as a strategy for socioeconomic change based on the strategic mining sector. Indeed, it was precisely through the campaign for democratic liberties that the Left had made significant progress since the end of the 1970s. Yet the formidable structural obstacles mentioned above, together with more conjunctural and political problems, impeded the realization of this promise during the 1980s.

Some sense of the scale of the setbacks suffered by the Left may be gleaned from comparing its position in October 1982 with that in October 1989. In 1982 a series of mass protests and strikes under the leadership of the Central Obrera Boliviana had played a central role in forcing the military to withdraw from the power that it had seized in the coup of July 1980. Although the dictatorship had also come under pressure from Washington because of its association with the cocaine trade, the workers' movement had maintained a resolute resistance to military government and had always threatened to repeat the mobilization of November 1979, when, within the space of a fortnight, it had combined with unprecedented campesino activism to destroy at birth an earlier dictatorship. Moreover, because the COB rather than the political parties had been the principal vehicle of the Left since 1952, it was now expected to ensure against any backsliding by the incoming administration of the Unión Democrática y Popular (Democratic and Popular Union—UDP), whose president was Hernán Siles Zuazo (1982–1985), over its proclaimed commitment to progressive social and economic policies.

The further fact that the UDP front encompassed the Partido Comunista de Bolivia and the Movimiento de la Izquierda Revolucionaria, which contained an important socialist current, seemed to augur well in that the Left was strongly represented both in government and out of it, covering the need to initiate and invigilate policy without being fully associated with either the administration or the opposition. The civilian Right, the military, and Washington had all been obliged to accept this unprecedented state of affairs, and it seemed more auspicious than that prevailing after the elections of 1980, when parties upholding some form of socialist platform had won 25 percent of the vote and thus provoked a military intervention before the UDP could take office. Indeed, in 1982 some on the Left, principally the PCB, called for new elections in order to secure proper constitutional reflection of their much enhanced position. The MIR, however, opposed this option on the grounds that "el hambre no espera" (hunger won't wait)—a position that enjoyed broad support within a populace that expected the combination of a "popular front" government and a workers' movement dynamized and legitimated by antimilitarist struggle to deliver substantial economic and political advances.

In October 1989 the Left stood outside the mainstream of national politics and was confronting the consequences of a second resounding electoral defeat, having secured less than 12 percent of the popular vote in May of that year and barely 8 percent in the election of July 1985. Moreover, the COB had lost much of its national authority, and after four years of a right-wing civilian government that had imposed a neoliberal deflationary program of exceptional severity it had proved unable to lead a concerted campaign of opposition despite a high level of popular discontent and activism. All the major parties that in 1982 might legitimately be considered either to be on the Left or to incorporate important left-wing currents—the PCB, the MIR, the Partido Socialista–Uno (Socialist Party One—PS-1), and the Movimiento Revolucionario Tupaj Katari de Liberación (Tupaj Katari Revolutionary Movement of Liberation—MRTKL)—had suffered debilitating divisions that had undermined the radical challenge at the polls and weakened the leadership of the COB. Closure of the country's major tin mines had all but eradicated the long-standing mine workers' union, the Federación Sindical de Trabajadores Mineros de Bolivia (Trade Union Federation of Mine Workers of Bolivia—FSTMB), and the campesino movement, which had joined the COB only at the turn of the decade, was badly split and distrustful of the Left. Along with the tens of thousands of newly unemployed who had voted for the Left in 1980 and habitually supported the COB, most peasants now either cast tactical votes for the least unsavory candidate from the three established right-wing parties that had a clear field or took a chance with new populist formations that had rapidly arisen to exploit the Left's failure to move beyond a purely denunciatory politics. Outside the realm of electoralism, popular organization had shifted significantly toward clientelist and civic bodies, where the traditional and "new" Right generally prevailed, and to a focus on plant or sector-based unionism, where narrow economic objectives predominated. It would be misguided to see this process as one of emergent, dynamic new social movements rather than as a shift in political orientation and a reduction in expectations. Nevertheless, some of the consequences for the organized Left were quite similar to those faced in other countries, not least in terms of accepting the problems of "co-opting" movements resistant—through choice or design—to becoming the site of ideological or programmatic competition.

Two factors are widely accepted as causing this tangible retreat of the Left: the severe economic crisis that broke in 1983 and the disastrous experience of the UDP government. Both phenomena sorely taxed the traditions and programs of a radical movement that had minimal experience in dealing either with hyperinflation or with a tractable civilian administration in which it had a partial interest. The resulting dilemmas were as complex as they were acute, and although this is not the place to explore the full scope of these experiences and the responses to them, some brief comment on the broad developments of the 1980s is necessary to convey a sense of the stark peculiarities of the Bolivian case.[1]

The performance and organization of the economy during that decade exhibited wide fluctuations. At one extreme, inflation under the UDP between 1982 and 1985 exceeded 12,000 percent. At the other, one of the world's most emphatic deflationary programs, imposed in August 1985 by the government of the Movimiento Nacionalista Revolucionario (Nationalist Revolutionary Movement—MNR) led by Víctor Paz Estenssoro, reduced inflation to less than 15 percent in the space of weeks at the cost of a profound recession, extensive unemployment, and radically reduced public spending. Throughout the 1980s the economy contracted by about a quarter. Tin mining, which had been the country's strategic export sector since the turn of the century and the principal economic activity of the public sector since 1952, all but disappeared following the collapse of the international tin price in October 1985 and the determination of the MNR to enforce the closure of unprofitable pits.[2] At the same time, there was an upsurge in the production of cocaine, which, although based on the legal cultivation of the coca leaf (almost exclusively by smallholders), was an illegal activity subjected to the laws of primitive accumulation. By 1986 cocaine revenue very probably exceeded that of all legal exports together, and the coca/cocaine subeconomy provided the means of subsistence for perhaps an eighth of the economically active population while employment in the mines had fallen by two-thirds to less than ten

thousand workers. These developments had exceptionally serious consequences for the Left, which had not only championed a reorganization of
the economy through industrialization and nationalization but also
drawn much of its programmatic culture from the miners' militant
trade unionism. Moreover, the close association of the Left—both in and
outside government—with the catastrophic state of the economy under
the UDP that had preceded the radical capitalist restructuring of the MNR
weakened socialist claims to possession of a viable alternative.

The experience of the UDP was traumatic on two counts. First, the two
largest avowedly radical parties (the PCB and the MIR) participated, by
virtue of holding posts in the cabinet, in a series of inept and ineffective
deflationary measures that simply spurred inflation and cut real wages by
about a third. Second, the COB, backed by the "revolutionary Left"
(dedicated to the armed overthrow of the state), crippled the government
with a succession of strikes and refusal to make concessions over its "ultimatumist" program of a moratorium on the external debt, widespread
nationalization under workers' control, and state control of foreign trade.[3]
By mid-1984 this dynamic had reached the point at which the now-
habitual devaluation of the peso was met by a general strike of three
weeks simply in order to secure a negotiated compensatory wage hike. In
October of that year, having acquiesced in the COB's demand to cease
interest payments on the debt and having accepted the de facto imposition of workers' control in the state mining corporation (COMIBOL), a
government bereft of reserves and relations with international finance
was confronted with a further major stoppage that openly challenged its
capacity to rule. When the strikers demanded complete implementation
of the COB's program, the UDP simply capitulated to the Right by
agreeing to advance elections by a year, in the clear knowledge that these
would yield a landslide victory for the advocates of "public order" and
neoliberal deflation.

For our present purposes the key feature of this scenario is that the
combination of "gradualist reformism" and "maximalist syndicalism"
drove each tendency to an untenable extreme, impaired the state of the
economy, and permitted the Right not only to take power but also fully to
exploit the mercantilist logic of possessive individualism in both the
backlash against inflation and the scurry for survival under restructuring.
As a consequence, the Left entered a period of bitter recrimination
between advocates of "capitulationism" and those of "ultraleftism."
These exchanges were undoubtedly sharpened by the fact that they
resulted from acute manifestations of each tendency under exceptionally
difficult circumstances. Before we turn to the impact of these tendencies
on the contemporary position of the Left, both of them have to be placed
in historical context. This is particularly important because the trajectory

of the socialist movement in Bolivia differs in both its chronological development and its ideological temper from that in neighboring countries.

The Influence of Historical Experience

Two crucial historical experiences shaped leftist thinking and behavior— the National Revolution under the MNR between 1952 and 1964 and the Asamblea Popular in early 1971.[4] The revolution may plausibly be described as "populist" in that the MNR depended heavily upon the rhetoric of class alliance, nationalized the major mines, introduced an agrarian reform and universal suffrage, and adopted a vague anti-imperialism while upholding an anticommunism that stopped only just short of outright proscription of the PCB. As a result of this hostility and the fact that the Cold War was at its zenith, the PCB was unable to pursue a popular-front alliance and was forced into an isolated position of "critical support" for the MNR. At the same time, it proved possible for an important current of socialists influenced by Trotskyism to take leading positions within the COB and develop a base inside the MNR by "entryist" tactics.[5] Although this tendency was soon embattled as the second revolutionary administration under Hernán Siles (1956—1960) was brought to heel by Washington, imposed an orthodox stabilization plan, and reconstructed the military (effectively destroyed in 1952), it was able to draw strength from the pursuit of a number of policies that had become enshrined as leitmotifs of the COB and enjoyed popular support.

Key among these were what might be termed the "transitional demands" of workers' participation in both the management of state industries (*cogestión*) and government itself (*cogobierno*). However, as the MNR withdrew its initial tolerance of some radical pressure, cogobierno was increasingly seen as collaborationism with state capitalism, and cogestión lost any managerial authority. When the COB and the MNR entered into outright conflict in the late 1950s, these mechanisms for popular power within the state and the leading sector of the economy were rendered redundant in practice but remained core issues of debate within a Left seeking to regain the momentum it had held in the early years of the revolution.

The experience of the MNR years fortified the orthodox Marxist critics of cogobierno—the PCB and the Trotskyist Partido Obrero Revolucionario (Revolutionary Workers' Party—POR), which attacked it as simply a device for co-optation. These parties recognized, however, both that the COB continued to be their primary sphere of organization and debate and that it was more than a simple trade union confederation, having operated in the early days of the revolution as something akin to a soviet or workers' council. The resulting elision of the distinct tasks traditionally ascribed to the revolutionary party and trade union was reflected in the Tesis Política promulgated at the COB's fourth congress in 1970. To all intents and purposes, this upheld a platform for socialist revolution that replaced cogobierno with a strong insistence upon class independence and the primacy of the COB as an organ of popular democracy with *cogestión mayoritaria* (workers' control) as a central plank.[6]

This partial but critical shift was rapidly put to the test in 1971 under the weak but progressively inclined military regime of General Juan José Torres. Torres, who had been impressed by the policies of the Velasco regime in Peru and was anxious to revive popular support for the "nationalism" of the 1950s to counter the threat of foquista guerrillaism, sought to reestablish cogobierno with the COB but was swiftly rebuffed by its leadership under Juan Lechín Oquendo.[7] Although Lechín was deeply distrustful of the PCB and remained within the orbit of a now-fractured MNR, both he and the leadership of the FSTMB were determined at all costs to avoid a repetition of the experience of collaboration in government that had so weakened the COB both as a trade union body and as a wider workers' institution bisecting state and civil society. As a consequence, they agreed upon the formation of an Asamblea Popular that would operate as a type of workers' parliament, with representation allocated to both unions and "revolutionary parties" (excluding the MNR) in recognition of the fact that this would create a state of dual power.

Despite their antagonism, both the PCB and the POR viewed the Asamblea within the traditions of the Russian Revolution and the classic prospectus for soviet power. For the majority of the COB leaders, who rejected the vanguardist ambitions of these orthodox parties, it represented a restoration of the promise of 1952 that had been corrupted by the MNR and that would complement the introduction of cogestión mayoritaria in COMIBOL—which itself incubated a revolutionary potential through its control of the commanding heights of the economy. These currents stood together against the self-proclaimed "revolutionary Left" composed of Maoists (the Partido Comunista de Bolivia, Marxista-Leninista [Communist party of Bolivia, Marxist-Leninist]—PCBM-L) and the Cuban-inspired advocates of the armed overthrow of the state.[8]

Perhaps the most crucial issue of programmatic contention was the role ascribed to the campesino movement, which was central to the strategies of Maoism and foquismo. The peasantry was treated with great suspicion by the COB and the orthodox Left, which not only attributed to it a subordinate revolutionary role but also were mindful of its comprehensive co-optation by first the MNR and then the military through the agrarian reform and clientelism. Peasant conservatism had played an important part in permitting the MNR to reverse the radical features of the revolution in 1956—1964, and it provided a secure base for the army to destroy the guerrilla campaigns of Che Guevara (1966—1967) and the Teoponte group of radicalized Christian youth (1969—1970). This record contrasted sharply with the militant resistance of the industrial proletariat represented by the FSTMB, which had included sufficient recourse to armed struggle to weaken the criticism that the urban workers had succumbed to the "peaceful road to socialism" as well as regressive economism.

Hence, the Asamblea divided into two broad blocs: the "conservatives" (the PCB, POR, and COB leadership), dedicated to proletarian primacy and the development of mass organization parallel to the institutions of the state, and the "ultras" (PCBM-L and what was shortly to become the MIR), who inveighed against such industrial elitism and demanded a rapid resolution of the question of state power through a politico-military offensive. As in the early 1980s, this familiar dispute over strategy was undertaken at the center of national life and with exceptionally high political stakes. Yet it had barely begun before a bloody coup led by Colonel Hugo Banzer imposed an authoritarian regime (1971—1978), drove the Left underground, and forced it to undertake far-reaching reconsideration of its strategy for the better part of a decade. It was during this period that the lessons of the revolutionary era, the short-lived experiment of the Asamblea, and the experience of antidictatorial resistance were distilled into the distinct currents on the Left that predominated during the chaotic transition to constitutionalism (1978—1982) and the UDP government. Many on the Bolivian Left, including militants of the PCB, who were exiled in Chile during the Allende government, held distinctly sober expectations of its survival, and its eventual overthrow did not greatly alter the broad conclusions that they had already drawn from the Banzer coup.

The Left in the 1970s and 1980s

Parliamentarianism had never secured a hegemonic hold over the Bolivian masses, being a distinctly subordinate feature of the revolutionary period and little more than a vanity under the succeeding dictatorship of General René Barrientos (1964—1969). This was one important reason that the COB was able in 1971 to take the initiative in convening a quasi-legislative body in the form of the Asamblea and that its restriction of participation to the unions and the Left was not widely challenged (except by the Torres regime and some peasant leaders). However, the precipitate overthrow of that effort to establish a vehicle for popular democracy prompted reconsideration of the narrowness of its constitution with respect both to the peasantry, which largely supported Torres, and the still formidable mass base of the MNR, which split over the Banzer coup

(Victor Paz backed the dictatorship while Hernán Siles went into opposition and formed the MNR Izquierda (MNR-Left—MNRI).

The PCB, for its part, laid stress upon the damage that the Asamblea did to the Torres regime before it was itself in a position to take on governmental powers, especially in terms of the military question. Less concerned with the rural population, where it had a very slight presence indeed, the PCB moved away from a position of "socialist unity" within the orbit of the COB toward a cross-class alliance on the grounds that this would provide some necessary "middle ground" against the *golpismo* (support for military coups) of the Right. In effect, the Communists reverted to the familiar protocols of popular-frontism, which was made possible by the existence of a multiclass opposition to dictatorship and which acquired an increasingly constitutionalist momentum as demands for civil rights accumulated. The corollary to this was that the PCB, which had been unable to pose a major challenge to Lechín in twenty years, sought to reduce the political role of the COB and effectively disregarded the anti-cogobierno thrust of the Tesis Política of 1970 despite the fact that it had played a major role in drafting it and retained a strong presence in the leadership of both the FSTMB and the COB. Equally, despite their historical enmity, the PCB and the MNRI shared an economic strategy founded upon the expansion of national capitalism and the development of industry on the basis of COMIBOL.[9]

The third main component of the UDP—the MIR—traversed much more political ground between 1971 and 1978, when the UDP was set up. Formed after the Banzer coup, the MIR brought together radicalized Christian Democratic youth close to the short-lived Ejército de Liberación Nacional (Army of National Liberation—ELN) guerrilla experience of 1969—1970, socialist intellectuals critical of the "outmoded" and "monolithic" approach of the orthodox Marxist parties, and a significant stratum of young people for whom the example of Che Guevara was more compelling than that of 1952. In practice the MIR never properly engaged in armed activity, which even in 1970 had failed to have an impact and was thenceforth largely eclipsed among the options of the Left except, notably in 1980, in defense of the mining camps against army attacks. Moreover, the MIR's weak base in the workers' movement and the very slight and heterogeneous influences manifest in its ideology prompted an early loss of leading figures to the PCB and subsequently a far greater emphasis upon radical nationalism than socialism. At root, under Banzer the MIR came to see itself as a "generational" formation destined to replace the MNR, which had brilliantly expressed the revolutionary content of nationalism in the late 1940s and early 1950s but then capitulated to Washington. The *MIRistas* were the most active and effective propagandists against the dictatorship, and, in a clear extension of their original guerrillaist inclinations, they concentrated heavily upon the issue of state power, albeit increasingly in terms of replacing dictatorship with democracy. This, together with the conviction that they would, through both a more modern character and greater moral standing, replace the *entronque histórico* (historical relationship) of the MNR, produced a kind of political "stagism" complementary to, if distinct from, that of the PCB. The resultant rhetorically driven left-wing populism was highly conducive to alliance with both the Communists and the MNRI. At the same time, it suppressed a number of key differences of outlook that broke into the open once the constraints of dictatorship were removed and absence of a clear programmatic focus became a political challenge rather than an operational asset.[10]

Although the MIR was a little less sectarian in its dealings with the rest of the Left than were the PCB and the POR (which lost much of its influence after 1971), its public persona was too activist-led and dependent upon denunciation to draw in more than a small but critical urban constituency of professionals and intellectuals that also rejected the inherited holistic rigidities of the orthodox parties but perceived the need to retain a clear Marxist core in a modern radical politics. During the Banzer period part of this educated middle sector coalesced in the PS-1 around the figure of Marcelo Quiroga Santa Cruz, an exceptionally talented speaker of upper-class and falangist background whose charisma threatened to dissolve the party in personalism. Yet Quiroga succeeded in developing a modest movement—in the late 1970s its electoral support far outstripped its organized base—of sufficiently resolute socialist principles that one Trotskyist group attempted, with limited success, to colonize it.[11] Perhaps the most distinctive feature of the PS-1's conduct was its recognition that parliamentary politics were a necessary but insufficient factor in building a socialist movement and that both the necessity and the insufficiency should be scrupulously demonstrated rather than idly asserted. This approach lay behind Quiroga's leadership of the congressional impeachment of Generals Barrientos (1967) and Banzer (1979), for which he paid with his life in the 1980 coup, and the steadfast refusal of the PS-1 to accept any electoral alliance that would dilute its program in popular-frontist minimalism. Thus, in early 1980 it alone of the major forces of the Left refused to participate in an all-party front dedicated exclusively to the defense of constitutionalism (in which the COB also participated).[12] During the 1980s this deep suspicion of alliances acquired a more sectarian character in that it was maintained, particularly in 1988—1989, in the face of efforts to establish a united Left slate. Nonetheless, the party was prominent in demanding electoral reform and at the end of the decade had established itself as the most consistent and effective critic of government corruption. Its new leader, Roger Cortez, proved an eloquent advocate of political morality when this appeared to be one of the Left's few remaining assets and a gravely underexploited resource.

What is notable about the leaderships of all the parties discussed above is that they were overwhelmingly composed of mestizo lowlanders, usually of urban background. Few spoke the indigenous languages of Aymara and Quechua, and most adopted a purely token respect for the causes of the campesino and *indio* that had acquired impetus with the collapse of the pact with the military under Banzer and, for the first time, offered the possibility of the majority of the electorate's being won over from the MNR-military clientelist axis. The Left failed to respond to this challenge, its lack of interest in and experience with the rural population fusing with an instrumentalist approach in reliance upon an alternative clientelism (most marked within the UDP through the MNRI's ties inherited from the 1950s). This was also true of the COB, which even at its seventh congress in 1988 insisted, as in 1971, upon proletarian primacy—the peasantry representing a mere 14 percent of delegates even though it constituted the great majority of the laboring population.[13] Aside from the residual "urbanism" already mentioned as a strong trait of both organized labor and the traditional vanguard parties, it should be noted that the tasks of organization in the Bolivian countryside are exceptionally demanding. The chief factor in this scenario, however, was the tension between the politics of class articulated in terms of the Hispanic republic and those of ethnicity based upon autonomy—if not independence—for the indigenous peoples or nations subsumed by imperial and republican colonization.

The emergence of this *indigenista* current—known as *katarismo* after the rebel leader Tupaj Katari, killed by the Spanish in 1781—was most marked among the Aymara and contained enough expressions of racism and millenarianism to justify some aspects of socialist caution.[14] Yet it also proferred an unparalleled opportunity to correct the urban, Occidental, and elitist characteristics of the Left's past conduct and beliefs. This was especially the case in 1979—1980, when the peasantry of the altiplano exhibited a rising radicalism in the formation of the Confederación Sindical Unica de Trabajadores Campesinos de Bolivia (Sole Trade Union of Rural Workers of Bolivia—CSUTCB), integration within the COB, and the staging of particularly efficacious roadblocks in protest against both dictatorship and devaluation.[15] (These were repeated under the Siles government and increased under that of Paz Estenssoro in opposition to the government's coca policy.) The strength and autonomy of this radicalism may certainly be exaggerated; it was clearly influenced by urban mobilization and soon fell prey to a debilitating parochial caudillismo that had been nurtured by decades of competition for state patronage. All the same, the general failure—often based on reluctance—of the Left to engage with this challenge beyond the bounds of rhetoric inhibited the construction of an authentic peasant-worker alliance under the UDP. It also constrained full exploitation of the state's offensive on coca in the late 1980s, when many former workers had undergone at least partial *campesinación* and had taken more than a vestige of trade union culture and radical politics into the countryside.

The difficulties inherited from a past urban bias should not, however, be confused with those emanating from what was in essence a new phenomenon, to which the COB did turn its attention in the late 1980s. This revolved around the class and ethnic recomposition of the population of the valleys compelled by the recession in the formal economy—both urban and rural—in the altiplano and the precarious dynamism experienced by a trade based upon subsistence agriculture (cultivation of the coca plant) but dependent upon processing into an illegal substance and commercialization by a mafia that made it subject to sanction by a foreign power.[16] The coca issue, therefore, restored the question of anti-imperialism to the political agenda in a manner that had not occurred with the debt. This was something of a paradox in that the United States had been relatively consistent in its opposition to dictatorship after 1978 and had contributed to the downfall of the military regime because of its association with the cocaine trade. Increased U.S. intervention after 1984—including the deployment of troops in 1986— provided an issue that allowed the Left to challenge the Right over national sovereignty and to introduce into its own politics a recognition of ethnic culture that had previously been subordinated by strenuous emphasis on class and nation-as-republic. It should be noted that some elements of the Right also attacked the United States on this question and that relations between the coca growers' organization and the COB were sometimes strained. Yet it is notable that the Left's campaign was free of many of the presumptions of the previous decade, exhibiting resourcefulness as well as sharpness on a matter that posed a number of acute dilemmas for policy.

The counterproductive legacy of the 1960s and 1970s for the Left was more pronounced in the altiplano, where katarismo foundered upon internal sectarianism (often based on regionalism and personalism) and was reduced as a political force first by tactical voting for the MNR (still associated with the agrarian reform) and then by the rapid expansion of what may be termed "cholo populism."[17] This was most forcefully represented by Conciencia de Patria (Conscience of the Fatherland—CONDEPA), which was based on Aymara migrants to greater La Paz and disseminated, largely through radio and television, an agile expression of the travails of an expanding underclass that had been ignored by the

Left as "lumpen" and that could no longer afford to restrict itself to a rural and ethnic vision. The ascendency of CONDEPA was confirmed by its sweeping victory in La Paz in the 1989 elections and complemented the national triumph of the traditional Right.

In 1980 the UDP had easily won in the capital, but now the Left paid the price for both its association with the economic conditions under Siles's government and its previous lack of work among the peasantry, significant elements of which were either directly or indirectly connected with the urban sphere to a much greater degree than had been the case a decade earlier. Moreover, whereas the Left had lost a natural constituency through "deproletarianization," it found it difficult to address a new one thrown up by *descampesinación*, remaining attached to a culture of mass meetings and pamphleteering that had little leverage with largely illiterate recent migrants lacking trade union experience and scavenging an individualist or kinship-based survival in the informal economy. Equally, katarismo was reluctant to embrace those elements of acculturation (*choloficación*) that tested its central indigenista nerve.

In this connection, note should be made of the signal absence in Bolivia during the past decade of an insurgent force comparable to Sendero Luminoso in Peru. Although at the end of the 1980s the depleted promise of katarismo and the depths of the recession had provoked some slight moves in this direction in the form of discrete terrorist acts by the Fuerzas Armadas de Liberación–Zárate Willka (Zárate Willka Armed Forces of Liberation), these were much less than might have been expected in the light of the failures of the orthodox Left and the degree of popular pauperization. Here a number of factors may be mentioned: the existence of survivalist opportunities in the coca circuit, the weakness of the ultra-Left in the countryside and, particularly, the eclipse of Maoism at the end of the 1970s through wholesale class collaboration, the legacy of the agrarian reform of 1953 in the altiplano, and the relatively low stigma attached to race compared with Peru.[18]

The Left's Emergence from the Experience of Power Sharing

The Left, therefore, entered the postdictatorial period in 1982 both in the same organizational form and on the broad understanding that it should be engaged to some degree in parliamentary politics. Even the POR, which entertained a particularly robust critique of "parliamentary cretinism," participated in local and national elections. Moreover, although the COB eventually drove the UDP to the wall in late 1984, it had previously taken care to modulate its pressure in the face of right-wing threats to constitutionalism. There were, as already indicated, widely differing views as to the extent to which socialists might progress within the confines of liberal democratic institutions and ideology, but on only two occasions did elements of the Left seriously consider reversing their position: in November 1979 (when the short-lived coup of Colonel Alberto Natusch enticed the PCB to explore a bonapartist pact, which was forestalled by popular resistance) and in March 1985 (when, in a final, bitter general strike against the UDP, the COB came close to repudiating the elections tabled for August as a *golpe constitucional* (constitutional coup) and thus at heart no different from any other golpe).[19] It should be added that in July 1986, a year after the MNR's stabilization plan was imposed, the COB staged an extremely well-supported national consultation on government economic policy and the deployment of U.S. troops. This initiative resembled more the traditional *cabildos abiertos* (public town meetings) than the Asamblea of 1971, but it did reintroduce into the political arena the possibility of "dual authority" and was fiercely attacked by the government as unconstitutional. For some this type of activity represented the best means by which to adjust to the contraction of the unions and the emergent importance of local bodies such as *comités cívicos* and *juntas vecinales* under conditions of constitutionalism. Although the COB did not attempt to repeat its national exercise, the incidence of cabildos abiertos, particularly in provincial towns, increased markedly with the frequent support of the Left.

After nearly a decade of civilian government and economic recession, a number of general features may be identified in the conduct and outlook of the Bolivian Left. First and most important is the decline of syndicalism through both an erosion of its social base and the defeats suffered by *autogestión* (worker control) that lacked any political prospectus. Insistence upon workers' control by the COB leadership in an effort to avoid repeating the defeats of the 1950s represented a return to reliance on the tradition of intransigent struggle that had served it so well over two decades of dictatorship. However, this was now shown to be insufficient and, indeed, dangerous insofar as its veto power raised more political questions than it was prepared to answer.[20] Secondly, the popular-frontist strategy was comprehensively discredited. This led to the division of the PCB after its fifth congress early in 1985 that laid the basis for subsequent disputes over the lack of democracy within the party but did not force the leadership into anything more than a limited critique of errors committed under the UDP.[21] At the same time, the MIR split into three factions: the MIR–Nueva Mayoría (New Majority) under Jaime Paz, which swung sharply to the right, retrieved many features of its Christian Democratic origins under the guise of social democracy, and came to office in August 1989 in alliance with Banzer;[22] the MIR-Masas (Masses) under Walter Delgadillo, which initially led the offensive against the

PCB within the COB; and the MIR–Bolivia Libre (Free Bolivia) (later Movimiento Bolivia Libre) under Antonio Aranibar, which formed the core of the left-wing electoral alliance (Pueblo Unido in 1985, Izquierda Unida in 1989) to which the various factions of the PCB and the MIR-Masas adhered.[23]

Third, the lack of a military threat to constitutionalism after 1985 and the consolidation of the Right on the basis of severe neoliberal deflation led the Left to place far greater emphasis upon socioeconomic change than on defense of the liberal democratic order. Nevertheless, the Right's extensive manipulation of the constitution prompted renewed attention, particularly on the part of the PS-1, to the importance of legal guarantees and the need to adjust the prescriptions of proletarian democracy inherited from the 1950s and cultivated under conditions of dictatorship to those of the nominal rule of law and a popular movement of unprecedented heterogeneity. This involved a questioning of the centralist practices of the COB more than of the parties themselves, which were notably reluctant to revise internal practices that remained largely determined by caudillismo in the guise of "democratic centralism." As a result, much of the reappraisal of received beliefs about the relation between socialism and democracy took place among independent intellectual groups.[24] This was also the case with respect to the issues of gender and the environment. The former had long received expression within the mining communities through the *comités de amas de casa*, which had led the mobilization against Banzer in 1978 and had extended, albeit in less emphatic fashion, to the campesina movement.[25] Yet these movements had exercised a strictly limited influence on the practice of the unions and parties and remained distant from the very small groups of urban and largely middle-class feminists. Despite the fact that Bolivia could lay claim to Latin America's first woman president other than by courtesy of marriage (Lydia Gueiler, 1979–1980), representation of women in the leadership of the Left was notably poor. It was, rather, the populist Right, such as CONDEPA, that exploited the fact that women were a majority of the labor force and lacked real protection of their rights, let alone the opportunity to escape the formidable sociocultural limits imposed on the basis of gender. Similarly, the ecological question remained subordinate, although at the end of the 1980s it acquired increasing importance as a result of state plans to eradicate coca, wanton exploitation of mineral resources for short-term gain both on the altiplano (particularly lithium) and in the lowlands (particularly gold), and the lack of restrictions on slash-and-burn agricultural practices, the microclimatic effects of which were substantial. Because the Left was obliged to turn its attention to the new locus of both economy and population in the rural sector, it was correspondingly forced to remedy its lack of interest in this sphere.

Finally, although the 1980s had witnessed the complete marginalization of the continent's most redoubtable advocate of permanent revolution (the POR), the developments of the decade provoked a fundamental questioning of "stagist" stratagems, not least because the MNR—long considered by many on the Left to be at least the surrogate of a "national bourgeoisie"—could no longer meaningfully be presented as a progressive and anti-imperialist force. This shift was not made explicit within the PCB leadership itself, but it was evident in the widespread acceptance that the political era opened by the 1952 revolution had come to an end. Since 1952 had broadly been interpreted as a kind of "bourgeois democratic revolution," the notion that it would have to be repeated defied credibility. Here it should be stressed that the experience and interpretation of national developments far outstripped external influences, which had never played a major part in determining the activity of the Left (with the partial exception of the POR as well as the PCB) in a landlocked mountainous country with particularly poor communications and very slight immigration in the twentieth century. In one sense these circumstances had restricted the "modernity" of the Left, but they also served to give a high profile to the cultural features of oppression and exploitation both within the country and from outside. Whereas katarismo placed greatest emphasis upon internal colonialism, there was a perceptible shift among other leftist currents toward engagement with those varied communitarian forces in the struggle against payment of the debt, the offensive against coca, the imposition of free market economics, and the progressive erosion of the gains of 1952. There was growing recognition of the fact that it was no longer feasible to undertake struggle simply along the lines of the organizations and ideology bequeathed by the revolution. However, the process of distinguishing between those elements that had been superseded by history and those that still retained validity for the construction of a socialist alternative in the post-tin and postdictatorial epoch remained exceptionally uneven and taxing.

Notes

1. For an overview of the main developments of the decade and their background, see James Dunkerley, "Political Transition and Economic Stabilization in Bolivia, 1982–1989," research paper, Institute of Latin American Studies, University of London, 1990.

2. The crisis in tin mining is analyzed in Latin America Bureau, *The Great Tin Crash: Bolivia and the World Tin Market* (London: Latin America Bureau, 1987).

3. There is as yet no detailed analysis of the economic policy of the UDP by the Left, although a sense of the objectives of those who were part of the government in its early phase can be gleaned from Rolando Morales, "La Crisis Económica," *Informe R* (La Paz), May 1985, and Horst Grebe López [of the PCB], "Notas críticas sobre la gestión económica de la UDP," in Movimiento Bolivia Libre, *Repensando el país* (La Paz, 1987).

4. A narrative account of this period may be found in James Dunkerley, *Rebellion in the Veins: Political Struggle in Bolivia, 1952–1982* (London: Verso, 1984).

5. The Trotskyist POR was responsible for drafting the 1946 Tesis de Pulacayo of the FSTMB that served a programmatic reference point for the COB in the early years of the revolution.

6. For details, see Dunkerley, *Rebellion in the Veins*, 168–196; Jorge Lazarte, *Movimiento obrero y procesos políticos en Bolivia: Historia de la COB, 1952–1987* (La Paz: ILDIS, 1988), 45–58, 143–147.

7. The complex personality and activity of Lechín, who headed the FSTMB from 1944 to 1986 and the COB from 1952 to 1986, is explored in Lupe Cajías, *Historia de una leyenda* (La Paz: Ediciones Gráficas, 1988).

8. The two positions are presented and reconsidered in René Zavaleta, *El poder dual en América Latina* (Mexico: Siglo XXI, 1974), and Guillermo Lora, *Bolivia: De la asamblea popular al golpe fascista* (Buenos Aires: El Yunque, 1972).

9. PCB, *IV Congreso: Documentos principales* (La Paz, 1980). The PCB's paper is *Unidad*.

10. One of the marked features of the MIR was a paucity of strategic political analysis, especially following the departure of René Zavaleta in the mid-1970s. Some sense of its perspectives at the start of the 1980s can, however, be gleaned from the essays in *Bases* (Mexico, 1980), and, very occasionally, from the party's paper *Bolivia Libre*.

11. Marcelo Quiroga Santa Cruz, *El saqueo de Bolivia* (Buenos Aires, Ediciones de Crisis, 1973); *Oleocracia o patria* (Mexico: Siglo XXI, 1982). The PS-1's paper was *Mañana el Pueblo*.

12. Marcelo Quiroga Santa Cruz, *Bolivia recupera la palabra: Juicio a la dictadura* (La Paz, PS-1, 1982). This tactic was later used by MIR–Bolivia Libre against the MNR. Antonio Aranibar and Alfonso Ferrufino, *Interpelación al gobierno del MNR* (La Paz, 1986).

13. COB, *VII Congreso: Documentos y resoluciones* (La Paz, 1988). This did not vary the position adopted at the previous congress dominated by the radical Left opposed to the PCB.

14. Javier Hurtado, *El Katarismo* (La Paz: Hisbol, 1986); Silvia Rivera, *Oprimidos pero no vencidos* (La Paz: Hisbol, 1984); Javier Albó "From MNRistas to kataristas to Katari," in Steve Stern, ed., *Rebellion and Consciousness in the Andean Peasant World* (Madison: University of Wisconsin Press, 1987).

15. René Zavaleta Mercado, *Las masas en noviembre* (La Paz: Juventio, 1983), reprinted in Zavaleta, ed., *Bolivia hoy* (Mexico: Siglo XXI, 1983).

16. Kevin Healy, "Coca, the State, and the Peasantry in Bolivia, 1982–1988," *Journal of Inter-American Studies*, 30, 2 and 3 (September 1989).

17. Carlos F. Toranzo Roca and Mario Arrieta Abdalla, *Nueva derecha y desproletarización en Bolivia* (La Paz: ILDIS, 1989).

18. In 1979 the PCBML, led by Oscar Zamora, allied itself with the MNR on the grounds that it represented the national bourgeoisie. Subsequently the party decomposed into a personalist vehicle for Zamora, who became minister of labor in the MIR–Acción Democrática Nacionalista (National Democratic Action—ADN) government formed in August 1989.

19. For 1979, see Pablo Ramos, *La democracia: Sus defensores y sus enemigos* (La Paz: Juventud, 1979), and Zavaleta, *Masas en noviembre*, which synthesizes for a specific conjuncture the author's efforts to apply ideas developed from Gramsci to Bolivian history and social structure: *Clases sociales y conocimiento* (La Paz: Los Amigos del Libro, 1988); *Lo nacional-popular en Bolivia* (Mexico: Siglo XXI, 1986). Zavaleta's tragically early death in 1984 deprived the Bolivian Left of its most outstanding intellectual.

20. See the important debates reprinted in FLACSO, *Crísis del sindicalismo en Bolivia* (La Paz, 1987). It is worth noting that in the mid-1980s the hunger strike became the preferred tactic of both the COB leadership and the unemployed. Perhaps there was no more striking symbol of the fortunes of the miners than the mock crucifixion of redundant workers demanding

severance pay in La Paz in 1989 when just four years earlier they had occupied the city center for ten days and cowed the government with frequent discharges of dynamite in the streets.

21. For the polemic over strategy, see *Unidad,* 639 (July 19, 1985), for the official line, and 641 (July 20–26, 1985), for the dissident line. Early in 1990 the PCB leadership came under renewed internal challenge of lack of democracy in the party.

22. Paz Zamora's *Bolivia: Una necesidad para los bolivianos* (La Paz, 1985), clearly prefigures the full shift to the Right effected in 1989.

23. In 1986 the Communist dissidents, organized as PCB-V Congreso (Fifth Congress Communist Party of Bolivia), joined with the MIR-Masas and a small group of independent intellectuals known as the Bloque Popular Patriótico (Patriotic Popular Bloc) to form the Eje de Convergencia (Convergence Axis), which successfully challenged the PCB for the leadership of the COB but was soon forced to modulate its aggressive line by the collapse of the 1986 miners' mobilization.

24. See, in particular, *Autodeterminación* (La Paz), 6 and 7 (December 1988), which contain an extensive debate on the state and prospects of the Left.

25. The best-known account of the movement of the women of the mines is Domitila Barrios de Chungara, *Let me Speak!* (London: Stage 1, 1978). It is notable that the 1989 IU program devoted some space to the women's question—an innovation for the Bolivian Left.

8

The Venezuelan Left:
From Years of Prosperity
to Economic Crisis

Steve Ellner

The Venezuelan Left—its positions, its locus in the political party system, and its prospects—has been thoroughly transformed as a consequence of political and economic changes and external factors since the mid-1980s. Up until then, leftists sought legitimacy and incorporation into the existing political system. Their electoral focus was demonstrated by the significance they attached to—and the meticulous analyses they provided of—variations at the polls of a mere one or two percentage points. This orientation in the 1970s and early 1980s was no doubt a reaction to the "ultraleftist" errors committed during the guerrilla warfare of the 1960s, when the Left attempted to enforce an electoral boycott. Nevertheless, at no time did leftists apologize for their decision to take up arms, which they now viewed as an honest, perhaps even necessary, mistake. In spite of the negligible recuperation of leftist parties in the 1970s in both organized labor and national elections, leftists did make a rich literary contribution in the form of a spate of provocative books, periodicals, and newsletters in which innovations in organization and strategy were debated.[1]

The sharp decline in oil prices in the first half of 1986 marked a turning point for the Left, as it did for the nation as a whole. Violent confrontations between students and security forces became a frequent occurrence,

The author is grateful for critical comments by Susan Berglund and Dick Parker, both of the Universidad Central de Venezuela.

as they had been in the 1960s, although they paled in comparison with the spontaneous mass disturbances during the week of February 27, 1989, which resulted in hundreds if not thousands of deaths. This popular protest compelled leftists to harden their stand toward the government and converge in their positions on concrete issues. They also moved somewhat away from their sectarian fixation on party identities, which had contributed to intraleft divisions. Simultaneously, perestroika not only encouraged the Partido Comunista de Venezuela (Communist party of Venezuela—PCV) to affirm its commitment to democracy but also led leftists in other parties to abandon their resistance to unity on the ground that the PCV defended totalitarianism. The efforts of leftists of the 1970s to explore and experiment with novel forms of democracy were far from exhausted by the 1980s. Now, however, the renovation current on the left had the entire nation behind it in its democratic reform impulse: the model of worker participation (cogestión) was embraced by organized labor, and "state reform" became a government catchword and even the name of a new ministry.

The willingness of the Left to unite, its more critical stands, and its success in disassociating itself from traditional Left stereotypes, all in a context of severe and prolonged economic crisis, paid handsome dividends at the polls. In the elections of December 1989, the Left elected three governors and broke the bipolarized pattern that had provided virtually monopoly status to the nation's two main establishment parties for over fifteen years. The "great electoral leap forward" that the largest leftist party, the Movimiento al Socialismo, had been striving to achieve since the 1970s finally became a reality, its candidates receiving 20 percent of the municipal vote—double that of five years before.

The Oil Boom and Its Immediate Aftermath

The first presidency of Carlos Andrés Pérez (1974–1979) was replete with surprises for Venezuela. The threefold increase in oil prices at the outset of his term transformed the nation in many ways, particularly in creating an ambience of material well-being and optimism. This was reflected in Pérez's proclamation that Venezuela had achieved "full employment"; the phrase, which became a political catchword exploited by his Acción Democrática party, not only indicated that levels of unemployment had been substantially reduced but reflected widespread acceptance of the myth that it had, for all intents and purposes, been eradicated. At the outset of his administration, Pérez introduced a series of proworker reforms and nationalistic policies including the Ley de Estabilidad Laboral (Labor Stability Law)—later watered down and renamed the Ley Contra Despidos Injustificados (Law Against Unjustified

Dismissals), the establishment of a minimum wage, price regulations on basic commodities, the nationalization of the iron and petroleum industries, and the pursuit of a vocally pro–Third World foreign policy. Pérez's left-leaning populism was not in keeping with the image stemming from the hard line he had adopted toward the insurgent Left as minister of the interior in the early 1960s. It also seemed unlikely following a recent split in AD, in which party conservatives retained control of the organization and its left-wing faction withdrew to form the Movimiento Electoral del Pueblo (People's Electoral Movement—MEP). Political observers were also surprised by the qualified support extended to the Pérez administration in 1974 by the "ultraleftist" MAS. The MAS had been founded in 1971 by Communists who had been among those most committed to the guerrilla struggle in the 1960s and were impatient with the traditional Left's relegation of socialism to the distant future.

The MAS's turnabout signaled a profound change in the Left's political strategy and discourse. MAS leaders now ruled out excessive reliance on mass mobilizations, arguing that Venezuela's privileged status as an oil producer translated into greater economic and political stability than existed elsewhere in Latin America. The MAS also dissolved parallel unions and entered the AD-dominated Confederación de Trabajadores de Venezuela (Workers' Confederation of Venezuela—CTV), which leftists had severely denounced in the 1960s for impeding class struggle and promoting party interests. In addition, the *MASistas* redefined the concept of socialism to emphasize democracy over changes in property relations. The MAS's commitment to democracy was not limited to theoretical formulations: it pioneered in organizational reform, the most far-reaching of which was the recognition of internal "tendencies" (a euphemism for factions) that were allowed to proselytize within the party, ran their own slates in internal elections, and received proportional representation at all levels of the party.[2]

The MAS was a pacesetter on the left. Other leftist parties also abandoned the notion that Venezuelan democracy was inextricably tied to the capitalist structure. As did with the MAS, they entered the CTV and, in spite of their limited representation at its congresses, were given positions on its executive committee. At first, leftist parties pledged themselves to struggle within the CTV to democratize and radicalize it and to eliminate corruption within its ranks. Nevertheless, in the course of time the leftists on the CTV's executive committee did not always forcefully pursue these objectives. Furthermore, the leftists coincided with AD's trade union leadership on certain basic issues, such as the need to deemphasize labor conflict in state-run industries and to avoid public questioning of the ethical conduct of fellow *CTVistas*, limiting criticism to internal discussion. By the late 1970s, the Causa R (Radical Cause) and a host of other marginal left parties that opposed these restraints made important inroads in conflict-ridden sectors, specifically in the steel company Siderúrgica del Orinoco (SIDOR) and other state-run basic industries in the state of Bolívar, as well as in the textile industry.[3] Contrary to the general impression conveyed by many leftists that labor harmony prevailed during the oil boom period, strike activity, while tapering off after 1973, was still considerably greater than during the 1960s.

Up until its 1985 congress, the MAS was greatly concerned with staking out an identity that would differentiate it from the PCV, from which it had emerged, and social democracy as represented by AD, which a minority of MASistas felt their party should approximate. According to many MASistas, such delineation was obstructed by the party's decision to choose an independent leftist, José Vicente Rangel, as its presidential candidate in 1973 and 1978. For the latter election, they pushed for the nomination of the MAS's principal theoretician, ex-guerrilla Teodoro Petkoff, arguing that this would stimulate the party to seek greater ideological clarity. Subsequently, Petkoff was selected to represent the MAS in the presidential elections of 1983 and 1988. The determination of MASistas to disassociate themselves from the traditional Left because of the nondemocratic implications of its doctrine led them to rule out a priori any electoral pact that included the PCV.

The MAS's approach, which rejected compromise on any of its positions in an attempt to appeal to voters on the basis of an undiluted program and ideology, was at odds with the united-frontism promoted by the PCV. As a result, in spite of considerable interest in a united leftist candidacy, the Left ran several presidential candidates in the elections of 1973, 1978, 1983, and 1988. In these elections (with the exception of that of 1978, in which there were four leftist candidates), the united-front strategy supported by the PCV and the MEP succeeded in drawing a host of smaller leftist groups that Petkoff contemptuously called "alphabet soup letters." In these three elections the MAS's only ally was the Movimiento de la Izquierda Revolucionaria (Movement of the Revolutionary Left—MIR), a 1960 split-off from the AD. While the fledgling MAS's 5.3 percent in the 1973 congressional elections was considered a breakthrough at the time, the party's vote in the three subsequent congressional contests, which ranged from 5.2 percent to 10.3 percent, was a disappointment to the MASistas, who were convinced of socialism's short-term prospects in Venezuela. The three other main leftist parties (the MEP, the MIR, and the PCV) fared even worse, the entire leftist vote in the presidential elections and congressional elections respectively being 9.4 percent and 12.5 percent in 1973, 7.8 percent and 11.7 percent in 1978, 7.5 percent and 13.6 percent in 1983, and 4.0 percent and 13.6 percent in 1988.

The stability of Venezuelan democracy during this period contrasted sharply with the situation in the rest of Latin America, mostly governed by military dictatorships and subject to considerable unrest. These conditions influenced Petkoff and other MASistas to view the Venezuelan road to socialism as largely free of violence and more akin to the democratic path mapped out by the Italian Communist party than what could be expected elsewhere in the continent. For this reason, the MAS was clearly in the forefront in the modification of socialist doctrine, emphasizing pluralism and rank-and-file participation, that other Latin American leftist parties would begin to stress only in the latter part of the 1980s, after democracy had been restored in their nations.

The Deepening of the Economic Crisis, 1986–1991

The recession that set in during the administration of Luis Herrera Campíns (1979–1984) of the Social Christian Comité de Organización Política Electoral Independiente (Committee of Independent Electoral Political Organization—COPEI), AD's main party rival, grew worse under the government of AD's Jaime Lusinchi (1984–1989) and the beginning of Carlos Andrés Pérez's second term (1989–1994). During the 1980s, the popular and progressive policies of Pérez's first administration were abandoned in favor of neoliberal economic formulas and a less defiant stand toward the United States, in spite of the previous reputation of all three presidents as being left-leaning or at least reformist. The MAS's positions shifted to the left, partly as a result of the election of hard-liner Freddy Muñoz as secretary-general at the party's national convention in 1985 and his reelection in 1990. At the time of the 1985 convention, most members of its social democratic faction left the party, after which it was less concerned about disputing AD's claim to the social democratic label. Pérez's conservative tendency after his reelection in 1988 and the MAS's move to the left were part of a veritable polarization in Venezuelan politics in which the "Center-Left" position ceased to be as attractive and promising as it had been in the 1970s, when Pérez and the MAS seemed to be converging on it from opposite directions.

The MAS's shift to the left must also be placed in a historical-international context. The MAS had always avoided a staunchly anti-United States position and made a conscious effort to balance criticism of Washington with that of Soviet foreign policy.[4] Underpinning its refusal to take sides in U.S.-Soviet disputes was the conviction that the Cold War impaired Third World interests. It opposed U.S. belligerence toward the Sandinista regime, for instance, because this thrust Nicaragua onto center stage in the East-West conflict and undermined that government's efforts to experiment with policies that did not accord with either U.S. or Soviet models. When the Soviet Union dropped out of the Cold War under Gorbachev, the MAS's denunciations of U.S. policies were no longer moderated or counterpoised by attacks on the other camp. At its 1990 convention, it hailed the ending of the Cold War: "The cessation of bipolarity has and will continue to have positive effects on all fronts. Options in the area of economic relations and international politics will be opened up in favor of plurality. . . . It will also reduce the obstacles to a 'new treatment' between the 'big' nations and the 'small' ones."[5]

The historical implications of this revised focus were apparent in the MAS's reaction to the U.S. attack on Iraq in 1991 and its criticism of both the Venezuelan government and the United Nations for failing to remain evenhanded in the dispute. Petkoff argued that, whereas the U.S. decision to enter the Korean War and the U.S. confrontation with the Soviet Union in the Cuban missile crisis had been justified by the risk of alteration of the international balance of power, such constraints were no longer operative and therefore the U.S. action amounted to no more than the naked assertion of hegemony in the Third World.[6]

Reactions in COPEI, AD, and the Left to privatization and other IMF-inspired economic policies in the 1980s were varied. The COPEI, under the leadership of the party's 1988 presidential candidate Eduardo Fernández, urged President Pérez to accelerate official plans for privatization, which included seventy state-owned firms. The PCV, the MAS, and other leftist parties rejected proposals to turn over operations in strategic industries to private interests, although they were not opposed to privatization per se. The PCV, for instance, accepted the privatization of certain companies as long as "it is carried out with absolute rectitude and does not contribute to a greater concentration of wealth . . . in favor of monopolies."[7] The Left also insisted that Congress set general guidelines for privatization, including worker input in the management of privatized firms—something that the CTV also called for. At first glance, it would have appeared that the Left had the same concerns as certain influential traditional sectors in both COPEI (particularly former president Rafael Caldera) and AD (especially members of the "orthodox" faction, which included former president Jaime Lusinchi) about the neoliberal bent of Pérez's economic policies. Nevertheless, by the late 1980s Caldera's influence in COPEI's leadership was marginal. More important, those AD leaders who resisted privatization were swayed by clientelistic imperatives to which the Left was not subject: state companies, in contrast to private ones, provided opportunities to AD and its members in the form of employment, contracts, and resources.[8]

Within the leftist camp divergences of opinion on other measures imposed by the IMF were evident. The Left, for instance, criticized the "shock treatment" embraced by the Pérez administration, whereby tariffs, preferential dollars for nonluxury imports, subsidies for the production of basic commodities, and the regulation of their prices were to be almost completely eliminated in a short period of time. The main thrust of the critique put forward by Teodoro Petkoff was that the strategy of opening Venezuela to foreign capital and imports had to be implemented gradually in order to limit adverse socioeconomic effects. Other leftists emphasized the need to go beyond the "easy" stage of import substitution, although few offered blueprints based on the state interventionism that had been considered a virtual panacea prior to the 1980s.[9]

Petkoff, Muñoz, and other leftists defended different criteria for the role of foreign capital in the nationalized oil industry. Petkoff viewed with favor the proposed joint venture for the exploitation of natural gas in the Peninsula of Paria, in which the state oil company was to hold only 40 percent of the stock. Petkoff pointed out that none of the company's foreign partners would have a greater share and that, in any case, Venezuela was to have veto power over all decisions. Muñoz, while also going along with the deal, adhered more strictly to the original terms of the nationalization of oil, which circumscribed the participation of private capital in the industry. In contrast, *MEPistas,* among others, refused to endorse the arrangement, arguing that it represented a step toward the denationalization of the industry.[10]

The more aggressive opposition of the Causa R to the government's economic policies nearly led it to a direct confrontation with SIDOR in the state of Bolívar, where the party's standard-bearer, Andrés Velásquez, was elected governor in 1989. The Sindicato Único de Trabajadores de la Industria Siderúrgica (Single Union of Workers of the Steel Industry—SUTISS) had been a stronghold of the Causa R since the 1970s, when Velásquez was elected its president, only to be ousted by the union's affiliate federations two years later. SIDOR was being prodded by its creditor the World Bank to carry out a plan of industrial reconversion that consisted of the closing of several plants and the immediate dismissal of three thousand workers. The Pérez government was also motivated by the prospect that the Bush administration's commitment to a hemispheric union would be translated into the lifting of voluntary restrictions on Venezuelan steel exports to the United States.

The Causa R–controlled SUTISS called several symbolic strikes and proposed that the three thousand jobs be preserved by eliminating overtime work, contracted work, and bureaucratic waste. The union also claimed that SIDOR's real aim was to streamline individual operations in order to privatize them. The Causa R, which in the 1970s had sharply criticized other leftists in SIDOR for overrelying on strikes, was now encouraged by its control of the governorship and threatened to call a general strike in the region. SIDOR, for its part, raised the specter of the militarization of the zone and the dismissal of the union's entire leadership. Governor Velásquez played a key role in persuading the Pérez administration to set up a commission with union and company participation to work out a plan to mitigate the negative effects of reconversion. The agreement created a labor exchange whereby discharged workers would be employed in other state firms in the region for two years, during which time they would receive 80 percent of their former salaries (SIDOR had wanted it to be reduced in time to 50 percent) and be covered by certain clauses in SIDOR's labor contract. In addition, workers who left SIDOR voluntarily would be granted double severance pay. Velásquez recognized that both sides had made important concessions and hailed the agreement as a breakthrough that improved upon similar arrangements in countries such as Spain.[11]

Another important issue to which the Venezuelan Left lacked a uniform approach was the problem of ecological disruption and preservation of national borders. In the late 1980s thousands of Brazilian miners, known as *garimpeiros*, illegally entered Venezuela's southern rain forest region in search of gold and diamonds. Not only did the use of mercury in the extraction of gold contaminate the Orinoco River system, but the miners' presence threatened the precarious existence of indigenous tribes. Individual leftists defended two diametrically opposed positions. On the one hand, the ex-MEPista national deputy Alexander Luzardo argued that the area's delicate ecological equilibrium would be upset if the population were to exceed two inhabitants per square kilometer. On the other, some leftists favored colonization schemes and the promotion of economic activity such as tourism as the only way to check Brazilian expansionism, purportedly sponsored by the armed forces of that nation. They questioned "ultraconservationism" and alleged that certain conservationist organizations were a cover for multinational interests seeking to exploit the region in a supposedly orderly manner. Leftist parties did not have a fixed stand. Most of them, however, were undoubtedly sensitive to the possibility that a vocal defense of the ultraconservationist strategy would leave them vulnerable to criticisms of failing to defend national boundaries and being antipatriotic. Prior to the 1970s, the Left in Venezuela and elsewhere in the continent, under the influence of "internationalism," had generally committed this error.[12]

The Left in the Nation's Democratic Setting

Some of the Left's positions on democratic reforms and party reorganization—as with the issue of privatization—were supported, at least in theory, by individual leaders of Venezuela's two main establishment parties. Interest in the deepening of the nation's democracy became increasingly widespread as the memory of the violence-ridden decade of the 1960s, which had convinced many that national security required strict controls on expression, faded and political stability set in. The MAS's structural reforms—including the decentralization of authority and the granting of autonomous status to internal electoral commissions and voting privileges to non-card-carrying "friends of the party"—were designed to demonstrate that the party's commitment to democracy was not confined to theoretical formulations such as repudiation of the dictatorship of the proletariat.

The most far-reaching organizational reform was the liberty given to internal "tendencies" to propagate ideas within the party, which was seen as a corrective to the orthodox Communist practice of suppressing minority opinions. In the party's 1985 congress, nearly all delegates were clearly identified with one of the tendencies, and because of their discipline Petkoff, who at the time remained aloof of the internal currents, was not elected a regular member of the party's executive committee. Some MASistas claimed that the selection of their national authorities in 1985 was to all intents and purposes based on the system of direct elections— much as are presidential elections in the United States, in which members of the electoral college are pledged to vote for a given candidate.

At the time of the 1985 congress, it appeared that the MAS had exhausted its reformist democratic impulse and that consensus existed on the need to retreat from the "legalization of tendencies" whose resultant factionalism was threatening to tear the party apart. Since 1985, the activities of the MAS's internal tendencies have been curbed in concrete ways: they no longer publish magazines and bulletins for internal circulation, nor are their positions articulated in public. Furthermore, the MAS's three major historical leaders (Petkoff, Muñoz, and Pompeyo Márquez) are no longer in charge of the tendencies they formerly led.

Nevertheless, since 1985 the MAS has continued to pioneer reforms in favor of the deepening of democratic structures and practices. Decentralization of decision making, part of the MAS program since the late 1970s, became the cornerstone of its strategy in the 1988 national elections. The MASistas called their campaign "bicentric" in that Petkoff shared the limelight he received as presidential candidate in order to promote the images of the party's congressional aspirants. This effort came to fruition in the 1989 municipal and state elections with the emergence of strong MAS gubernatorial candidates who were clearly identified with the interests of their respective states in Aragua, Zulia, Táchira, and Lara.

The MAS's 1990 internal elections were noteworthy for several reasons. Muñoz and his only rival for secretary-general, Victor Hugo D'Paola, had both been leading members of the same tendency. This situation signaled the abatement of the ongoing, often bitter struggle among factions that had characterized the party nearly since its founding in 1971. Furthermore, ideological and even programmatic issues were largely absent from the internal campaign. Muñoz's supporters hailed the secretary-general for having checked factionalism and guided the party to its much-acclaimed success in the 1989 elections. Petkoff, who actively campaigned on behalf of D'Paola, recognized Muñoz's merits but pointed out that the MAS had to set an example for Venezuelans, whose skepticism toward parties and politicians was demonstrated by an increase in abstentionism amounting to 54 percent in 1989. He pointed out that if reelected Muñoz might end up occupying the secretary-generalship for ten years, thus contradicting the MAS's commitment to rotation in office and its opposition to the tight control by political cliques (known as *cogollitos*).

Finally, in 1990 for the first time in Venezuelan history primaries were held for party authorities, including the national and statewide posts of secretary-general and president. At the same time, MASistas were given the opportunity to vote for delegates to the national convention either by slate or nominally. In several states neither of the two main slates emerged triumphant for all leadership positions, which demonstrated that a large number of MASistas split their votes. Furthermore, the "independent" Argelia Laya was elected president (becoming the first woman president of an important political party in Venezuela) with more votes than were received by Muñoz. Some MASistas considered this voting behavior a healthy sign in that it indicated that party members were forming their own independent criteria and drew the conclusion that solidified tendencies at the national level were in the process of disappearing.

The MAS's reforms served as a model for other political parties in Venezuela. By the late 1980s, proposals that copied aspects of its reorganization and practices were put forward in AD and COPEI, although resistance from the cogollitos in both parties placed in doubt their short-term implementation. Thus, for instance, a "renovation" current in AD associated with President Pérez called for such organizational changes as proportional representation for minority slates, sharp reduction in the number of *delegados natos* (who automatically attend party conventions without having been elected), the granting of the right to vote to "friends of the party," and the electoral commission's autonomy vis-à-vis the party's executive committee. The renovators' proposal to hold primaries to elect party authorities was turned down in favor of nomination at conventions by delegates elected by the membership. The defeat of the plan discredited the claim of its architect Carlos Canache Mata that AD throughout its history had always been in the forefront in the struggle for democracy and that it was currently ahead of the MAS in internal organizational reform.[13] One of COPEI's top leaders, Gustavo Tarre, in a book critical of his party's failure to keep pace with popular support for the deepening of democracy, admitted that the MAS's regionalization and decentralization had made possible the triumph of its candidate over that of COPEI in Aragua in the 1989 gubernatorial elections.[14]

Other leftist parties moved in the same direction as the MAS. The MIR abandoned its intransigent positions of the 1960s and, shortly before the 1988 elections, merged with the MAS. In 1990, the PCV implemented direct elections for party authorities at local and regional levels. At the same time, rank-and-file Communists were given the opportunity to nominate some of the members of the party's central committee.

At the PCV's eighth congress in August 1990 neither renovator Héctor Mujica, a former presidential candidate, nor old-timer Pedro Ortega Díaz received a majority of votes for the presidency, and therefore it was decided that the position would rotate between the two. Ortega Díaz and other orthodox Communists opposed the proposed self-criticism of the party's endorsement of the 1968 Soviet invasion of Czechoslovakia that had set off the MAS split. Ortega pointed out that this proposal, as well as Mujica's blanket support of perestroika, repeated the previous Communist error of uncritically accepting models and policies from abroad in their entirety.[15] The renovators, for their part, hoped that their self-criticism would convince ex-dissidents to rejoin the party. They proposed a unity congress to amalgamate existing leftist parties and, similarly, the dissolution of the Communist-run Central Unitaria de Trabajadores de Venezuela (United Center of Workers of Venezuela—CUTV) in order to create a united workers' confederation.

The favorable outcome of the 1989 elections, in which the opposition emerged triumphant in nine of the nation's twenty gubernatorial contests, including seven of Venezuela's eight most populated and industrialized states, encouraged interest in broad-based unity. In most areas the MAS and the PCV supported common candidates. In addition, in four states virtually the entire opposition, including COPEI, endorsed the winning gubernatorial candidate. In agreeing to these electoral pacts, COPEI put aside its traditional anticommunism and the MAS replaced the go-it-alone approach that it had embraced in previous elections.

The victory of the MAS's Carlos Tablante in Aragua and Andrés Velásquez in Bolívar put in evidence the primary importance of the struggle against corruption and identification with regional interests in the outcome of the elections. As vice-president of the Chamber of Deputies, Tablante had been a major protagonist in the inquiry into the illicit sale of preferential dollars by the state foreign-exchange agency Recadi, which led to indictments against President Lusinchi's minister of interior as well as his private secretary. Velásquez's Causa R skillfully focused national attention on issues related to SIDOR and other heavy industries controlled by the state-run Corporación Venezolana de Guayana (Venezuelan Guayana Corporation—CVG) in Bolívar. The Causa R accused the politically appointed heads of CVG-affiliated companies and other government officials (including AD's candidate for governor) of favoring their own private companies with contracts. It also attacked the CVG for overextending its authority and, in the process, eclipsing local and state governments.

The triumph of the socialist MEP's candidate in Anzoátegui was made possible by the support of a host of political parties; as governor he was forced to satisfy the clientelistic appetites of his COPEI allies. In contrast, the victories of both Tablante and Velásquez were largely due to their own reputations rather than to party backing. Indeed, Tablante disappointed some MASistas by refusing to favor them in top positions as part of his declared war on clientelism. He also created special boards of bidding and purchases consisting of upstanding citizens to award state contracts to businesses without political considerations. Tablante and his followers, known as the "Force of Aragua," attempted to draw ideological conclusions from his experiences in the governorship. They argued for a model of government based on a nonsectarian approach that incorporated all citizens into the decision-making process independent of their political affiliations. This task, rather than socialism, had to be the MAS's priority goal.[16] Tablante's critics in the MAS argued that the Force of Aragua exalted administrative skills at the expense of class analysis and socioeconomic objectives.

Governor Velásquez, for his part, refused to modify his unpretentious style; thus, for instance, he avoided formal attire and drove a car rather than using a chauffeur. He continued the practice, which had become a veritable tradition in the area, of speaking at informal gatherings of workers outside the SIDOR plant. The Causa R sponsored public assemblies, which they had previously organized for the workers at SIDOR, in neighborhoods and towns to facilitate popular input into decision making at the gubernatorial level. The Causa R, whose coupling of politics and imagination had always been its trademark, undertook a campaign initiated by Velásquez of collecting fifty cents from every citizen in order to finance a professional audit of the past AD state administration.

Velásquez, Tablante, and a number of other governors and mayors (including COPEI's charismatic governor of Zulia) called for the implementation (at least in local and state contests) of uninominal elections, in which voters select candidates individually rather than by slate. They pointed out that they themselves had been elected on the basis not of identification with their respective parties, but of voter confidence in their personal integrity and political competence. The uninominal system, which threatens to undermine the dominant role of political parties, was opposed by Venezuela's major parties (although more recently AD has expressed qualified support for it). The MAS, for instance, argued that elimination of slates would deny minority parties proportional representation (as is the case in the United States) and would thus reduce if not completely do away with the Left's legislative presence. Nevertheless, Tablante's position was supported by some MASistas who claimed that forcing voters to take into consideration the candidate's qualifications and not his party affiliation would strike a blow at party machines and thus represent an important step in favor of the perfection of democracy. Indeed, at the MAS's 1990 convention, several leading MASistas ran for party positions independent of any of the slates and urged delegates to abandon the outworn practice of voting for lists elaborated by others without considering the merits of each candidate.

Critical Appraisals of the Venezuelan Left

The disturbances that broke out simultaneously throughout the nation on February 27, 1989, in response to IMF-imposed price increases took the entire nation by surprise. Many commentators pointed out at the time that the violence was a testimony to the CTV's loss of leadership and credibility and its failure to channel mass discontent. In fact, the same observation could have been applied to the Venezuelan Left. Over the previous two decades the Left had concentrated its efforts along electoral lines and had learned to play by the rules of the democratic system, even helping to reform them in constructive and creative ways. Nevertheless, it had neglected the task of establishing tight links with popular organizations and engaging in grass-roots organizing. Illustrative of the shortcoming of this approach was the Left's failure to make inroads in organized labor: in the CTV congresses of 1975, 1980, 1985, and 1990, AD retained an absolute majority, and the representation of the combined parties of the Left declined from 19 percent to 15 percent.

The events of the week of February 27 led some leftist intellectuals and activists to criticize the Left's performance and call for a reconsideration of the strategy based on electoralism. They pointed out that the disturbances demonstrated the potential for a mass movement in favor of thoroughgoing change and that the principal impediments to such an achievement were the Left's mistaken policies and priorities. Some drew the conclusion that organizations in civil society including neighborhood associations and unions, acting largely outside the realm of political party influence, would be the main instruments for radical change in Venezuela. Others placed a premium on the Communist practice prior to the 1960s of sending cadres to chosen locations and industries to organize around bread-and-butter issues. This tradition was allegedly maintained by the handful of former Communists who founded the Causa R in the early 1970s and who engaged in grass-roots politics in priority areas without attempting to project the image of their nascent party. In an attempt to revitalize the tradition, several national PCV leaders (including José Manuel Carrasquel, president of the CUTV) voluntarily stepped down from their bureaucratic positions in order to establish themselves in the rank and file in the nation's interior. Belonging to the renovation current of their party, these *PCVistas* maintained that the main lesson of perestroika was the danger of the ossification of leadership and its isolation from ordinary working people.[17]

Other leftists argued that neither trade unions nor neighborhood associations were sufficiently autonomous to conduct revolutionary struggle on their own and displace leftist parties. They defended unity from above in the form of interparty agreements as the first step toward increasing the Left's effectiveness at the grass-roots level.[18] This position was embodied in the proposal of a unity congress in 1991 for the purpose of forming a united party or front, which was endorsed by the MEP, the PCV, a group of dissident Communists, and several other small groupings. Only the MAS, which had generally spurned intraleftist unity, and the Causa R, whose explicit policy was to reject endorsement of its candidates by other parties, failed to show interest in the meeting.

The differences in leftist perceptions of civil society are understandable given the changes that have taken place in recent years. Although Venezuelan civil society is weak in comparison with others in Latin America, assertions of autonomy and independent action have become increasingly pronounced. Most neighborhood associations are controlled by AD and to a lesser extent COPEI. Nevertheless, in the latter half of the 1980s a movement within these organizations emerged in opposition to party interference and in favor of uninominal elections in order to curb party control of local government. At the same time, militant protests against the deficient public services in individual communities became a daily occurrence in Caracas and other large cities. In university elections after 1985, slates of independents mostly with a radical orientation triumphed over those identified with political parties at the Central University and elsewhere.[19] In organized labor the most important strikes were led by federations of professional workers in the state sector (grade school and university teachers, medical personnel, laboratory technicians), which were largely independent of the CTV and therefore less subject to outside control than most trade unions. Finally, in 1990, independent women's groups organized protests outside of congressional offices in defense of the provisions in the new labor law regarding paid leave of absence and absolute job security for female workers following childbirth, which had come under heavy attack from business spokesmen.

The greatest achievement of the Left in the period under study has been the legitimacy and credibility conferred on it by its commitment to democracy, which has effaced the negative stereotypes engendered by the guerrilla fiasco of the 1960s. This success made possible the electoral gains in 1989 that transformed Venezuela's political landscape. It can be expected that the congressional-presidential elections in December 1993 will break the AD-COPEI bipolarization of national expectation and attention. On the negative side is the Left's electoralism and neglect of grassroots political work. If this shortcoming is not corrected, leftist parties run the risk of being left on the sidelines in the face of spontaneous popular protests at the same time that discontent is being channeled through the two main establishment parties. Throughout its history the Venezuelan Left has shown an exceptional capacity to reflect on previous errors and change its strategy in an effort to correct them. Given this pattern, it may be expected that with the resurgence of popular movements in the post–oil-boom years the Left will modify its priorities, which up until now have been biased in favor of electoral politics.

Notes

1. Steve Ellner, "Diverse Influences on the Venezuelan Left: Five Books by Venezuelan Leftists," *Journal of Interamerican Studies and World Affairs*, 23, 4 (November 1981):483–493.

2. Steve Ellner, *Venezuela's Movimiento al Socialismo: From Guerrilla Defeat to Innovative Politics* (Durham: Duke University Press, 1988); Jorge A. Giordani, *La propuesta socialista del MAS: ¿Hacia un reformismo de izquierda?* (Valencia: Vadell Hermanos, 1989).

3. Daniel Hellinger, "Venezuelan Democracy and the Challenge of *Nuevo Sindicalismo*," paper presented at Thirteenth International Congress of the Latin American Studies Association, Boston, October 23–25, 1986.

4. Steve Ellner, *New York Times*, August 25, 1981, A-19.

5. *Punto*, January 24, 1991, my translation.

6. *Punto*, January 24, 1991.

7. *Tribuna Popular* [PCV newspaper], August 10–16, 1990, 5.

8. This point has been made by various prominent analysts, including José Antonio Gil Yepez, the journalist Alfredo Peña, and even the AD leader Héctor Alonso López. See *El Nacional*, February 24, 1991, D-2; May 5, 1991, D-2.

9. Petkoff, interview, Caracas, March 7, 1991; *El Nacional*, June 8, 1980, D-16.

10. *El Nacional*, September 12, 1990, D-7.

11. Andrés Velásquez, speech delivered in Barcelona, December 13, 1990; Tello Benítez (former secretary-general of the steelworkers' union), speech delivered in Puerto La Cruz, February 6, 1991.

12. Alexander Luzardo, interview, Caracas, August 8, 1991; *Punto*, October 11, 1990, 13; October 25, 1990, 8–9; Ellner, *Venezuela's Movimiento*, 81.

13. *El Nacional*, May 8, 1990, A-4; May 22, 1990, A-4.

14. Gustavo Tarre Briceño, *Carta abierta a los copeyanos (que puede ser leída por quienes no lo son)* (Caracas: Ediciones Centauro, 1990), 83–84.

15. Pedro Ortega Díaz, interview, Caracas, August 14, 1990.

16. Carlos Tablante, "El MAS es la Fuerza de Aragua," speech at MAS's Seventh Regional Convention in Maracay, October 1990, mimeo.

17. José Manuel Carrasquel, interview, Barcelona, February 25, 1991; *Pablo Medina en entrevista* (Caracas: Ediciones del Agua Mansa, 1988), 24.

18. Eustoquio Contreras (secretary of organization of the MEP), interview, Barcelona, March 2, 1991.

19. Luis Gómez Calcaño, "Introducción," in Gómez Calcaño, ed., *Crisis y movimientos sociales en Venezuela* (Caracas: Editorial Tropykos, 1987), 15.

9

The Argentine Left Since Perón

Donald C. Hodges

Is some political pattern discernible in the evolution of the Argentine Left since the death of President Juan Domingo Perón on July 1, 1974? Broken down into its components, this question reduces to what has happened to the principal sectors of the Argentine Left: the populist, the national, and the socialist.

Representing the interests of a broad majority, populism in Argentina rests on a truce between industrial capital and organized labor aimed at their common enemy—the landed and financial oligarchy. Although a multiclass movement, its leftwing advocates a new deal for labor based on collective bargaining, a welfare state with a strong public sector, a fifty-fifty division of national income between labor and capital as an alternative to profit sharing, and a corresponding share of political power. While the main populist party has increasingly come under the sway of its right wing since Perón's death, a majority of Peronist trade unionists in the leadership of the Confederación General del Trabajo have been consistently faithful to his ideology of justicialism (a compound of "justice" and "socialism"). Justicialism stands for a mixed economy but one that continually evolves toward socialism as labor's share in the national income, seats in Congress, and control over the provincial governments exceed the fifty-fifty mark.[1]

The Peronist Left is broad enough to include not only populists but also a self-styled national Left. Within the Peronist movement during the 1960s, the conviction that a consistent nationalism must ally itself with the socialist Left and with the socialist countries against U.S. imperialism and the multinational corporations received its classic exposition in the writings of John William Cooke. As do the corresponding movements in Bolivia and Peru, the Argentine national Left believes that the struggle against economic dependence can ultimately succeed only through a socialist revolution with nationalist overtones.[2] Within the Peronist party, the national Left embraces the various tendencies associated with Cooke's Revolutionary Peronism, but it is not an exclusively Peronist phenomenon. Of Marxist origin, the national Left dates back to a 1940s split from the Trotskyist Fourth International led by Jorge Abelardo Ramos. Thus it also includes his Frente de Izquierda Popular (Popular Left Front—FIP). But despite their socialist and Marxist leanings, all sectors of the national Left have consistently chosen to ally themselves with the Peronist rather than the socialist Left.

The socialist Left differs from the national Left in its commitment to an independent strategy for socialism by stages unencumbered by populist constraints. With few exceptions, Argentine socialists are Marxist-Leninists, but although communists in name they are not egalitarians concerned with equalizing wages and leveling the salaries of managers and professionals.[3] Although differing on how to acquire political power, they would use it to expropriate the multinationals, to nationalize the land along with large and middle-sized enterprises, and to lay the groundwork for workers' self-management. Socialists are not always true to their calling, but at one time or another the socialist Left has included the Partido Comunista de Argentina (PCA), the neo-Trotskyist Movimiento al Socialismo (Movement Toward Socialism—MAS), the ex-Trotskyist Partido Revolucionario de los Trabajadores (Revolutionary Workers' party—PRT), its now-defunct Ejército Revolucionario del Pueblo (People's Revolutionary Army—ERP), and their various splinter groups.

Lessons of the Historic Defeat of 1976–1982

In Argentina the restructuring of the Left during the 1980s responded not only to the seven years of military dictatorship beginning in 1976 but also to the advances of the world socialist movement and the Latin American revolution in particular. The influence of Unidad Popular, the popular-front experiment in Chile (1970–1973) hegemonized by the Communist and Socialist parties, encouraged the socialist Left to emulate the Chilean experience.[4] The unity of the Left that undergirded the Cuban Revolution of 1959, the Sandinista Revolution of 1979, and the promise of victory by the Farabundo Martí National Liberation Front in El Salvador was another pole of attraction.

These positive incentives toward a unified Left were not, however, the most compelling ones. The single most important factor in restructuring the Argentine Left was the historic defeat of 1976–1982. This sanguinary episode, which decimated the Left, went hand in hand with a system of state terrorism aimed at eradicating Marxist cultural as well as political-military subversion. Reflections on its causes gave birth to a spate of books beginning in 1982, a literature about the Left's defeat aimed at recovering from the "holocaust," ensuring that it would never recur, and correcting mistaken assessments of the Argentine situation and corresponding strategic errors.[5]

The military dictatorship concentrated on stamping out not only the insurgent Left but also its legal and political structures. In the conviction that armed subversion was nourished by the national Left as well as by the Communist and Trotskyist parties, the armed forces were determined to cripple them. As a condition of preventing a recurrence of the million and more votes amassed by the socialist Left in the March 1973 elections and the landslide victory of the Frente Justicialista de Liberación (Justicialist Liberation Front—FREJULI) with the support of most of the socialist parties in September 1973, the military regime overrode the constitution to ban all political activity. It also systematically discredited the ideologies of the Left. That these military policies bore fruit is confirmed by the convergence of the political Right that contributed to the electoral victory of the Radical party in October 1983.

The principal lesson drawn from this defeat by most sectors of the Left is that strength comes from unity but not with parties that have moved over to the Right.[6] Although there is still a debate about whether the Peronist party is a party of the Left, the differences between it and the Radical party are not what they used to be, and therefore an alliance with mainstream Peronism is increasingly perceived by socialists as self-defeating. Thus the Argentine Left now recognizes not only the imperative of unity but also its perils.

The critical point in a populist government arrives when the masses begin to question its intentions and threaten to desert it for not keeping its promises, thereby encouraging military intervention. Thus another lesson of defeat is that populist governments have to respond to the expectations of organized labor or face the prospect of being overthrown. One Argentine leftist expressed the dilemma this way: "When the governments of these past seven decades promoted policies of 'transformation' . . . and made evident they had popular support, coup-mongering did not appear on the political scene to 'dissuade' them. It appeared in the political calendar when, on the contrary, the institutional governments did not complete those transformations or abandoned them."[7]

Two widely respected Peronist intellectuals, José P. Feinmann and Alvaro Abós, broke with the Peronist party and refused to vote for it in the 1985 congressional elections because the Peronist option had atrophied and ceased to represent the national interest. Although it still whistled a populist tune, the party had become stymied by its right wing.[8] Just as

Argentina had ceased to be the same country it was before the March 1976 coup, so the Peronist party had compromised its populist substance while retaining its populist image. To Feinmann it seemed that "todos unidos perderemos" (together we shall all lose), and to Abós that "para crecer, hay que romper" (to grow, we have to split).[9]

Feinmann stressed the urgency of an anti-imperialist policy on which the entire Argentine Left could agree, the "formation of a national front . . . including all the social and political sectors objectively opposed to imperialism."[10] On the premise that "the contradiction between the proletariat and the bourgeoisie is a secondary contradiction in the dependent countries," this front would not be a workers' front with socialism as its objective.[11] Yet no less a revolutionary than Lenin advocated a coalition in which the socialist Left might have to play second fiddle.[12] That was the kind of coalition promoted by the PCA in March 1973. Hegemonized by the moderate leftist Intransigent party, the PCA's Popular Revolutionary Alliance polled almost nine hundred thousand votes compared with some seventy-four thousand for the Partido Socialista de los Trabajadores (Socialist Workers' Party—PST), the Trotskyist forerunner of the MAS that pursued an independent strategy.

There was a reasonable chance that the socialist Left might some day prevail in such an alliance, but in September 1973 both the Intransigent and the Communist party supported Perón's candidacy for president in an electoral coalition that neither party could ever hope to dominate. At that point Communist party strategy became a caricature of Lenin's and an independent strategy began to pay off. The PST more than doubled its vote of six months earlier by polling 181,000 votes, more than 1.5 percent of the total. Although the FIP improved its standing considerably in September compared with a meagre 49,000 in March, it was at the cost of joining an alliance with the Peronists and effectively abandoning its socialist project. At least the PST had the prescience to realize that both the populist and the national Left had been induced by the prospect of seats in Congress to table their socialist agendas and that Peronism no longer contained a solution to economic dependence. Only recently, in response to the historic defeat of 1976–1982, has the Communist party also acknowledged the force of this predicament.[13]

Convergence of the Socialist Left

After rethinking its former strategy, the PCA responded to an appeal by the MAS by launching the Frente del Pueblo (People's Front—FREPU) in September 1985. The MAS itself was an instance of socialist convergence in response to the military dictatorship. Formed in 1982 through a merger of the PST and other socialists, it spurned the strategy of alliances with the populist Left.[14] Instead, it called for the "political unity of the workers in a new massive Workers' Party" and for the organization of a revolutionary front limited to the organizations of the working class.[15] The FREPU formed the nucleus of such a front.

The FREPU aimed to overcome the "false option" at the polls between the Radical and Peronist parties. With memories of their persecution, imprisonment, and torture under the government of Isabel Perón still fresh, many in the Peronist Left had voted for the Radical presidential candidate, Raúl Alfonsín, in October 1983.[16] They could not forget that the military's dirty war against subversion had been authorized by Isabel Perón in a presidential decree of February 1975, fully a year before her fall. But Alfonsín's human rights record hardly sufficed to command their enduring allegiance; hence their support for the FREPU's independent alternative in 1985.

In the congressional elections of November 1985, with the support of the disenchanted Peronist Left and the illegal PRT, the FREPU polled some 250,000 votes. Its comparatively poor showing induced the PCA to broaden the alliance by wooing elements of the national Left. In May 1987 a new front was launched, the Frente Amplio de Liberación (Broad Front of Liberation—FRAL), based on a seven-point program, a "new alternative that includes Peronists, Radicals, Intransigents, Communists, Humanists, Socialists, Christians, and ecologists . . . that expresses the project of national liberation against dependence, that revindicates authentic democracy with social justice and popular participation."[17] Since the MAS refused to endorse the new front, which it viewed as a betrayal of working-class unity and an impediment to building an independent labor party, the PCA relied on the Humanist party and splinter groups from the Intransigent, Peronist, and Radical parties to float the new organization. Among the signatories of the FRAL's program were also a newly formed Green party and the illegal PRT, under the cover of its legal front.

The Broad Front fared even worse than its predecessor. By mid-1987 the Humanist party had deserted the FRAL to run an independent campaign, while the July 26th Peronist Movement returned to the Peronist fold. Consequently, in the September 1987 congressional elections the FRAL polled only 224,000 votes. Its response was to broaden the front by wooing officials of the Radical party. In mid-1988 a tiny sector of the Radical leadership agreed to form a coalition with the Communists but only on its own terms. Since the PCA was offered a meager 20 percent of the contested seats, a Center-Left coalition never materialized.[18]

The PCA then resumed negotiations with the MAS, by then predisposed to a renewed alliance owing to the defection of its left wing. But a coalition with the MAS was not the PCA's first choice. By tradition, it would have preferred to resume its alliance with the Intransigent party in the kind of front first proposed by the latter in May 1975, a broad front of the populist, national, and socialist Left similar to the Broad Front in Uruguay.[19]

At its third Congress in 1988 the MAS reaffirmed its commitment to a government of workers. Its electoral ambitions were better served, however, by a broad front with the Communists than by a united front with minuscule pro-Trotskyist parties to its left. Consequently, it reneged on the resolution voted at its previous congress and proposed that the FRAL's successor, the Frente de Izquierda Unida (United Left Front— FIU), should be limited to a "struggle for national and social liberation."[20] It also hoped to impose Luis Zamora, the MAS's main theoretician, as its candidate for president. But the PCA prevailed, thanks to superiority in money, apparatus, and access to the mass media, and because the Communists hoped to attract the votes of nonsocialists the FIU's program contained no Leninist slogans.

The shift of the PCA toward an independent strategy made socialist convergence a reality, but an about-face followed in response to the poor electoral showings of 1985 and 1987. After the defection of its left wing, the MAS too abandoned a strategy of socialist convergence. Thus both have gravitated toward an alliance with new parties and political groupings whose socialism is either nominal or merely lukewarm.

The Impact of Perestroika

No discussion of the convergence of the electoral Left would be complete without considering the role of perestroika. By disputing Communist dogmatism and the claim of Communists to be the only genuine representatives of the workers' interests, perestroika appeared to promote a convergence of socialist parties. But that was not its principal impact.

As the new political line adopted at the twenty-seventh congress of the Soviet Communist party in March 1986, perestroika had an adverse effect on revolution-prone movements in Latin America. First, it meant the affirmation of Western-style democracy, a political and economic pluralism at odds with nearly sixty years of Stalinist and neo-Stalinist forced marches. Second, it signified a renewed struggle against "Left Communists" and "Trotskyites" in the conviction that "promoting revolutions from outside, and even more so by military means, is futile and inadmissible."[21] Together, they would be translated into a repudiation of both the forcible imposition of socialism in Eastern Europe and the export of the Cuban and Nicaraguan revolutions with the help of local political-military vanguards. As interpreted by its critics in Argentina, perestroika heralded the abandonment of the PCA's celebrated "left turn," the abandonment of an independent strategy for the working class.[22]

Perestroika responded to a crisis not only in Marxism-Leninism but also in Marxist ideology. Marx believed that economic growth was compatible with workers in control, the abolition of the market, and social protection from the cradle to the grave. Perestroika is an admission that once the industrial infrastructure has been built or rebuilt, as in the wake of World War II, these other objectives may become impediments to growth. By 1970 the centralized command economy had resulted in economic stagnation coupled with chronic shortages and a failure to innovate, and the absence of negative incentives to work such as the fear of dismissal and the threat of unemployment contributed to low productivity and lack of responsibility on the job. Thus, as a condition of modernizing the economy, the fetters on the operation of market forces and material incentives began to be scrapped. In Argentina as in the Soviet Union, the response to this Marxist dilemma was disenchantment not with socialism but with its mismanagement. However, only several Trotskyist parties remained true to their Marxist origins by continuing to defend centralized planning.

The partisans of perestroika want economic growth and modernization but also a bigger slice of the economic pie for professional and managerial cadres. Although they have yet to repudiate Lenin openly, Marxist-Leninists long ago trashed his principle of equality of burdens and equality of benefits. This accounts for the shelving of his interpretation of the first stage of communism. The change in name of the parties in Eastern Europe—from "Communist" to "Socialist"—amounts to a recognition that the reform-minded intelligentsia does not want to "work equally . . . and get equal pay" any more than do party bureaucrats.[23] Challenging them in Argentina, as in the Soviet Union, are the perestroika sceptics—the neo-Bolsheviks and social Luddites who look to Che Guevara, not to Gorbachev, as their hero.[24]

In Argentina, Moscow's adoption of perestroika took the Communists by surprise. The Soviets' new line scarcely figured in the proceedings of the party's sixteenth congress. It was at this congress that the PCA abjured its past reformist errors and its failure to support the Guevarist vanguards of the 1970s. A united front with the parties on its political left became official policy as opposed to a popular front hegemonized by the populist parties on its right.

What did Moscow think of the PCA's new "revolutionary line"? Victor Volski, director of the Latin American Institute of the Soviet Academy of Sciences, was on hand to give his opinion to the Argentine press. Interviewed by *La Razón* (November 21, 1986), he said it was dangerous to support the policies of the extreme Left. Although he supported what he called a policy of "global revolution," by that he meant peaceful revolutions from below and above through movements in the Third World over which Communists had virtually no control. Volski even questioned the FREPU's call for a moratorium on debt payments on the ground that it might provoke a counterrevolution.

In response to Moscow's criticism, the PCA scrapped the FREPU and launched the FRAL, without the MAS's support, and then the FIU with the help of a changed MAS relieved of the impediment of its left wing. Perestroika made the difference. It contributed less to socialist convergence than to a coalition of Communists with other sectors of the Left. As a result, the polarization of the socialist Left (between those who favor an exclusively socialist front and those who promote a broader alliance) continues to be a fact of Argentine political life.

The Eclipse of the Insurgent Left

The most vociferous champion of the broad fronts sponsored by the PCA and the MAS was the Movimiento Todos por la Patria (All for the Homeland Movement—MTP). Since its founding in March 1986 it had become the most intrepid defender of the democratic process. As the political arm of the monthly *Entre Todos*, whose first issue appeared in December 1984, it had the structure not of a political party but of a supra-party movement of the Left. Founded by former cadres of the ERP, backed and fronted by political moderates, the MTP hoped to attract all sectors of the Left that cherished national and social liberation and were willing to fight for it: Peronists, Radicals, Intransigents, Christians, Socialists, Communists, Independents.[25] But the bulk of its members and supporters remained in the dark concerning its secret intentions. To their dismay, they learned in January 1989 that its leaders had been using the MTP as a front for a political-military vanguard aimed at uniting the insurgent Left.

This strategy had been masterminded by the ERP's former commander, Enrique Gorriarán Merlo, with the Frente Sandinista de Liberación Nacional (Sandinista National Liberation Front—FSLN) as his model.[26] The MTP was launched as a social movement comparable to the Mothers of the Plaza de Mayo and other human rights groups linked to the Left.[27] As did these movements, it cut across party lines; in contrast to them, it was manipulated by a camarilla of former guerrillas who had only momentarily abandoned the armed struggle. As Gorriarán noted in an interview in Cali, Colombia, where he was then in hiding: "We believe . . . in a synthesis of the progressive wings of the traditional parties with what survived of the revolutionary movement of the last decade, plus the new generation and the sectoral organizations that emerged during recent years, all united in a great political and social movement prepared to lead the struggle for genuine national liberation with everything that this implies."[28]

Today, we know what this implied: a revival of Che Guevara's strategy of armed struggle adapted to the new conditions in Argentina after 1983. "What is our duty?" asked Guevara. "To liberate ourselves at any price . . . a liberation that will be brought about in most cases through armed struggle and will, in our America, almost certainly have the characteristic of being a socialist revolution."[29] To succeed, such a struggle had to be supported by all sectors of the Left. Consequently, in the absence of military dictatorship, Gorriarán sought a pretext in the defense of democracy.

In preparation for this event, Gorriarán organized the nucleus of an international vanguard with links to other national movements committed to armed struggle.[30] To finance the struggle, he embarked on a series of "expropriations." The first such action in 1986 involved the kidnapping for ransom of a businessman in southern Brazil, followed by that of a Chilean colonel, the publisher Luis Sales in São Paulo, and in 1989 the Brazilian businessman Abdilio Diniz, for whom the guerrillas demanded sixty-five million dollars. This last operation was crushed by Brazilian police intelligence through the capture and torture of its local leader, a Gorriarán disciple.[31] The international composition of the guerrillas adds credibility to a report by Uruguayan military intelligence that Gorriarán proposed to extend his organization to a sizable part of South America in conjunction with the Tupamaros, the followers of the slain Brazilian guerrilla leader Carlos Marighela, and Chile's Movimiento de Izquierda Revolucionaria. Among those captured in Brazil were five Chileans affiliated to the MIR, two Canadians, two Argentines belonging to the MTP, and only one Brazilian.

Because its commitment to armed struggle was tied to a populist program, Argentine military intelligence described the MTP as an example of "social-democratic militarism" aimed at installing a "Swedish-style socialism."[32] This perception of the MTP was also shared by influential sectors of the Left.[33] In fact, the MTP supported the FREPU-FRAL-FIU series of electoral alliances but perceived its role as that of the armed fist of a united Left in defense of the constitutional government. Whatever the defects of Argentine democracy, said the MTP, it had to be defended as a condition of broadening it and bringing about a fundamental change in the social structure. As a first step, it began organizing cadres for an eventual showdown with veterans of the Malvinas war, the *carapintadas* (painted faces) responsible for the military rebellions of Holy Week 1987, January 1988, and December 1988. But in proposing an armed response to military rebellions, the MTP's leadership ran afoul of its membership and suffered a split in December 1987 in which it lost most of its activists. At issue was its vanguardism, its vertical structure of authority, and the alleged sectarianism of its leaders.[34]

In response to the first military uprising in April 1987, Francisco Provenzano and his comrades in control of the MTP concluded that the advance of the military was irreversible without an armed counter-response. A former ERP militant, Provenzano argued that no matter who might win the elections in 1989, sooner or later the increasing aggressiveness of the military was bound to culminate in a coup. As early as April 1985, when I interviewed him, he was obsessed with an armed showdown with the military. Convinced that he and others like him were slated for extinction, he believed that armed struggle was the best defense.

Matters came to a head with the publication of a second interview with Gorriarán in August 1988 with a foreword by Tupamaro leader Raúl Sendic. Encouraged by what he called the "democratic explosion" in Argentina, Gorriarán outlined his strategy for uniting the insurgent Left:

> In our country there are many revolutionaries who, from different organizations, have struggled for the same ultimate objectives. . . . I mean those who belonged to the Argentine Liberation Forces, the Peronist Armed Forces, the Montoneros, the Popular Commandos of Liberation, the Workers' Power Revolutionary Organization, the PRT-ERP, and others. Many of those comrades gave their life for those objectives of liberation, but others are alive. Those who are alive have the duty . . . to unite their combative experience, this time from within a single political organization.[35]

Although the new organization would resemble Peronism in its ideological smorgasbord, it would have a "revolutionary leadership."[36] In other words, it would function as a political-military vanguard.

Did the former cadres of the insurgent Left respond to Gorriarán's invitation? Although the PRT worked closely with the MTP leadership, it would have nothing to do with Gorriarán's armed strategy. By then it was committed to an electoral option shared with other ex-combatants of the 1970s. In short, Gorriarán's appeals for unification of the insurgent Left fell on deaf ears.

But that was not enough to stop the MTP in its tracks. Within three years of its founding, the moment of truth arrived. To the third military rebellion in December 1988 the MTP responded with an advertisement in a major newspaper that for the first time included Gorriarán's name at the head of those who would "resist the coup."[37] This was followed by an attempted bank "expropriation" suggestive of links to the MTP and by an article in *Entre Todos* giving Provenzano's interpretation of the popular mobilization against the December uprising. Democracy was not the only issue, he maintained, but also "the people's defense of lives against the threat of genocide . . . [and] the search for paths that will lead to a fundamental change."[38]

One such path was the counterresponse of January 23, 1989. In anticipation of a fourth military rebellion from units of the Third Infantry Regiment stationed at La Tablada on the outskirts of Buenos Aires, the

MTP launched a preventive attack on the barracks. The assault lasted almost thirty hours, resulting in the partial takeover of the military base by more than fifty guerrillas. Twenty-eight of the assailants along with nine soldiers and two policemen died in the attack. Another eighteen guerrillas surrendered, but in a revival of the tactics of the dirty war Provenzano and five others were executed without trial.

Whatever the guerrillas' intentions, popular support for the operation failed to materialize, and the assault was universally condemned by the MTP's allies. Meanwhile, the Right used it as an excuse for reviving national security legislation and launching a witch-hunt against the Left. It was said that international terrorists were involved in the assault. A week later these suspicions were confirmed in an announcement from Uruguay by the hitherto unknown Frente de Resistencia Popular (Popular Resistance Front—FRP) claiming credit for the operation. From a second statement by the FRP on March 12, 1989, one learns that two Paraguayans and a Brazilian were killed in the assault and that a Bolivian died after being taken prisoner. Thus Gorriarán was accused of responsibility for the entire episode.

With its founders dead or imprisoned, *Entre Todos* collapsed as a political venture while the Guevarist Left had to return underground to carry on its project for a "fundamental change."[39] It was not the first time and perhaps would not be the last. It is fair to say that from its inception the MTP, along with the Mothers of the Plaza de Mayo and the Ecumenical Movement for Human Rights, helped to sustain a subterranean Left whose shared objectives of the "defense of life" and "fundamental change" presupposed an independent strategy for socialism—a strategy of profit sharing aimed at immediate inroads on the rights of private ownership as a source of human exploitation. Although opting for a fundamental change different from that of the Communists, these social movements went to greater lengths than the Communists in promoting social transformation.

Results and Prospects

There is no longer a viable populist option in Argentina. The 1980s were marked by severe setbacks in economic and social fields, leading to its characterization as a "lost decade" not only for Argentina but for most of the countries of Latin America and the Caribbean.[40] What was happening in Argentina was part of a worldwide phenomenon: "everywhere in the industrialized democratic world the old manual working class was in decline, trade union membership was falling, old class loyalties were crumbling."[41] Although this was far from heralding the end of the socialist age, it meant that populists were scrapping the welfare state and that socialists too were sponsoring measures aimed at privatizing and deregulating the economy.

The populist premise of a community of interests between the organized proletariat and the national bourgeoisie producing for the local market had collapsed in the face of persistent economic decline. There was no escaping the fact that a strategy of development undermines a populist coalition by cutting into wages as a condition of accumulation, whereas a strategy of mass consumption undermines it by cutting into profits.[42] Faced with this Hobson's choice, President Carlos Saúl Menem opted in 1989 to take the path of Isabel Perón by giving priority to economic growth, market forces, and the private sector.

Left populists too were reversing their historical emphasis on statist and welfare policies. The CGT split in October 1989 over support for Menem's new program, popularly referred to as *thatcherismo*. This should not have come as a surprise, for the populist Left in Western Europe and Latin America during the 1980s was a Thatcherite Left that agreed in principle with the British prime minister's policies of privatization, reduced government spending, and a moratorium on income redistribution.[43]

As matters turned out, however, the Argentine Left was an exception to the global shift to the right of the trade unions, for the *menemistas* were defeated in their bid to control Argentine labor. In 1985 the CGT had adopted a 26-point program that was both statist and redistributionist, a program that continues to have the overwhelming support of labor's rank and file. It also enjoys the backing of other sectors of the Argentine Left. First, they agree with the CGT's call for a moratorium on servicing the foreign debt and for the nonpayment of whatever portion may be decided to be illegitimate. Second, they agree with the CGT's resolve to expand the public sector and system of workers' self-management. Third, they agree with the CGT's strikes for higher wages and its program of redistribution. Finally, they agree on the revival of public works and welfare benefits to be financed by the state.[44]

By March 1990 the Argentine Left had further agreed on the following concrete steps: price controls on basic consumer goods, an end to the privatization of public enterprises, an end to streamlining the public administration through downgrading positions and reducing personnel, and massive wage increases.[45] Ironically, the populist CGT rather than the PCA-MAS had become the nucleus of a united workers' front in Argentina. Said the PRT after abandoning its independent strategy for socialism:

> The Front we need to curb the monopolies and bring about social changes of different magnitude must include all the popular, democratic, anti-imperialist, and revolutionary forces. It must bring together the representative organizations of the whole people, of laborers and employees, the urban petty

bourgeoisie, poor and middle peasants, the poor and marginal urban and rural populations, workers on their own account, and even sectors of the middle bourgeoisie uncompromised by the interests of the monopolies.[46]

While other sectors of Peronism had moved to the Right, most of the CGT had made a left-turn. Yet even Menem's policy of selling off state-owned enterprises, firing government workers, and reducing corporate taxes had another side to it. For he also promised to restore labor's share of the national income, estimated at less than 32 percent in 1987, to its former peak of 50 percent during the 1950s.[47]

But did Menem really stand for a reinvigorated populism? At most he can be credited for dismantling a bureaucratic-infested and inefficient welfare system, which was being financed mainly through sales taxes that weighed most heavily on the workers. Taxes on profits in 1989 represented less than 5 percent of the total, compared to 24 percent in Mexico, 50 percent in the United States of America, and 68 percent in Japan, while some 10 percent of public spending consisted of subsidies to private industry.[48] Under such conditions, the Populist State had become a caricature of its former self by taxing the poor and subsidizing the rich.

On the debit side of this ledger, the process of privatization and reliance on market forces was making Argentine industry bankrupt instead of competitive, while "recreating the basis of the Oligarchical State."[49] Periodically challenged by military dictatorships since 1955, the Populist State never really had a chance to prove itself. What failed were the efforts to implement the model whenever economic liberals took over the management of the state and the economy.

This is not to say that populism might have worked or that it may still have another chance to prove itself. For there are only two realistic scenarios for Argentina covering the next few decades, and a populist revival is incidental to both of them. First, the country may continue to drift or muddle along with a capitalism that discourages investment, an armed establishment that periodically threatens to intervene, a labor movement that is less than socialist, and a socialist Left that is politically ineffectual. Furthermore, a temporary capitalist recovery may be made possible by technological modernization of a few key industries capable of competing on the world market, by renewed concentration on agricultural exports where Argentina enjoys a comparative advantage, and by a bipartisan accord between the Peronist and Radical parties capable of breaking the stalemate with organized labor without military intervention.

In the latter event, there may be a marked shift from populist to socialist ideologies in response to labor's disillusionment with a Peronist party that is only nominally Peronist. As for Perón's goal of a fifty-fifty division of the national income between labor and capital, the setback to organized labor during the military process convinced many Argentine labor leaders that this half-and-half solution was already obsolete. Thus, in a report on comparative wages undertaken by a commission of twenty-five trade unions, labor's share was unfavorably contrasted with that in Canada and Australia, where it had already passed the 60 percent mark—approximately twice the share in Argentina at the time. To these figures should be added those for the United States, which recorded the same percentages as early as 1929 and by the time of the report boasted a 75 percent share for labor compared with a total of profits, including net interest and rents, of 25 percent![50] That the United States meets Perón's criterion for a socialist new order must be a bitter pill for the Peronists. At the same time, it suggests that something is seriously wrong with Peronist ideology and that the Argentine Left may be acquiring a palate for more potent medicine.

Notes

1. Donald C. Hodges, *Argentina, 1943–1987: The National Revolution and Resistance* (Albuquerque: University of New Mexico Press, 1988), 16–17, 136–139, 279–280.

2. Enrique Zuleta Alvarez, *El nacionalismo argentino* (Buenos Aires: La Bastilla, 1975), 2:619–657.

3. Donald C. Hodges, *The Bureaucratization of Socialism* (Amherst: University of Massachusetts Press, 1981), 77–173.

4. *Juventud Intransigente: Apuntes para la liberación* (Buenos Aires: Editorial Apuntes para la Liberación, 1985), 10–24; and, representing the new line of the PCA, Claudia Korol, *El Che y los argentinos* (Buenos Aires: Dialéctica, 1988), 145–166.

5. The literature of counterdefeat of the insurgent Left includes Envar El Kadri and Jorge Rulli, *Diálogos en el exilio* (Buenos Aires: Foro Sur, 1984); Roger Gutiérrez, ed., *Gorriarán: Democracia y liberación* (Buenos Aires: Reencuentro, 1985); Samuel Blixen, ed., *Treinta años de lucha popular: Conversaciones con Gorriarán Merlo* (Buenos Aires: Contrapunto, 1988); Julio Santucho, *Los últimos guevaristas* (Buenos Aires: Puntosur, 1988); Miguel Bonasso, *Recuerdo de la muerte* (Buenos Aires: Bruguera, 1984); Juan Gasparini, *Montoneros: Final de cuentas* (Buenos Aires: Puntosur, 1988); Roberto Mero, ed., *Conversaciones con Juan Gelman* (Buenos Aires: Contrapunto, 1988); Roberto Cirilo Perdía and Fernando Vaca Narvaja, *Existe otra Argentina posible* (Buenos Aires: Olguin, 1986).

6. See Jorge Luis Bernetti, *El peronismo de la victoria* (Buenos Aires: Legasa, 1983); Mora Cordeu et al., *Peronismo, la mayoría perdida* (Buenos Aires: Sudamericana/Planeta, 1985); Mona Moncalvillo and Alberto Fernández, eds., *La renovación fundacional* (Buenos Aires: El Cid, 1986); Alberto Kohen, *La izquierda y los nuevos tiempos* (Buenos Aires: Antarca, 1987), 3–4, 168–170, 190–193; and Alvaro Abós, *El posperonismo* (Buenos Aires: Legasa, 1986), 77–81, 120–121, 132–133.

7. Carlos A. Brocato, *La Argentina que quisieron* (Buenos Aires: Sudamericana/Planeta, 1985), 200, my translation.

8. Abós, *El posperonismo*, 11–13, 67–69; José Pablo Feinmann and Carlos "Chacho" Alvarez, "Diálogos con Alberto Fernández," in Moncalvillo and Fernández, *La renovación*, 152–154, 179–180.

9. Abós, *El posperonismo*, 132–133; Feinmann and Alvarez, "Diálogos," 159–160.

10. José Pablo Feinmann, "¿Adonde va el peronismo?" *Unidos* (December 1984):29, my translation.

11. Feinmann, "¿Adonde va?" 22, my translation.

12. V. I. Lenin, "Two Tactics of Social-Democracy in the Democratic Revolution," in *Selected Works* (New York: International Publishers, 1967), 1:516–518.

13. Kohen, *La izquierda*, 4, 193–198, and the prologue by Isidoro Gilbert, i–iv.

14. MAS, *Participemos en las elecciones para llamar a la movilización obrera y popular contra el pago de la deuda externa* (August 12, 1983), 5. See the program adopted at the second national congress of the MAS in March 1985, *Programa del MAS* (Buenos Aires, 1988), 2, 31, 36.

15. *Programa del MAS*, 5; Nahuel Moreno and Mercedes Petit, *Conceptos políticos elementales* (Buenos Aires: Antidoto, 1989), 41.

16. José Osvaldo Villaflor [former labor secretary of the Fuerzas Armadas Peronistas (Peronist Armed Forces—FAP) and, after the military process, the vice-secretary of the Printers' Union], interview, Buenos Aires, January 17, 1985; Raimundo Ongaro [secretary of the Printers' Union], interview, Buenos Aires, January 26, 1985. In the congressional elections of November 1985, Villaflor was a candidate of the FREPU.

17. FRAL, *Programa y declaración de principios* (May 1987), 2, my translation.

18. Jorge Altamira, *La estrategía de la izquierda en la Argentina* (Buenos Aires: Prensa Obrera, 1989), 200.

19. See Hodges, *Argentina, 1943–1987*, 129–131.

20. Mario G. Cravero, "El Frente de la Izquierda Unida propondrá la fórmula Luis Zamora–Néstor Vicente," *El Informador Público* (September 30, 1988):7.

21. Mikhail Gorbachev, *Political Report of the CPSU Central Committee to the 27th Party Congress* (Moscow: Novosti Press Agency, 1986), 15–16.

22. Altamira, *La estrategía*, 108.

23. Lenin, "The State and Revolution," in *Selected Works*, 2:344–345.

24. See Leon Aron, "Waiting for Yeltsin," *The National Interest* (Summer 1990):43–45; Boris Yeltsin, *Against the Grain* (New York: Summit Books, 1990), 157–169.

25. From the epigraph of the head-piece of *Entre Todos*.

26. Gutiérrez, *Gorriarán*, 44–46, 67–68.

27. On the resistance of the "Mothers," see Jean-Pierre Bousquet, *Las locas de la Plaza de Mayo*, 5th ed. (Buenos Aires: El Cid, 1984).

28. Gutiérrez, *Gorriarán*, 45–46, my translation.

29. Rolando E. Bonachea and Nelson P. Valdés, eds., *Che: Selected Works of Ernesto Guevara* (Cambridge: M.I.T. Press, 1969), 173, 179.

30. "Próximo cambio de gobierno," *El Informador Público* (February 9, 1990).

31. "Gorriarán Merlo al frente de un rebrote subversivo en Sudamérica," *El Informador Público* (January 12, 1990):2.

32. Guillermo Cherashny, "Gorriarán Merlo, detectado en Montevideo por los servicios de inteligencia uruguayos," *El Informador Público* (August 25, 1989).

33. Mario G. Cravero, "Según la izquierda, el MTP nunca formó parte de ella," *El Informador Público* (February 10, 1989); Altamira, *la estrategía*, 239–242.

34. Cravero, "Según la izquierda."

35. Blixen, *Treinta años*, 376, my translation.

36. Blixen, *Treinta años*, 381–382.

37. *Clarín* (December 8, 1988).

38. Pablo Hernández, *La Tablada: El regreso de los que no se fueron* (Buenos Aires: Fortaleza, 1989), 97–98, my translation.

39. Hernández, *La Tablada*, 74, 76, 98–99.

40. United Nations Economic Commission for Latin America and the Caribbean (ECLA), *Notas sobre la economía y el desarrollo* (December 1990), 20.

41. Peter Jenkins, *Mrs. Thatcher's Revolution: The Ending of the Socialist Era* (London: Jonathan Cape, 1987), 335.

42. Hodges, *Argentina, 1943–1987*, 182–183.

43. Seymour Martin Lipset, "The Death of the Third Way," *The National Interest* (Summer 1990), 25–31, 34.

44. CGT, "Un llamado a todos los argentinos," in the documentary appendix to Perdía and Vaca Narvaja, *Exista otra Argentina posible*, 262–264.

45. "Ubaldini rallies support," *Latin American Regional Reports, Southern Cone* (April 9, 1990):2.

46. "¿Qué frente necesitamos?" *El Combatiente* (November 1987), special supplement:4.

47. Carlos Saúl Menem and Eduardo Duhalde, *La revolución productiva* (Buenos Aires: Peña Lillo, 1989), 13–14, 41–48, 80–85, 92–96.

48. Hugo Chumbita, *El enigma peronista* (Buenos Aires: Puntosur, 1989), 149.

49. Chumbita, *El enigma*.

50. See Hodges, *Argentina, 1943–1987*, 279–280.

10
Left Political Ideology and Practice

Ronald H. Chilcote

"Ideology" is any given set of values, beliefs, expectations, and pre-scriptions about society. Ideologies have evolved in a past and continuing association with the process of capitalism and industrialization and the consequent economic and social problems that accompany that process. They tend to address utopian goals—problems of human existence—and to be delineated in unrealistically utopian terms, whether they envision a free market or a classless society.

This chapter aims to survey ideological trends in Latin America by first briefly examining the legacy of political ideas that has guided the political thought and action advanced by classical writers and identifying tradi-tional ideological tendencies and then tracing the evolution of these ideas and noting new developments since the death of Salvador Allende in September 1973.

Traditional Ideological Currents

Left ideology has stimulated the formation of diverse political and revolutionary movements and political parties in Latin America.[1] During the nineteenth and early twentieth centuries anarchist, anarchosyndical-ist, and socialist currents were influential among leftist intellectuals and immigrant workers and others associated with the labor movement. The ideas of Marx, Lenin, Trotsky, Gramsci, Stalin, and Mao especially stimulated the Left.

Among the important Marxist intellectuals in Latin America were José Carlos Mariátegui of Peru, Julio Antonio Mella of Cuba, and Luis Emilio

Recabarren of Chile. All three of these thinkers questioned Stalinist orthodoxy on the necessity of a national-bourgeois and democratic party, and all three were associated with the founding of Communist parties and labor movements in their respective countries. Stalinism, in particular, was associated with the evolution of the traditional Communist parties in the region, founded in the wake of the Russian Revolution. These parties generally aligned themselves with progressive forces favoring socialism through the electoral process, although there were examples of armed struggle (in El Salvador in 1932 and Brazil in 1935), and they often supported bourgeois democratic regimes (in Mexico in 1934 to 1940, in Bolivia in 1952, in Guatemala in 1944–1954, in Costa Rica in 1948, and in Venezuela in 1958).

The theory and practice of the Stalinist parties in Latin America were dependent in large measure on the policies of the Third International, founded in 1919. Communist parties, formed in Argentina and Mexico (1919), Chile and Uruguay (1921), and Brazil (1922), emerged out of anarchosyndicalist and socialist currents led by workers and intellectuals, many of them European immigrants. Generally, the Comintern and later the Cominform determined the political line of the Latin American parties, with the Partido Comunista Brasileiro (Brazilian Communist Party—PCB) serving as a prime example of this link, while the Partido Comunista de Chile, influenced by the popular-front policy of the seventh congress of the Comintern in 1935 and its own participation in a popular front in 1938, was especially instrumental in forging the project of Unidad Popular around Salvador Allende during 1970 to 1973. The pro-Soviet parties usually projected a two-stage revolution, first a bourgeois democratic or national liberation to confront imperialism and the domestic ruling classes (oligarchic, semifeudal, and monopoly capitalist forces) and second a socialist revolution. This revolution might be implemented through armed struggle (advocated by the Partido Guatemalteco del Trabajo [Guatemalan Labor Party—PGT] and the Partido Comunista de Venezuela during the 1960s), electoral participation, or a combination of the two (practiced by the Colombian Communists from 1966 to 1976). The Cuban Revolution stimulated revolutionary activity in some countries (Guatemala and Venezuela during the 1960s, in particular), and the victory of Salvador Allende and the Unidad Popular fostered a strategy of broad popular fronts (as especially employed in Chile from 1970 to 1973 and in Uruguay in anticipation of the November 1971 elections). According to one observer, the Soviet-oriented parties were "relatively adept . . . at adjusting strategy and tactics to shifting national and international conditions while seeking to avoid what they consider the extremes of moderate reformers of the right and ultra-revolutionists of the left."[2]

After Stalin's death in 1953 and the denunciation of his personality cult, the traditional parties splintered, some groups being influenced by Maoism and others by allegiance to Stalinism and reaction to revisionism. Beginning early in the 1960s, Maoist and Marxist-Leninist movements were prominent in Brazil and Peru. Usually, youth elements of the established Communist parties broke away to form Maoist organizations and generally advocated a two-stage revolution through a worker-peasant alliance and the leadership of a proletarian Marxist-Leninist party. These parties encouraged the formation of united fronts of the proletariat, the semiproletariat, and the petty bourgeoisie threatened by imperialism. Such alliances were not to include the "rightist" or revisionist Communist parties sympathetic to the Soviet Union or the "ultraleftist" Trotskyists and some Castroist movements.

During the early 1960s national liberation movements influenced by Fidel Castro and Che Guevara appeared in most Latin American countries. Guevarism was premised on the principles that popular forces can defeat a regular army, that revolutionary conditions can be created through the insurrectional foco, and that armed struggle should take place in the countryside of backward countries. This theory allowed Che to deemphasize the vanguard party during the insurrectional period and concentrate on a military and political struggle. He believed in continental revolution to defeat imperialism reminiscent of Trotsky's permanent revolution. Castroism was characterized by the strategy of a united front in support of a liberation struggle in which unity of forces rather than leadership by a vanguard party was a principal object. The idea stemmed from the 26th of July Movement founded by Castro in March 1956, its name commemorating his abortive attack on the Moncada Barracks in Santiago in 1953. Castroism thus tolerated populist politics in an initial stage of struggle, while Guevarism became a second stage emphasizing popular support for guerrilla struggle through the coalition of peasants and workers. Whereas Fidel had included the national bourgeoisie and petty bourgeoisie in the Cuban Revolution, Che denied their revolutionary potential.

The death of Guevara, the demise of his rural revolutionary movement in Bolivia, and the liquidation of the urban guerrilla movements in Brazil and Uruguay did not deter revolutionary movements elsewhere. The Sendero Luminoso in Peru, for example, emerged from the radicalizing experience of sons and daughters of Quechua-speaking peasants at the University of San Cristóbal de Huamanga during the 1960s. Upon graduation they dispersed throughout the sierra as teachers and education workers and carried their revolutionary ideology directly into communities. According to one observer, "the new ideology followed from peasants being placed within exceptionally intense social networks (university and family), rather than ideological conversion leading to a wave of new senderista recruits."[3]

Revolutionaries in Central America were successful in recruiting peasants, in Nicaragua using the remnant network of Augusto César Sandino's 1930 guerrilla movement and building, in the words of the Sandinista leader Henry Ruíz, "en cadena," calling upon kinship and god-parenthood ties. Guerrilla movements in Guatemala and El Salvador recruited peasants through religious base communities, the solidarity exhibited within Indian communities, and other networks of common cause and mutual contact. Timothy P. Wickham-Crowley has analyzed this link between peasant networks and guerrilla movements, noting that peasant participation usually was the consequence of the channeling of peasant insurrection through the apparatus of the guerrilla organization: "the concatenation of both the guerrilla network and the peasant network served to strengthen the insurgency both militarily and socially, and the disruption of either or both could lead to a sharp decline in guerrilla fortunes."[4]

Trotskyism has carried some weight in Latin America since about 1929, when Leon Trotsky went into exile and opposition to the emerging Communist parties appeared. The principal lines of early Trotskyism revolved around Juan Posadas, Jorge Abelardo Ramos, and Nahuel Moreno in Argentina, Mário Pedrosa in Brazil, Luis Vitale in Chile, Sandalio Junco in Cuba, and Guillermo Lora in Bolivia. A central issue of Trotskyism related to national liberation—a line supported by Ramos, whose movement constituted a left wing of Peronism envisaged as an anti-imperialist front. A proletarian tendency, however, opposed any alliance with nationalist movements unless hegemony of the proletariat were ensured. These and other political positions divided Trotskyists not only in Argentina but elsewhere during the 1950s. In 1963 Trotskyists joined with the Movimiento Revolucionario 13 de Noviembre (13th of November Revolutionary Movement—MR-13) in Guatemala to proclaim the socialist nature of revolution and to build a workers' party from the guerrilla movement. In Peru two Trotskyist tendencies appeared in 1960, one led by Ismael Frías that sought association with the reformist APRA and the other involving Hugo Blanco and the organization of militant peasant unions in the La Convención area of the Andes. Although both movements eventually were repressed, Peruvian Trotskyists demon-strated that peasant militias could be closely linked to the needs of the masses, in contrast to the confrontational strategy of guerrilla warfare modeled on the experience of the Cuban Revolution.

The failure of the Chilean experiment under Salvador Allende was a blow to sympathizers everywhere who had hoped for an alternative peaceful means of implementing socialism in the Third World. The Unidad Popular emphasized radical reformist policies, carried out in a bourgeois parliamentary context and in the face of a conservative military that controlled arms. A national plebiscite provided legitimacy for nationalization of the U.S. copper industry; the takeover of private banks and some monopolies was carried out under obscure legislation enacted during the brief 1932 revolutionary intervention of socialist military officers under Marmaduke Grove and others, and the expansion of agrarian reform was based on legislation implemented by Allende's predecessor, the Christian Democrat Eduardo Frei. The radical wing of the Socialist party favored a strategy of "advancing so as to consolidate," whereas the Communists pushed for a policy of "consolidating so as to advance." Allende turned to the latter alternative, and policy thereafter tended to be conciliatory.

In Havana during June 1975 the Cuban Communist party held a continental congress uniting it with all the old pro-Soviet parties. The meeting brought an end to the Cuban effort, represented especially in the 1967 Tricontinental Congress, to form an alternative to the traditional international communist network. In a retrospective acknowledgment of the popular front in Chile, the resolutions of the seventh congress of the Comintern, the formation of antifascist and anti-imperialist fronts during World War II, and even the abortive UP in Chile, the 1975 congress proclaimed the possibility of future fronts and alliances. At the same time, efforts to export or replicate the Cuban Revolution were acknowledged to have failed, and it was recognized that class struggle and actions of the mass vanguard would evolve through lines other than those set forth by the Cuban leadership. By 1979 the strategy of coalition was acceptable even to the recalcitrant Chilean MIR, which called for a convergence with the Communists. Although in 1981 the Chilean Communist party adopted a policy in favor of armed struggle and its Manuel Rodríguez Patriotic Front actually initiated armed action, most Left parties joined with the Christian Democratic center to pressure the Pinochet dictatorship to relinquish power and permit elections. Thus, the failure of the Cuban effort to establish a continental revolution inspired by the example of Che Guevara, the crushing of the urban-based movements in the early 1970s, and Cuba's gravitation toward a Soviet model contributed to the convergence of the orthodox Communist parties and the radical Cuban alternative.

Recent Ideological Trends

In response to the stagnation of traditional radical ideas and the intransigence of the movements and vanguard parties that espoused them, some Left intellectuals turned in new directions. The radical ideologies usually focused on some concept of imperialism, and after World War II intellectuals began to note changes in the international order. For example, large multinational or transnational firms were appearing in Latin America; their activities no longer concentrated on a single commodity within a country (petroleum in Venezuela or tin in Bolivia) but cut across national economies and markets. Theotônio dos Santos associated this development with a "new dependency" and demonstrated the need to examine internal structure for an explanation of backwardness; he contrasted this new form with the colonial and industrial dependencies that characterized earlier historical periods.[5]

The new dependency was partially influenced by earlier currents. One emanated from the Argentine economist Raúl Prebisch of the UN Economic Commission for Latin America, who advanced a theory of unequal exchange based on relations between the capitalist center and the backward periphery of Latin American nations; another stemmed from the work of the law professor Silvio Frondizi, the intellectual leader of a small group named Praxis that opposed the Stalinist line of the Argentine Communist party and included some Trotskyists within its ranks. The economist Paul Baran had inspired Latin American intellectuals with his account of backwardness and forms of surplus in his 1960 work *The Political Economy of Growth*, a best-seller in Latin America. Influenced by Baran and by Brazilian intellectuals during the early 1960s, the economist André Gunder Frank advanced his well-known thesis on capitalist development of underdevelopment.[6] These studies of underdevelopment and dependency were complemented by slightly different lines of thinking, including the internal colonialist thesis of the Mexican sociologist Pablo González Casanova, the associated and dependent capitalist development suggested by the Brazilian political sociologist Fernando Henrique Cardoso, and the notion of subimperialism of the Brazilian political economist Ruy Mauro Marini.[7]

These ideas were occasionally assimilated into the platforms of revolutionary parties. The Mexican Communist party entertained a theory of dependency as an explanation for underdevelopment. The Cuban historian Francisco López Segrera incorporated a dependency perspective into a prize-winning book on Cuba.[8] Although during the early 1960s dos Santos and Marini were associated with the revolutionary Política Operária (Political Operation), which had Trotskyist and Marxist leanings, dos Santos later (in the 1980s) joined the Partido Democrático Trabalhista (Democratic Workers' Party—PDT), led by the progressive politician Leonel Brizola, and Cardoso organized a rival social democrat Partido Social Demócrata Brasileiro (Brazilian Social Democratic Party—PSDB). Both the PDT and the PSDB were affiliated with the Socialist International.

Radical intellectuals also turned away from orthodox perspectives as authoritarian regimes gave way to democratic openings during the early 1980s. Labor strikes and a general economic crisis led to democratic elections and a new constitution in Brazil, and the military regime in Argentina collapsed in the face of defeat in the war with the British over the Falklands-Malvinas in 1982. Uruguay gradually evolved toward representative democracy, and by the end of the decade the Pinochet regime in Chile had stepped down. During this period the Marxist discourse of intellectuals and practitioners began to shift toward a new understanding and a "post-Marxist terrain." The shift was led by Ernesto Laclau, an Argentine residing in England who had once attacked Frank's thesis of capitalist underdevelopment for its emphasis on capitalist relations of exchange rather than production.[9] Laclau now argued that the working class had not evolved into a revolutionary movement, that economic class interests were relatively autonomous from ideology and politics, that the working class held no basic position within socialism, that the objectives of socialism transcended class interests, and that the struggle for socialism consisted of a plurality of resistances to inequality and oppression. Laclau saw a need for blocs of Left-Center political forces to ensure a political majority within a fragmented multiparty setting, popular reforms to satisfy the demands of the popular classes of workers and peasants, and an end to political sectarianism and intolerance. The new discourse was particularly popular in the Southern Cone nations of Argentina, Chile, and Uruguay, where the realities of mainstream politics appear to have obscured the revolutionary rhetoric, with the result that terms such as "class struggle," "working class," "dictatorship of the proletariat," and even "Marxism" were dropped from Left dialogue. A class analysis was excised from a socialist perspective once the working class was no longer viewed as essential for its revolutionary potential. Further, politics were seen as autonomous of economics, and classes and class struggle were displaced by an emphasis on political pluralism, political organizations, and interest groups.

Democracy: Representative and Participatory

The decade of the 1980s witnessed a search for democracy, generally of a formal, representative kind under governments elected to power in the period of transition from dictatorship and authoritarianism. The parliamentary systems provided for the reemergence of the traditional parties, necessitating a shift in tactics on the Left toward conciliation and accommodation. In Brazil the legalization of the Communist party and its radical offshoots necessitated alliances to the left and the right in order to ensure representation in Congress.

New leftist political parties also appeared, and two examples serve to illustrate their impact. The Partido dos Trabalhadores, founded in 1979, marked the beginning of a new era of the workers' movement in Brazil (see the chapter by María Helena Moreira Alves in this volume). Michael Löwy has characterized it as "the building of a mass party that expresses the political independence of the working class and working people; a democratic, pluralist, militant party, free of all ties to the dominant classes and their state, with a clearly anticapitalist program; a party in solidarity with workers' struggles throughout the world yet independent of the politics of any particular post-revolutionary state."[10] In 1989 the PT sponsored Luís Inácio da Silva as its presidential candidate and nearly ushered into office the first Latin American worker to serve as president. To the right of the PT, intellectuals within the PSDB led by Fernando Henrique Cardoso called for democratic socialism through social and economic reform. Although Cardoso believed in periodic elections to legitimate those who governed, he did not advocate democratization by pressure from below. Direct democracy, he felt, was useful when formal party-based representation broke down, but democracy generally prevailed when the people had confidence in established institutions. This view was extended by his wife, Ruth Cardoso, who argued that political parties and not social movements force the democratization of the democratic state.[11] Such an assumption may have been influenced by Fernando Henrique's personal involvement in party life and in Congress, but it also reflected the dependence of parties on the state in Brazil and the marginalization of popular movements outside the parliamentary system.

Beyond the traditional and new leftist parties that appeared in the 1980s, popular movements also exercised influence at the informal and grass-roots level. In his provocative analysis of new cultural trends in Latin America, David Lehmann has focused on the grass-roots influence of liberation theology, which he believes has weakened Marxist class analysis, the dependency perspective, and revolutionary change while assimilating these tendencies within it. He has also argued that the authoritarian regime may have pressured Left intellectuals to turn toward post-Marxism, resuscitate social democracy, and reconsider liberal democracy. His own analysis attempts to bridge the gap between post-Marxist democratic theory and the grass roots in the struggle for social justice.[12]

Social conflict in Latin America today often takes nontraditional forms such as neighborhood councils in poor communities, Catholic base communities, women's organizations, ethnic associations, and so on. Tilman Evers shows that, although it is often assumed that these new forms of struggle substitute for activities or repressed labor movements and political parties, many of them are not new but decades old.[13] For example,

Fernando Ignacio Leiva and James Petras argue that during the military regime in Chile "the shantytown has eclipsed the factory and neighborhood organizations have displaced trade unions as the locus of political action."[14] This shows that through the development of new types of organization, action, and mobilization, the unemployed and urban poor "have been at the forefront of the popular struggle challenging authoritarian rule, transforming themselves from victims to protagonists, from social outcasts to social actors."[15]

Liberation theologians turn to principles of Christianity that they identify as egalitarian and socialist. Enrique Dussel has argued, "In theory there is no reason why we cannot contemplate the implementation of socialism."[16] Manzar Foroohar argues that progressive Christians, in support of the poor and working classes, have found biblical justification for involvement in the struggle against exploitative capitalist regimes in Latin America: "The division in the Catholic Church over liberation theology has its roots in the ongoing class struggle in the Third World countries. The question is centered not on the doctrinal purity of the factions but on their sociopolitical alliances."[17]

In Venezuela, the Movimiento al Socialismo emerged from the PCV in 1971 to redefine the democratic road to socialism and attract large numbers of people. Their model envisaged a democratic and peaceful course in which socialism would be possible in the short run but not through the two-stage revolution in which socialism is realizable only after national liberation. The MAS favored decentralization of economic decision making and worker participation at the factory level. It rejected bureaucratic socialism and the concept of a working-class vanguard and popular-frontism, but it supported pacts between leftist and nonleftist parties to achieve important objectives.[18]

The Left in Power

The question of the vanguard has been reassessed by the Chilean Marxist scholar Marta Harnecker, who argues that class struggle has a dual character, democratic and socialist: "Revolutionary vanguards—postponing their strategic project of socialism only in order to be able to fight with greater efficacy for it—had to take the leadership of all those oppressed by ruling regimes by raising the democratic banners of peace, bread, land, liberty, sovereignty, and the defense of oppressed nationalities, depending on the specific situation in each country."[19] Democracy, she believes, also has a twofold character, bourgeois in the restoration of bourgeois democracy and popular in the building of proletarian democracy. She notes that, because the forces of the Right block the Left from popular victories through legal means, other roads, including the military-political one, to revolutionary and full participatory democracy may be necessary. The strategy must be adapted to the conditions of each country rather than blindly following the models of others, for "the error of many parties and movements in Latin America is that they have placed the problem of the organizing structure above the requirements of struggle, when it should be the reverse."[20] The vanguard is not the same as the party, she insists. Many are misled into believing that the attainment of a single leadership is tied to organic unity or a single party when in fact there may be many revolutionary organizations or parties, necessitating a collective or shared vanguard. Leadership of the masses is not based on law and control from above: "No organization can simply proclaim itself the vanguard either before or after the seizure of power . . . political leadership is something that must be won on a daily basis, in the struggle for the seizure of power as well as the building of a new society."[21]

The transition to and consolidation of socialism implies meeting the basic needs of all people, ending poverty, satisfying requirements for nutrition, health care, housing, and education, and ensuring employment and redistribution of income. Ultimately socialism involves the socialization of the means of production under public rather than private ownership, but there is little consensus over the extent of state or other collective forms of ownership. Social democrats and democratic socialists may be willing to postpone the issue of ownership and concentrate on redistributive taxation and social welfare programs. Traditional Marxist-Leninists may advocate that power must reside with the vanguard party. In both instances, existing conditions may require either participation in an electoral process or resort to revolutionary means. Thus, although the transition to socialism is largely an economic undertaking, it has a political dimension as well. Essential is the dominance of a coalition of class and political forces interested in attaining socialism through either the peaceful takeover or through the revolutionary seizure of state power and the consolidation of that power.

Several examples illustrate this transition.[22] In the case of Cuba the struggle for liberation began early in the nineteenth century, was advanced in the independence wars against Spain, and ended with the overthrow of the dictator Fulgencio Batista in 1959. The seizure of state power initially involved an insurrectionary strategy aimed at mass uprising; the attack on the Moncada military garrison failed but became the impetus for a successful campaign of military action in the countryside and urban resistance. The consolidation of state power involved the opening of participation to all segments of society, the articulation of the interests of the peasant-workers' coalition supporting the revolution, and the establishment of a new ideological basis. It also necessitated agrarian and other reforms, redistribution of wealth throughout society, and provision of basic needs. Finally, it required mobilization of the population against the resistance of bourgeois class interests and a U.S. campaign of diplomatic pressure, economic blockade, and covert war. The development of a socialist economy was first carried out through the strategy of "moral incentives" advocated by Che Guevara as a means of stimulating voluntary work and commitment to the revolution, but the results were mixed. Differences in levels of consumption were mitigated, but centralization of planning had reduced workplace democracy and created economic problems. After the failure of the 1970 sugar harvest, Cuba turned toward material incentives such as production bonuses and overtime pay to deal with absenteeism and laziness in the workplace. An attempt to open up political space was initiated with the experiment of democratic elections in Matanzas province during 1974, and organs of "people's power" were established throughout the island, each electoral unit being based on the neighborhood rather than the workplace. This effort at limiting the bureaucracy and decentralizing administration allowed for some popular participation and expression of popular grievances but did not result in a self-managing economy or a decentralization of power at high levels. Linda Fuller found that union leaders were chosen through a regularized electoral procedure and unions were relatively autonomous and essential to workers' efforts to control production: "The picture . . . is one of more autonomous unions, with a more powerful presence in worksite decision making, with particular areas of primary authority, which anticipate that conflicts between the interests of their members, the party, and management will arise and need to be resolved in the daily course of production."[23]

After 1970 Cuba experimented with two strategies, one highly centralized, with egalitarian distributive policies, and the other decentralized and recognizing individual and collective involvement in the political economy. At issue was whether socialist development would avoid the tendency toward tolerating dominance by a privileged technical and managerial bureaucracy and allow the masses to practice participatory democracy. Harnecker provides a glimpse of participatory experience through a series of interviews with Cubans at many levels and in many walks of life.[24] Throughout the late 1970s and into the 1980s, however, the economy became highly centralized and corrupt, prompting the leadership in 1985 to implement a rectification process that at the political level resulted in "a new civility" and a "participatory political culture."[25] Carranza reports that the reorganization of the Soviet economy had an impact on external trade, forcing Cuba to redefine its participation in the world market and to make adjustments in domestic production in order to alleviate discomfort and dissatisfaction among the people.[26] Faced with this crisis in the international and national economy, however, Cuba chose not to roll back the standard of living of most people and actually increased some of the social achievements of the revolution (spending on education and health, for example, increased by 45 percent). At the same time Cuba continues to search for more political space to confront tensions, contradictions, and outcomes.

In the case of Nicaragua the struggle for state power aimed to overthrow the Somoza family and the well-trained national guard left behind by U.S. marines in 1933; it also sought to avenge the assassination of the revolutionary hero Augusto César Sandino. The FSLN, founded in 1961, initially operated as guerrilla bands along the Honduras-Nicaragua border, later emphasized political work in the cities, and ultimately came to power through sporadic attacks on military outposts and mass uprisings against the repression of the Somoza national guard. Three tendencies prevailed within the FSLN, one oriented to prolonged military struggle in the countryside, another to organization of urban workers, and a third to converting mass opposition into popular insurrection. Once in power, the FSLN attempted to reorganize the economy, provide for the basic needs of people, and mobilize the population against counterrevolutionary attacks sponsored by the United States. Nationalization was limited largely to former holdings of the Somoza family, and the economic program recognized the importance of the private sector in stimulating the capitalist forces of production. State policy encouraged private enterprise while attempting to redistribute resources in the interests of peasants and workers. Efforts to encourage a mixed economy complemented the establishment of a pluralistic political system through democratic elections held in November 1984. The revolution attempted to implement a strategy of "socialist populism" within a politics of human rights and needs but without adopting the economistic view that socialism is ultimately determined or revealed by one's relation to the means of production. According to Doug Brown, under Sandinismo a new socialist politics based on a rights discourse evolved as a product of Western capitalist experience and the traditions of stable democracies.[27] Illya Luciak has examined the Sandinista grass-roots movements that he believes fundamentally changed conditions in the countryside: "Sandinista democracy, based on new relations of production, has benefited the worker and peasant classes."[28] Steve Ellner has commented that collective leadership and a novel form of popular participation were reflective of changing conditions throughout the world. The Sandinistas, he argues, came to power through assault in a country that lacked a tradition of democracy, yet they supported pluralism, elections, and popular organizations in a process reminiscent of the Gramscian approach to hegemony—a concept associated with gradual and peaceful transition to socialism in Europe.[29] Continued U.S. aggression and support for the Contra war against the Sandinistas disrupted the economy, creating hardships, and threatened the political pluralism within a Sandinista ideological hegemony. The contradictions of the counterrevolution also served to stimulate the underlying class struggle and slow down the movement toward a socialist economy. The project of formulating a radical democracy ultimately suffered a serious setback with the electoral defeat of the Sandinistas early in 1990 by opposition forces under Violeta Chamorro.

Conclusion

Latin America has provided a variety of ideas and experiences, some influenced by classical Marxist thought and revolutionary successes and others emerging from the particular conditions and needs of peoples in search of a socialist outcome. The democratic openings in the Southern Cone and the collapse of dictatorships everywhere during the 1980s were accompanied by the decline (Brazil) and demise (Mexico) of monolithic communist theories of semifeudalism and the prospects for alliance with a national bourgeoisie. Theories of dependency and underdevelopment were obscured by the rise of democratic regimes, and the new ideas associated with revolutionary movements of various tendencies, including the Maoist and Trotskyist parties, eventually faded with the collapse of dictatorships everywhere. The establishment of parliamentary systems, the resuscitation of traditional political parties, and the formation of new ones necessitated diversity, a new dialogue toward pluralism, Left unity, broad alliances and coalitions, and a new intellectual discourse, much of it post-Marxist. The openings provided political space for the participation of new grass-roots and popular organizations, including neighborhood associations, church-based communities, ecological movements, and feminist and gay groups.

What is the future of political struggle in Latin America? Will the drive toward an improved society, whether capitalist, socialist, or some post-form, be peaceful (as in Chile in 1970–1973 or the Southern Cone in the late 1980s) or violent (as in revolutionary Mexico, Cuba, Nicaragua)? Once a strategy has been adopted, what kind of system is likely to evolve? If the authoritarianism and central control characteristic of corporatist fascism, bureaucratic authoritarianism, and the national security state are to be avoided, what kind of democracy (formal or informal, representative or participatory, indirect or direct) should be pursued? Will the new social movements (ecologist, pacifist, feminist) participate meaningfully in civil society, or will they be marginalized, dispersed, and rendered powerless by the political parties, the labor movement, or other traditional forces? What of the role of the traditional (financial, commercial, industrial, agrarian) bourgeois class and of new class forces (especially the new middle class of the state sector) in the reorganization of capital? Will the focus for a changing society be social classes or institutional forces or perhaps some combination of the two? Will the labor movement stand opposed to capital, or might it align itself with capital to improve local conditions in particular situations? What is the impact on labor of the recomposition of capital at both the national and international levels? In the development of the capitalist forces of production, should the transition be democratic or autocratic? What kind of socialism (social democracy, democratic socialism, revolutionary socialism) should be adopted? Finally, in either the capitalist or the socialist transformation, what of the role of the state bureaucracy, corporate groups, and bourgeois parliamentary forces? What are the prospects for popular unity (popular fronts and united fronts) and class alliances as opposed to the fragmentation or co-optation of popular forces? If goods and services are to be distributed in some egalitarian manner, how are human needs to be met (planned system or free market)? How do individual preferences relate to collective activity?

These are but some of the important questions being addressed by the Left in Latin America today. Its central problem is the transition to a better society through democracy and socialism. Among the obstacles are the bourgeois economic interests that may be decisive in stemming the tide toward socialism as the new regimes turn from radical alternatives to bourgeois parliamentary and social democratic forms and the political parties overshadow the popular and revolutionary movements. Indirect formal representative forces may obstruct direct participatory democracy. Talk of pluralism premised on individual choice, bargaining, and compromise may undermine the possibilities of alliances and coalitions of popular movements outside the political party system and interfere with the goal of achieving a "new" society. Excluded also may be the working class as the agent deeply involved in carrying out the transformation.

Szymanski reminds us that Marxism in crisis is but a cyclical reflection of the society at large.[30] The apparent exhaustion of Marxism among the popular social movements and political parties in Latin America during the early 1990s may signal an eventual resurgence of Marxist thinking adapted to new and changing conditions. Indeed, ideas and ideological currents historically have corresponded to such cycles of activity. This proposition can be simply illustrated by reference to patterns of contradictions in historical experience. One contradiction appears in cycles of democratic openings (1920s, 1940s to 1950s, 1970s, and 1980s) and authoritarian closures (1930s, 1960s, and 1970s). Another is evident in situations of revolutionary socialism (insurrection, resistance, guerrilla warfare) and evolutionary capitalism (peaceful reformism, nationalism). A further contradiction is seen in perspectives that emphasize stable institutional cohesion (church, military, bureaucracy, political parties) in contrast to class interests based on a division of labor (financial, industrial, commercial, agrarian bourgeois versus the proletariat and peasantry) or simply the traditional contradictory relationships between capital and labor, capitalism and social systems, and dominant and popular social forces. The level of the productive forces and the seemingly insurmountable problems of external and internal debt, inflation, and unemployment also hinder progress toward a different society. In the face of these problems today, part of the Left in Latin America is retreating from Marxism while favoring a pluralism of interests extending beyond the vanguard party and working class to other parties and social movements. In contrast, other leftists continue to work within the categories and principles of Marxism while searching for a socialism adapted to the changing conditions of particular situations, without reliance on the stifling model of centralist bureaucratic socialism that ignored autonomous popular participation.

Notes

1. Donald Hodges, *The Latin American Revolution: Politics and Strategy from Apro-Marxism to Guevarism* (New York: William Morrow, 1974).

2. William E. Ratliff, *Castroism and Communism in Latin America, 1959–1976: The Varieties of Marxist-Leninist Experience* (Washington, DC: American Enterprise Institute for Public Policy Research/Stanford: Hoover Institution on War, Revolution, and Peace, 1976), 85.

3. Timothy P. Wickham-Crowley, *Exploring Revolution: Essays on Latin American Insurgency and Revolutionary Theory* (Armonk, NY: M. E. Sharpe, 1991), 131.

4. Wickham-Crowley, *Exploring Revolution*, 138.

5. Theotônio dos Santos, "The Structure of Dependence," *American Economic Review*, 60 (May 1970):231–236.

6. André Gunder Frank, "The Development of Underdevelopment," *Monthly Review*, 18 (1966):17–31.

7. Pablo González Casanova, "Internal Colonialism and National Development" in Irving Louis Horowitz, et al., *Latin American Radicalism* (New York: Vintage Books, 1969), 118–139; Fernando Henrique Cardoso and Enzo Faletto, *Dependency and Development* (Berkeley: University of California Press, 1979); Ruy Mauro Marini, "World Capitalist Accumulation and Sub-Imperialism," *Two Thirds*, 1 (Fall 1978):29–39. Elsewhere I have characterized Marini's view as revolutionary and socialist because of its assumption that radical change was necessary to alter the exploitative conditions in Latin America, whereas I have described the perspectives of González Casanova and Cardoso as reformist, nationalist, and supportive of capitalist development. Ronald H. Chilcote, *Theories of Development and Underdevelopment* (Boulder: Westview Press, 1984).

8. Francisco López Segrera, *Cuba: Capitalismo dependiente y subdesarrollo (1510–1959)* (Havana: Casa de las Américas, 1972).

9. Ernesto Laclau, "Feudalism and Capitalism in Latin America," *New Left Review*, 67 (May-June 1971):19–38.

10. Michael Löwy, "A New Type of Party: The Brazilian PT," *Latin American Perspectives*, 14 (Fall 1987):454; David Lehmann, *Democracy and Development in Latin America: Economics, Politics, and Religion in the Post-War Period* (Philadelphia: Temple University Press, 1990), 74.

11. Ruth Cardoso, "Movimentos sociais urbanos: Balanço crítico," in Bernardo Sorj and María de Almeida, eds., *Sociedade e política no Brasil pós-64* (São Paulo: Brasiliense, 1983).

12. Lehmann, *Democracy and Development in Latin America.*

13. Tilman Evers, "Labor-Force Reproduction and Urban Movements: Illegal Subdivision of Land in São Paulo," *Latin American Perspectives,* 14 (Spring 1987):187–203.

14. Fernando Ignacio Leiva and James Petras, "Chile's Poor in the Struggle for Democracy," *Latin American Perspectives,* 13 (Fall 1986):5. See also Philip Oxhorn, "The Popular Sector Response to an Authoritarian Regime: Shantytown Organization Since the Military Coup," *Latin American Perspectives,* 18 (Winter 1991):66–91; and Cathy Schneider, "Mobilization at the Grassroots: Shantytowns and Resistance in Authoritarianism," *Latin American Perspectives,* 18 (Winter 1991):92–112.

15. Leiva and Petras, "Chile's Poor," 5.

16. Enrique Dussel, *History and the Theology of Liberation: A Latin American Perspective* (Maryknoll, NY: Orbis, 1976), 137.

17. Manzar Foroohar, "Liberation Theology: The Response of Latin American Catholicism to Socioeconomic Problems," *Latin American Perspectives,* 13 (Summer 1986):55.

18. Steve Ellner, "The MAS Party in Venezuela," *Latin American Perspectives,* 13 (Spring 1986):81–107.

19. Marta Harnecker, "The Question of the Vanguard and the Present Crisis in Latin America," *Rethinking Marxism,* 3 (Summer 1990):45.

20. Harnecker, "The Question of the Vanguard," 55.

21. Harnecker, "The Question of the Vanguard," 63.

22. Ronald H. Chilcote and Joel C. Edelstein, *Latin America: Capitalist and Socialist Perspectives of Development and Underdevelopment* (Boulder: Westview Press, 1986).

23. Linda Fuller, "Changes in the Relationship among the Unions, Administration, and the Party at the Cuban Workplace, 1959–1982," *Latin American Perspectives,* 13 (Spring 1986):28.

24. Marta Harnecker, *Cuba: Dictatorship or Democracy?* (Westport: Lawrence Hill, 1980).

25. Rafael Hernández and Haroldo Dilla, "Political Culture and Popular Participation in Cuba," *Latin American Perspectives,* 18 (Spring 1991):38–54.

26. Julio Carranza Valdés, "The Current Situation in Cuba and the Process of Change," *Latin American Perspectives,* 17 (Spring 1991):10–17.

27. Doug Brown, "Sandinismo and the Problem of Democratic Hegemony," *Latin American Perspectives,* 17 (Spring 1990):57.

28. Illya Luciak, "Democracy in the Nicaraguan Countryside: A Comparative Analysis of Sandinista Grassroots Movements," *Latin American Perspectives,* 17 (Summer 1990):72.

29. Steve Ellner, "The Latin American Left since Allende: Perspectives and New Directions," *Latin American Research Review,* 24, 2 (1989):162.

30. Al Szymanski, "Crisis and Vitalization in Marxist Theory," *Science and Society,* 49 (Fall 1985):327–340.

11

Guerrilla Warfare in the 1980s

Richard Gillespie

During a decade that saw the Latin American Left taking diverse new initiatives in response to changing domestic and international circumstances, guerrilla warfare in the 1980s remained an important aspect of left-wing activity. The appeal of violence was by no means universal. While in certain countries armed struggle acquired fresh support, elsewhere there was an eschewal of violence by left-wing groups that had taken up arms in the 1970s. In contrast to the 1960s, when virtually every Latin American country saw some kind of attempt to implant a guerrilla foco, no continental trend in political violence was visible two decades later. Yet it would be a mistake not to attempt a continentally focused analysis of the guerrilla phenomenon in the 1980s, for similarities did exist at the supranational level, and the Left was collectively reacting to various recent events and new circumstances.

By the start of the 1980s, there was substantial consensus on the Left regarding the failure of foquismo, although there was disagreement over its nature. While some groups criticized only the crude foquismo presented in Régis Debray's *Revolution in the Revolution?* and sought to dissociate Guevara from it,[1] others condemned vanguardism, militarism, and voluntarism more broadly. Since 1959 rural guerrillas had suffered defeats or setbacks in Peru, Colombia, Bolivia, Venezuela, and Guatemala—to list just the best-documented cases—and urban guerrillas had been destroyed in Argentina, Uruguay, and Brazil.

The rural guerrillas of the 1960s had been thwarted by security forces sensitized to the guerrilla "threat" by the Cuban success whose task was facilitated by the lack of preparation, sophistication, and unity of the guerrilla movements themselves and the irresolute involvement or hostility of the traditional Left. In Venezuela and elsewhere the guerrillas had isolated themselves by declaring war on elected civilian governments that possessed substantial popular legitimacy.

A new lease on life was given to armed insurgency by the appearance toward the end of the decade, in countries with predominantly urban populations, of the urban guerrilla. The general appeal of armed activity was greatly reinforced by the early "Robin Hood" activity of the Uruguayan and Argentine organizations; this renewed the romantic image of guerrilla warfare derived from Guevara, which had become somewhat tarnished by defeat. However, despite having attracted widespread support among the youth of Uruguay and Argentina, the urban guerrillas were eventually defeated. Their activities provoked forms and levels of repression that made it impossible for insurgency to undergo the envisaged transition from guerrilla foco to people's army in the cities. Some guerrilla groups had always regarded this transition as unrealizable and therefore saw urban warfare as merely preparatory to the establishment of a rural front. But here they came up against many of the practical problems that rural guerrillas had faced in the 1960s, such as being forced into military confrontations before adequate logistical and political preparations could be made and sometimes lacking a terrain suitable both topographically and demographically for guerrilla warfare. Moreover, moving into the countryside, while a way of evading intense urban repression, also meant evading the reality of large urban populations for whom rural guerrillas were of no great relevance.

Whereas urban guerrilla movements succumbed to repression without having resolved their strategic problems,[2] predominantly rural guerrilla movements managed to survive in Colombia and Central America. Even here, however, the 1970s were generally a decade of reorganization, adaptation, and careful preparation by insurgents who had suffered setbacks in the 1960s. Meanwhile, in South America the early part of the decade saw insurgents having to compete with the attractions of populist and nonviolent alternatives, notably the "Chilean Road to Socialism," and as the decade advanced the spread of military regimes increased the hazards of involvement in guerrilla warfare and made recruitment much more difficult. In several countries, guerrilla warfare had been almost abandoned by 1979, when the Sandinista success in Nicaragua provided a fresh vindication of armed struggle. As the 1980s commenced, the Latin American Left was being pulled in different directions as it responded to a series of damaging defeats but also to a recent and tangible success.

Responses to Defeat

Whereas quite broad sectors of the Latin American Left, including some Communist parties, became more committed to insurgency in response to the Sandinista victory, other groups faced the 1980s with greater caution and pragmatism than in the past. Those who had lived under repressive military regimes in Brazil, Uruguay, and Argentina or who had survived them in the loneliness of exile were reluctant to resume activities that might offer the military a new pretext for intervention. Many of them were ready to acknowledge that urban guerrilla activities in the 1970s, although not the main or only reason for military interventionism, had made some contribution to the destabilization of civilian political regimes in addition to claiming the lives of thousands of revolutionaries.[3] Having been preoccupied in recent years with personal survival rather than grand designs for radical social change, their political ambitions remained circumscribed in the 1980s. Their appreciation of political democracy had increased dramatically as a result of the experience of dictatorship; moreover, they were aware that Latin American militaries retained substantial power even after the election of civilian authorities. Proponents of further guerrilla violence in these countries were extremely isolated.

The most prevalent 1980s tendency within the previously insurgent Left involved attempts to enter or reenter the political arena. This took two radically different forms, one peaceful, the other violent. The former, pioneered by a sector of the Venezuelan Left,[4] involved the renunciation of armed struggle and the establishment of new political parties or attempts at accommodation with existing political forces. This occurred where urban guerrilla movements had suffered a clear defeat in the past and hoped to take advantage of liberalization to gain legal status and greater legitimacy. The survivors of guerrilla experiences were by now middle-aged, reluctant to risk all for a political objective, and conscious of the emergence of a younger political generation with concerns and illusions different from their own.

These forces had been so dramatically weakened by repression and had suffered so badly that there was no great danger of further reprisals by their enemies. The main problem faced by the ex-combatants was that potential allies regarded them as political liabilities. Thus the Movimiento de Liberación Nacional–Tupamaros (National Liberation Movement–Tupamaros—MLN-T) in Uruguay, which renounced violence on condition that there be no reversion to military rule, found that the more moderate components of the Frente Amplio (Broad Front) initially barred their entry.[5] Only after it split in 1989 was admission into a weakened alliance granted, after which the Left's breakthrough in Montevideo in the municipal elections later that year offered some vindication of the MLN-T participationist strategy.

Meanwhile, in Argentina the few hundred Montonero survivors sought reintegration into the Peronist movement by presenting a new political face as Peronismo Revolucionario (Revolutionary Peronism) in 1985. In their pursuit of acceptance, former Montoneros renounced violence, sought the forgiveness of the pope for their misdeeds, and even proposed celebrating a "reconciliation mass" with the leaders of the last military junta, but again they had to wait for political acceptance. Indeed, their faction was formally expelled in 1988 by a Justicialist party that was preoccupied with defeating Alfonsín's Radicals at the next election. The former guerrillas' conciliatory behavior was influenced by the imprisonment of several dozen of their companions, yet this was arguably not the only reason that "revolutionary Peronists" were heard calling for the release of Videla and other dirty-war officers: the pronounced militarism of the Montoneros in the late 1970s had led the guerrilla elite to resemble its military counterpart in certain respects,[6] and a degree of empathy between the Montonero and army "commanders" must have existed by this time. The Montoneros paid heavily for their conciliatory discourse, earning condemnation from diverse sectors of the Left and the Mothers of the Plaza de Mayo as well as losing dissident members.[7]

Former guerrillas seeking to reenter the political arena are prone to division. Differences surface after years in which political debate has been severely constrained by strict military discipline and compartmental organizational structures, and parts of the organization may be seduced by the prospect of holding public office through an accommodation with established political forces. The Montonero leadership split in 1990 after two former guerrilla leaders pardoned by President Menem had come out in forthright support of the government's radical break with traditional Peronist policies and declared themselves available for public office despite the continuing imprisonment of Montonero leader Mario Firmenich. Perhaps even more important in this case was a struggle among former guerrilla leaders for control of the organization's tens of millions of dollars.[8]

The other way of seeking entry into the political arena has been by force of arms. Much of the guerrilla violence in the 1980s has been "tactical" rather than "strategic," in the sense of providing pressure for change within the system rather than being designed to initiate a people's war through which insurgents would seek a revolutionary seizure of power. Tactical violence, aimed at securing a broadening of political participation and other reforms, cannot always be clearly differentiated from strategic guerrilla violence. A campaign of violence may commence with an uncompromising strategy but become less ambitious when the guerrilla war fails to realize its aims or a reformist government comes to power. Central America offers two examples here, with both the Farabundo Martí National Liberation Front "final offensive" in early 1981 and the contemporaneous guerrilla escalation in Guatemala aiming at victory in the aftermath of the Sandinista triumph but with violence subsequently being aimed at bringing opponents to the negotiating table. The FMLN's pursuit of compromise has been seen in successive moderations of its demands since 1981[9] and in periodic cease-fires and negotiations with the authorities, although its offensive in October–November 1989 demonstrated that major military initiatives could still be undertaken in the face of governmental intransigence. The Unión Revolucionaria Nacional de Guatemala (Guatemalan National Revolutionary Union—URNG) showed its desire for compromise in 1986 by scaling down its military activities for a year following the restoration of civilian government, but guerrilla attempts to negotiate with President Vinicio Cerezo were resisted by generals who thought they scented victory.

In South America, insurgents also showed flexibility when faced either with new governments promising reform or with transitions from military to civilian rule. After a campaign of urban violence against U.S. targets, Peru's Movimiento Revolucionario Túpac Amaru (Túpac Amaru Revolutionary Movement—MRTA) suspended armed activity when Alan García was elected in 1985 but recommenced it when he completely ignored their gesture and members began deserting to join Sendero Luminoso.[10] In neighboring Ecuador, the Alfaro Vive, ¡Carajo! group actually dissolved itself following negotiations with the newly elected Center-Left government of Rodrigo Borja in 1989, amidst speculation that the move, in addition to being a response to domestic developments, was related to concurrent efforts by the group's Colombian mentor, the Movimiento 19 de Abril, to abandon warfare for parliamentary politics.[11]

Several of the Colombian guerrilla organizations, among them M-19 and the Fuerzas Armadas Revolucionarias de Colombia, reached agreements with the successive governments of presidents Betancur and Barco during the 1980s, but their political integration was shown to require rather more than a pact between the government and guerrilla commanders. The most obvious problem was the existence of death squads sponsored by right-wing military officers and drug barons, which had claimed the lives of over a thousand members of the FARC-backed Unión Patriótica by the end of the decade and assassinated three of the candidates for the 1990 presidential election, including the M-19 and UP nominees. Although considerable electoral success was providing former guerrillas with a fruitful, if hazardous, role in the political system by 1990, the transformation of guerrillas into politicians was not an easy one. Apart from the loss of security, it was impossible for integrationists to provide some former rebels with the same standard of living they had known as members of guerrilla movements, several of the Colombian guerrilla organizations being renowned for multimillion-dollar budgets financed by kidnap ransoms, other forms of extortion, and in some cases "protection" money from drug traffickers.[12] Moreover, many of the former insurgents had abandoned their studies in order to join the guerrillas and thus were lacking in the professional skills that could have facilitated their economic integration.

Colombia experienced a combination of tactical and strategic guerrilla violence in the 1980s, the most intransigent group being the Castroite Ejército de Liberación Nacional, which even killed a bishop in 1989. There was also this kind of mix in Chile, where a much weakened Movimiento de Izquierda Revolucionaria maintained its traditional Guevarist faith in strategic armed struggle while the Communist party announced the "armed rebellion of the masses" with more tactical intentions in 1980. When an evolutionary, electoral transition from authoritarian rule materialized toward the end of the decade, armed activity gave way to broad democratic collaboration under the leadership of the Christian Democratic party.

Responses to Success

The insurgent Left in the 1980s was reacting not only to past defeats and experiences of authoritarian rule but also to the Sandinista triumph in Nicaragua. The second successful Latin American revolution in twenty years gave a new boost to armed struggle. Nicaragua became an automatic point of reference for the Latin American Left, not least because of the return of small contingents of guerrillas from other countries that had served as "internationalists" in the anti-Somoza struggle. The lessons they took back to their countries were several. The first of these was that while the effectiveness of armed struggle had been confirmed, it should not be regarded as an exclusive form of action: the "strategy of victory" in Nicaragua had combined guerrilla activity with mass protest and insurrection, and Sandinista plans had been adapted dextrously in response to popular initiatives during the insurrection.[13] Second, the Nicaraguan message echoed a more traditional call for revolutionary unity and a policy of broad alliances. Third, the long-standing gulf separating Marxists from Christians had been bridged by liberation theology, which had helped a group of university origin to win support among the peasantry and middle classes in particular. Finally, as had the Cuban Revolution but much more patently, the recent revolution had shown the value of revolutionaries' assuming the nationalist heritage of their country, with all the legitimation that this promised.

The "Nicaraguan effect" was strongest in parts of Central America for reasons of propinquity and because groups from these countries were able to establish secure headquarters in Managua after the revolution. Indeed, in El Salvador in 1981 the so-called final offensive by the FMLN saw guerrillas being swept along by a subsequently acknowledged "triumphalism" and forgetting, as had the early emulators of Castro, that "revolution revolutionizes the counter-revolution"—in this case in the form of a major counterinsurgency effort by the United States. Sandinista (and Cuban) influence was seen in 1980–1982 in the establishment of new umbrella bodies designed to coordinate and eventually unify the guerrilla forces of El Salvador, Guatemala, and Honduras. Of these, the most effective was the FMLN, whose component forces gradually adopted a common strategy, mainly provided by Joaquín Villalobos's Ejército Revolucionario del Pueblo after the Fuerzas Populares de Liberación (Popular Liberation Forces—FPL) had declined through internal conflict.[14] There was even progress toward the creation of an FMLN party, although the political benefits of this were offset by the virtual break of the guerrilla front with its erstwhile political ally, the Frente Democrático Revolucionario on the eve of the 1989 election: an FMLN offensive was blamed by the FDR and Democratic Convergence leader Guillermo Ungo for the coalition's poor share of the vote (3 percent).[15]

In Guatemala, there was less strategic cohesion within the URNG, as a result of which its component forces continued to operate in different parts of the country rather than jointly. Still less coordination was achieved by the Unified National Directorate of the Honduran Revolutionary Movement, which mainly acted as a negotiating body in peace initiatives rather than a general staff for the guerrillas. Yet, if largely symbolically, the Nicaraguan influence was present in Honduras in the way that new groups adopted the names of national heroes and peasant leaders such as Francisco Morazán, Lorenzo Zelaya, and "El Cinchonero" (Serapio Romero) and substituted national liberation programs for Marxist-Leninist pronouncements.[16]

The Latin American Left in general was moved to take fresh initiatives by the Sandinista victory. Nicaragua's experience had a major impact on the behavior of a number of Communist parties, whose movement was undergoing diversification even before the advent of perestroika. Communists were confronted with a second Latin American social revolution in which their party had conspicuously failed to play a vanguard role. The fear of being marginalized as guerrilla forces advanced was particularly strong in El Salvador, where Communists belatedly joined forces with more established guerrillas, and in Guatemala, where new factions of the Communist Partido Guatemalteco del Trabajo joined the armed struggle. In this process of unification, the Communists could point out that the guerrillas had made some concessions by abandoning the crude foquismo of the 1960s, but overall the process demanded serious Communist self-criticism.[17] More important than acknowledging that they had failed to play a vanguard role in recent decades was the reason for this: the old belief that a democratic, anti-imperialist revolution had to precede a socialist one. Referring to "two triumphant armed revolutions" and two unsuccessful peaceful left-wing initiatives (Chile and Uruguay), the Salvadorian Communist leader Schafik Handal influenced many Latin American Communists with his criticism of the old conception of revolutionary stages and his contention that the conditions for successful armed struggle were now present.[18]

Responding both to Handal's arguments and to the breadth of popular sympathy for the Sandinistas, some Communist parties, as in the 1960s, adopted a rhetorically positive line on violence without actually taking up arms. This was the case of the Argentine party, which also found in common admiration for the Nicaraguan revolution one of the grounds for electoral cooperation with parties influenced by Trotskyism (just as shared sympathies for Cuba had facilitated bridge-building between Trotskyists and Stalinists in Peru and Mexico somewhat earlier). In South America Communist engagement in armed activity became a reality in Chile only after the party's change of line in 1980, and here as in Nicaragua a national hero was now invoked as a symbol of struggle, the Communists' new guerrilla organization being called the Frente Patriótico Manuel Rodríguez.

However, the "Nicaraguan effect" should not be exaggerated, especially in the South American cases, for a number of domestic factors were also present. Other suggested reasons for the Chilean Communist party's shift in 1980 were a degree of self-criticism of the party's behavior under Allende following the 1973 coup; the replacement of cadres who had been killed, imprisoned, or gone into exile by new, younger militants engaged in clandestine activity; moves by the Pinochet regime to institutionalize and perpetuate itself in 1980; and the changing social composition of the party as high unemployment reduced its traditional working-class base and as Communist militants acquired leading roles in the emergent movement of *pobladores* (shantytown dwellers) in the early 1980s.[19]

The potential advantages of Communist involvement in guerrilla movements were a strengthening of Left unity, the expansion of the guerrilla periphery into new areas such as industrial trade unionism, and an extension of the international networks that the guerrillas could exploit. In practice, Communist involvement in guerrilla movements seems to have provided only temporary reinforcement. The weighty tradition of reformist activity in the party no doubt influenced the behavior of at least some of the Chilean Communists who readapted to electoral practices and cooperation with democratic forces in 1988–1989.[20] Moreover, from the mid-1980s on perestroika exercised a moderating effect on or within a number of Communist parties, while Cuban moves in the other direction (the "rectification process") and the Socialist International's higher Central American profile helped to undermine much of the early 1980s' strengthening of revolutionary unity.[21]

Particularly disorienting for the guerrilla Left was Cuban-Nicaraguan divergence over perestroika, the Sandinistas' adoption of orthodox economic policies (described by Castro as "the most right-wing in Central America"), and the Cuban purge of General Arnaldo Ochoa and others in mid-1989.[22] At the same time, by 1990 elected civilian government was a reality in virtually the whole of Latin America, leaving guerrillas extremely uncertain about their future role. They were aware that predecessors who had ignored transitions from authoritarianism to democracy had paid a heavy price in Venezuela after 1958 and in Argentina in 1973–1976. On the other hand, given the fragility of civilian government in places and the even more widespread state of economic calamity, a return to military rule or increasing reliance by elected governments on repressive methods could not be ruled out. Unfortunately, although Guevara had warned against initiating guerrilla warfare against elected governments, he had left behind no advice on how to respond to democratization once the guerrilla struggle was under way.

Guerrilla Activity in the 1980s

The 1980s saw important guerrilla campaigns in Peru, El Salvador, Colombia, Guatemala, and Chile.[23] Of these, the only sustained urban activity was in Chile, although M-19 in Colombia and the MRTA in Peru began as urban guerrillas and in Peru and the Central American cases rural guerrillas increasingly undertook urban attacks as the decade progressed in order to demonstrate regime vulnerability, undermine enemy morale, and deploy urban sympathizers. The urban guerrillas in Chile took care not to escalate their struggle into a full-scale military confrontation with the security forces, as had occurred in Argentina and Uruguay a decade earlier. Acts of resistance such as sabotage rather than military assaults were the mainstay of FPMR activity, and perhaps even more than the Montoneros had in the mid-1970s the Front used masked *milicianos* belonging to mass organizations as opposed to well-trained *guerrilleros* for its activities. There were some elite-level operations such as assassination attempts (including a nearly successful one on Pinochet) and kidnappings of enemy officers to obtain intelligence and seek to sow disunity among the military, but there was more persistent involvement in mass protests and strikes.[24] Following Argentina in 1969–1973, the Chilean experience confirmed that urban guerrilla tactics have some utility in a resistance struggle, especially if applied at a time of growing popular assertiveness, but they once again failed to lead up to the insurrectionary finale that the guerrillas had envisaged.

The guerrillas that were primarily rural-based had much firmer roots than did the pioneers in the 1950s and 1960s. In Peru Sendero Luminoso's founders had been preparing for armed struggle in the fertile conditions of Ayacucho since the mid-1960s, long before the first armed action was undertaken in 1980. They had chosen their zone well: a remote, predominantly Indian region that had been so neglected by Lima that insurgency could prosper regardless of the democratic credentials of the government in the capital. Indeed, that neglect and the elite's contempt for the Indian population were so great that the state initially responded to Sendero with great lethargy and acted decisively (but clumsily) only when the insurgency was well advanced.[25]

Although the guerrilla movements had their origins in the intelligentsia (except in Colombia, where the movement was a peasant-based descendant of the 1940s *violencia*), they were much more adept at rooting themselves than were the earlier foquistas. In Peru Sendero was able to use its influence and temporary control of the University of San Cristóbal de Huamanga to develop community action programs in Ayacucho, and the teacher-training activities of the university provided a particularly useful means of infiltrating Indian communities. Both here and in Guatemala guerrilla organizations (Sendero, the Organización del Pueblo en Armas [Organization of the People in Arms—ORPA], and the Ejército Guerrillero de los Pobres [Guerrilla Army of the Poor—EGP]) spent a long time simply winning the confidence of the indigenous population, learning its languages and customs, before attracting enemy attention by commencing hostilities.[26] Sendero was particularly cautious and kept its ideology and program largely secret until 1987. Moreover, it was compartmentalized in small cells in order to avoid the concentration of guerrillas that had made the 1960s focos so visible and vulnerable.

Whereas the mass activity of some guerrillas was directly subordinated to the development of people's war, others were prepared to concede considerable autonomy to sympathetic mass organizations. In Guatemala only the EGP adopted the latter approach, but in El Salvador it was common practice.[27] This is one of the reasons the Salvadorian guerrillas were able to mobilize so much urban support through movements such as the Bloque Popular Revolucionario, which was linked to the FPL in the late 1970s when it claimed a hundred thousand members and numerous small union affiliations. The transfer of large numbers of urban militants to the rural FMLN forces contributed to the Salvadorian rebels' capacity to mount their offensive in 1981. However, this transfer of militants, together with increased repression, had the effect of weakening urban popular movements over the next few years.

Enemy tactics were certainly a factor influencing the subsequent course of events. The Guatemalan military had acquired considerable counterinsurgency expertise since the 1954 coup, and in General Efraín Ríos Montt it found a commander and president sufficiently ruthless to turn the tide against the guerrillas in the early 1980s. Repressive tactics—

aerial bombing of guerrilla zones, forcible concentration of the Indian population and its involvement in civil patrols, etc.—were particularly effective here. With an atrocious record of human rights violations since 1954, the Guatemalan regime had less to lose from international condemnation than the others. However, the army campaign was not exclusively based on slaughter: following a massive use of repressive violence in 1982–1983, the army's distribution of food and undertaking of limited rural development programs in Quiché and Huehuetenango also helped force the guerrillas onto the defensive by creating peasant dependency upon the military.[28]

In contrast, in Peru the initial counterinsurgency drive proved counterproductive in that it not only came late but was entirely repressive in nature—considerable violence against the Indian population of Ayacucho and attempts to organize civilian patrols, as in Guatemala, but no "beans" to offset the "bullets." Colombia was a different case altogether, the insurgency being too deep-rooted and the terrain too difficult for the state to contemplate swift and effective military action against the guerrillas, who, moreover, were by this time acting on multiple fronts.[29] Indeed, under presidents Betancur and Barco, much of the decade was devoted to the difficult pursuit of a peace settlement that would persuade guerrillas to renounce violence in return for being allowed to participate in the political system.

Of the guerrilla movements discussed here, only Sendero managed to gain ground throughout the 1980s. It spread first through the southern Andean highland departments of Ayacucho, Huancavelica, and Apurimac before moving into the coca-cultivating Upper Huallaga Valley in the mid-1980s, eventually coming out on top there in a conflict with the rival MRTA.[30] Sendero's subsequent deals with drug traffickers, involving the guerrilla protection of landing strips and processing laboratories, brought them an estimated fifty thousand dollars a day from a business that was quite compatible with the objective of undermining U.S. strength.[31] The second half of the 1980s saw Sendero become increasingly active in Lima and begin to threaten the strategic Mantaro Valley, from where it could severely disrupt Lima's food, energy, and mineral supplies. Signs of increased U.S. intervention in Peru at the end of the decade indicated just how far Sendero had progressed, while the split in the Izquierda Unida in 1989 and its electoral reverse in 1990 suggested that further recruitment to Sendero and the MRTA would not be difficult.

At the same time, reports of disagreements within Sendero and desertions from it were indicative of a real crisis in the organization arising from a fundamental strategic failure. Despite its territorial expansion, Sendero's vision of establishing liberated zones with people's committees in the countryside from which a people's army could begin to encircle the towns has not materialized. Rather, its recruitment and activity in the second half of the 1980s were predominantly urban.[32] It has been much more pragmatic in the development of insurgency than the dogmatic and strident tone of its few programmatic documents would suggest,[33] but by 1990 there was a deep division in the organization over whether the classic Maoist revolutionary model was appropriate to Peru or whether a major strategic reformulation was needed in response to the country's predominantly urban character. Not helping the case of those favoring a change was the 1989–1990 failure of Sendero's tactics of the "armed strike" and boycott of elections when extended from rural strongholds to Lima.

The fortunes of guerrilla wars elsewhere were rather more mixed, even though on two occasions in El Salvador—in 1981 and 1989—the FMLN seemed close to the seizure of power and U.S. backing for the regime was absolutely crucial in withstanding rebel offensives. What is important about the Salvadorian experience is that, despite very substantial U.S. military aid, including the training of elite army batallions specially prepared to fight guerrillas, access to modern technology failed to give the military the advantage. For example, claims that the introduction of OV-1 Mohawk spy planes would make guerrilla warfare obsolete because of their capacity to detect night-time movements by groups of just twelve guerrillas proved wrong, while the bulk of the Salvadorian army remained incompetent and very slow to respond to intelligence reports, the FMLN perfected the art of subdividing its forces into small units that could still be concentrated very quickly for major attacks.

Although on several occasions the Salvadorian guerrillas attacked enemy strongholds, the more fragmented Colombian guerrillas had to be militarily less ambitious. Yet the Colombian insurgents did attain greater influence in their country's politics than during the 1970s. In part, this was because of the greater potential for their reincorporation into the system,[34] but it was also because insurgents here used the classic guerrilla advantages to the fullest. Militarily, there was no great increase in the size of guerrilla forces. Indeed, the massacres carried out by the Frente Ricardo Franco (a breakaway from the FARC) in the mid-1980s were symptomatic of crisis and enemy success: more than two hundred members of this guerrilla force were "executed" by order of their own leaders, accused of being enemy agents.[35]

Nonetheless, Colombian guerrillas were able to exert political influence. When President Betancur's peace initiative broke down in 1985, the rebels put greater pressure on the government for concessions by taking unitary initiatives. In addition to announcing that most of the guerrilla forces were forming a Coordinadora Nacional Guerrillera (National Guerrilla Coordinator—CNG), M-19 took the lead in launching a Batallón

América incorporating fighters from neighboring countries. In fact, the CNG coordinated only a handful of joint guerrilla attacks on army patrols, and the Batallón had little more than symbolic participation by Peruvian MRTA and Ecuadorian Alfaro Vive guerrillas, but this raising of the ante may well have had some effect on a government that was clearly incapable of confronting both the guerrillas and the drug cartels simultaneously. Under President Barco, the guerrilla kidnapping of establishment figures and capture of enemy soldiers seems also to have encouraged new attempts at conciliation by the government.[36]

Colombia saw nothing like the military offensives staged by the FMLN, yet M-19's appreciation of the impact of symbolic violence and of the propaganda value of displays of audacity and panache led this guerrilla force to mount several assaults that made it seem far more important than its numbers warranted (it being clearly smaller than the FARC). Both the taking of diplomatic hostages during the occupation of the Dominican Republic's embassy in 1980 and the less successful attack on the Palace of Justice in 1985 captured world attention and highlighted the state's inability to guarantee security. Meanwhile, even the smaller guerrilla forces were able to take advantage of Colombia's lawlessness, whether to extort money from landowners, take over the operation of remote gold mines (said to be worth 2 to 3 million dollars a month), or cause major damage (put at 450 million dollars for 1988) to the Caño Limón–Puerto Coveñas oil pipeline.[37] Thus, although in no way effectively challenging state power, insurgents in Colombia did become a big enough problem to make the government go beyond its original offer of mere amnesty for the rebels; in the latter years of the 1980s positive ways of facilitating their reintegration into the political system were sought.

Prospects

By the early 1990s the international crisis of communism had sown doubts in many guerrilla minds about the viability of their activity. The electoral defeat of the Sandinistas in Nicaragua and the growing isolation and economic problems of the Cuban regime—points of reference for all Latin American insurgents apart from perhaps the autarkic *senderistas*—created great uncertainty within the armed Left about what could be done with political power even if it were attainable by means of armed struggle. Whether the Colombian, Salvadorian, and Guatemalan peace initiatives would succeed or not, their very existence suggested that the Guevarist tradition was now in decline.

Although such a watershed *may* have been reached by 1991, it seems highly improbable that armed rebellion of some variety will not persist. Even the more optimistic prognoses about economic revival envisage widespread social deprivation throughout Latin America for years to come, especially as the size of the state is drastically cut back in several countries. Already there have been serious cases of rioting and looting in the Dominican Republic, Venezuela, and Argentina as desperate people have reacted against IMF-approved austerity packages. With such a vast reservoir of social distress, it would be surprising if armed groups of left-wing, populist, or even anarchic orientation were not to feature in the politics of the 1990s.

Nonetheless, guerrilla movements will need to adapt if they are to remain influential. Although the extent and significance of external sponsorship have often been exaggerated, the international crisis of communism has clearly left several guerrilla movements with a need either to find new international sources of support or to increase their domestic sources of sustenance. Some guerrilla organizations have still to absorb the "lessons" of the Sandinista victory in Nicaragua and might benefit in future from the adoption of more sophisticated "combined" strategies and a more flexible approach to tactics and alliances. Others may be tempted to resort to a more extreme approach. One possibility is that terrorism may come to play a much more prominent role. Insurgents may decide that their predecessors were simply not ruthless enough and become far less discriminate in their use of violence. They may be encouraged here by the progress made by Sendero Luminoso, which (in contrast to the foquistas of the 1960s) has attacked whole communities of peasants that refused to cooperate. There have been occasional hints of Sendero-type imitation in Bolivia, while in Argentina in 1978–1979 there were a number of armed holdups by so-called *gurkhas*, ex-guerrillas who no longer entertained hopes of winning over "workers in uniform" and who commenced their assaults by killing police guards in cold blood.[38]

The latter incidents could equally form part of a different trend, with guerrilla veterans, finding no political function for themselves, turning to common crime, whether bank raids, kidnappings, extortion, or the cocaine business. The dividing line between political insurgency and rural banditry has always been rather thin in the case of the long-standing violence in Colombia. It is extremely doubtful whether all the guerrillas who have become accustomed to financing multimillion-dollar organizational budgets by means of violence against landlords and, more recently, "protecting" drug traffickers and their installations in Peru and Colombia are going to lay down their arms for political reasons.[39]

There is, however, a final scenario in which guerrillas might feature within a more general state of anomie, and for the authorities this must be the most alarming one. The rising rate of violence by youth gangs in Brazil and Colombia cannot simply be identified as further criminal evidence of the crisis of state authority, for there is at least an element of class war in

the way in which gangs of unemployed youths have sought to appropriate the wealth of rich (and not so rich) families by means of kidnappings.
It is hard to imagine how politicized such activity might become and
whether organized guerrilla groups might be able to intervene in it to
further their own purposes. However, these examples, together with that
of the FPMR in Chile and the composition of the assault group that took
over the La Tablada barracks outside Buenos Aires in 1989,[40] suggest that
the marginal sectors traditionally ignored by the Left could become an
important source of political violence in the 1990s. If the Left is to gain
influence among such sectors, it will have to dispense with any lingering
Leninist notions of mass organizations as subordinate bodies whose
development is secondary to the task of building the revolutionary
vanguard. To exert influence upon the marginal sectors, the Left will need
to respect their autonomy and personality and adopt strategies and
programs that accommodate their specific needs.

Notes

1. See María Isabel Rauber, *Vanguardia y revolución (Reflexiones sobre la experiencia latino-
americana)* (Havana: Centro de Estudios sobre América, 1989), written by a former member of
Argentina's Ejército Revolucionario del Pueblo.

2. Richard Gillespie, "The Urban Guerrilla in Latin America," in Noel O'Sullivan, ed.,
Terrorism, Ideology, and Revolution (Brighton: Wheatsheaf, 1986).

3. See, for example, "Hablan los Montoneros," *Somos*, September 20, 1989.

4. Steve Ellner, *Venezuela's Movimiento al Socialismo: From Guerrilla Defeat to Innovative
Politics* (Durham: Duke University Press, 1988).

5. *Latin American Weekly Report*, August 14, 1986, October 2, 1986, March 23, 1989.

6. Richard Gillespie, *Soldiers of Perón: Argentina's Montoneros* (Oxford: Clarendon, 1982),
Chapters 5 and 6.

7. *Página 12* (Buenos Aires), October 11–13, 1989; *Sur* (Buenos Aires), November 1, 1989,
March 9, 1990.

8. "Hablan los Montoneros," *Somos* (Buenos Aires), September 20, 1989; *Clarín* (Buenos
Aires), March 5, 1990.

9. For successive programs, see the FDR-FMLN *Boletín Informativo* (Mexico), 22 (1981);
Communist Affairs (London), 1, 3 (1982); *Granma Weekly Review*, November 7, 1982, February
19, 1984.

10. *Latin American Weekly Report*, December 17, 1987.

11. *Latin American Weekly Report*, February 9, 1989.

12. Malcolm Deas, "The Colombian Peace Process, 1982–85," in Giuseppe Di Palma
and Laurence Whitehead, eds., *The Central American Impasse* (London: Croom Helm, 1986),
106–107.

13. Humberto Ortega, interview, "Nicaragua—The Strategy of Victory," in Tomás Borge,
et al., *Sandinistas Speak* (New York: Pathfinder, 1986), 52–84; José Luis Coraggio, *Nicaragua:
Revolution and Democracy* (Boston: Allen and Unwin, 1986), 62.

14. Richard Gillespie, "Salvadoran Rebels Divide to Unite," *Communist Affairs*, 3, 3
(1984):313–315; James Dunkerley, *Power in the Isthmus: A Political History of Modern Central
America* (London: Verso, 1988), 481–484.

15. *Mexico and Central America Report* (London), May 4, 1989.

16. "The Honduran Revolutionary Movements," *Communist Affairs*, 1, 3 (1982):655–662.

17. For a different view, see Antonio Ybarra-Rojas, "The Changing Role of Revolutionary Violence in Nicaragua, 1959 to 1979," in Michael Radu, ed., *Violence and the Latin American Revolutionaries* (New Brunswick: Transaction, 1988): here the FSLN victory is attributed to its alleged final adoption of the position of the communist Nicaraguan Socialist party. The problem with this view is that *in practice* that party had always been reformist. In the same volume, Vladimir Tismaneanu, in "Communist Orthodoxy and Revolutionary Violence," sees Communist party involvement in guerrilla warfare as being mainly a result of Soviet-Cuban initiatives and convergence—a contention that ignores Soviet-Cuban differences in 1983 concerning the events in Grenada and the split in the Costa Rican party.

18. Schafik Jorge Handal, "Power, the Character and Path of the Revolution, and the Unity of the Left," *Communist Affairs*, 2, 2 (1983):236–245.

19. Carmelo Furci, *The Chilean Communist Party and the Road to Socialism* (London: Zed, 1984), 165–168; idem, "The Chilean Communist Party (PCCh) and its Third Underground Period, 1973–80," *Bulletin of Latin American Research*, 2, 1 (1982):87–92.

20. Violence against the state had never been broadly supported by the Chilean Left, and the recent commitment to it has provoked debilitating divisions in both the PCC and the MIR. On these, see Benny Pollack, "The Dilemmas Facing the Chilean Left Following the Plebiscite of 1988," *Journal of Communist Studies*, 5, 2 (1989):222–227.

21. Richard Gillespie, *Cuba after 30 Years: Rectification and the Revolution* (London: Cass, 1990); Eusebeio M. Mujal-León, *European Socialism and the Conflict in Central America* (New York: Praeger, 1989).

22. *Mesoamérica* (San José), February 1990, 4.

23. For information on all the active Latin American guerrilla organizations, see my entries in Roger East, ed., *Communist and Marxist Parties of the World*, 2nd ed. (London: Longman, forthcoming).

24. For a critical account of FPMR activity, see Genaro Arriagada, *Pinochet: The Politics of Power* (Boston: Unwin and Hyman, 1988), Chapter 8.

25. Raúl González, "Ayacucho: Por los caminos de Sendero," *Quehacer*, 19 (1982):19; Lewis Taylor, *Maoism in the Andes: Sendero Luminoso and the Contemporary Guerrilla Movement in Peru*, University of Liverpool, Centre for Latin American Studies, Working Paper 2, 1983; David Scott Palmer, "Rebellion in Rural Peru: The Origins and Evolution of Sendero Luminoso," *Comparative Politics*, 18, 2 (1986):127–146; idem, "Terrorism as a Revolutionary Strategy: Peru's Sendero Luminoso," in Barry Rubin, ed., *The Politics of Terrorism* (Washington, DC: Johns Hopkins Foreign Policy Institute, 1989).

26. Eduardo Galeano, José González, and Antonio Campos, *Guatemala: Un pueblo en lucha* (Madrid: Revolución, 1983); George Black, *Garrison Guatemala* (London: Zed, 1984), Chapters 4 and 5; Richard Gillespie, "Anatomy of the Guatemalan Guerrilla," *Communist Affairs*, 2, 4 (1983); Rigoberta Menchú, interview, "The Indian Struggle Became a Class Struggle," *Communist Affairs*, 2, 2 (1983).

27. Dunkerley, *Power in the Isthmus*, 368–400; *The Long War: Dictatorship and Revolution in El Salvador* (London: Junction, 1982), Chapters 6 and 9; Richard Gillespie, "From Farabundo Martí to FMLN," *Communist Affairs*, 1, 1 (1982); Jenny Pearce, *Promised Land: Peasant Rebellion in Chalatenango, El Salvador* (London: Latin America Bureau, 1986).

28. Dunkerley, *Power in the Isthmus*, 496.

29. Jorge P. Osterling, *Democracy in Colombia: Clientelist Politics and Guerrilla Warfare* (New Brunswick: Transaction, 1989), Chapter 7.

30. Raúl González, "Sendero vs. MRTA," *Quehacer*, 46 (1987); *Latin American Weekly Report*, December 17, 1987, March 2, 1989.

31. *Latin American Weekly Report*, April 13, 1989.

32. Raúl González, "Sendero: Duro desgaste y crisis estratégica," *Quehacer*, 64 (1990).

33. Colin Harding, "Notes on Sendero Luminoso," *Communist Affairs*, 3, 1 (1984):46; idem, "Antonio Díaz Martínez and the Ideology of Sendero Luminoso," *Bulletin of Latin American Research*, 7, 1 (1988), 71.

34. Deas, "The Colombian Peace Process," 108–109.

35. Osterling, *Democracy in Colombia*, 319–322; *Latin American Weekly Report*, January 10, 1986.

36. *Latin American Weekly Report*, June 23, 1988, September 15, 1988.

37. *Latin American Weekly Report*, May 25, 1989, June 29, 1989, July 6, 1989.

38. "El fantasma de la guerrilla," *Somos*, December 21, 1988.

39. *Latin American Weekly Report*, April 13, 1989, April 27, 1989; Osterling, *Democracy in Colombia*, 325–332.

40. *Latin American Weekly Report*, April 20, 1989.

12

Trade Union Struggle and the Left in Latin America, 1973–1990

Dick Parker

In the early stages of trade union organization in Latin America, as in the developed capitalist countries, most worker struggles were clearly identified with the Left. As has been recognized by one of today's most prominent Christian trade union leaders, the initiators of trade union organization were anarchists, socialists, and communists.[1] With the decline of anarchism in the 1920s, Left influence in the unions was incorporated into the Marxist tradition and, during several decades, dominated by the Communist parties.[2] What most clearly distinguished Left presence in organized labor was the attempt to promote a type of union activity that, rather than limiting itself to the immediate demands and necessities of its members or accommodating itself to the logic of capital, sought to subvert that logic and open up the prospect of an alternative order based on socialist principles.

The overall political objective inevitably placed the relationship between the party and the union at the very heart of the discussions over union strategy. Within the Marxist tradition, this relationship took on particular importance once it became evident that trade union activity per se did not generate revolutionary consciousness.[3] What came to be identified as a Leninist model of subordination of trade union activity to party political objectives became a source of permanent tension. The Leninist model itself was subject to an inherent contradiction between the natural "economistic" dynamic of trade union activity and long-term political goals. The linkage of union activity and revolutionary strategy not only assumed the existence of capable political leadership but also required class autonomy in the face of those political forces interested in the overall stability of the system. To the extent that the Marxist Left identified itself as the vanguard of the working class, the subordination of union activity to its political strategy was conceived of as perfectly compatible with the autonomy of the class. Nevertheless, there would be a permanent tension between the "autonomous" impulse of trade union activity, whose class base could hardly be questioned, and the political direction of Left parties, whose class orientation could always be placed in doubt.

In Latin America, this classic dilemma of the Left was particularly acute because union activity has traditionally been dominated by political militants—in part because of the structural weakness of the unions, in part because the state assumed the supervision of labor relations in the early stages of the development of the working class.[4] Labor relations were to be based less on collective bargaining with the employer than on state regulation and intervention, less on the organizational strength of labor in the workplace than on the capacity of union leaders to influence government policy. This situation not only accounted for the notorious influence of party militants in the unions; it also reinforced the potential weight of reformist or populist parties capable of negotiating with the state on behalf of the unions without questioning the basic structures of power. Furthermore, the import-substitution industrialization initiated in the 1930s lent itself to government policies that not only sought the consolidation of an internal market for mass-produced products (on the basis of a constant increase in the net income of the wage-earning population) but also favored labor organization as a way of gaining political support.

In general, in those countries that were most advanced in the industrialization process in the 1940s and 1950s, reformist or populist influence in the unions grew rapidly at the expense of the Left. In Mexico, the Confederación de Trabajadores de México, organically linked to the governing party, consolidated its control of the trade union movement to such an extent that Left influence has not recovered even today. Peronist ascendancy in the Argentine Confederación General de Trabajo (General Confederation of Labor—CGT) was also to have long-term implications that would severely limit the possibilities of a recovery of the Left, although in Argentina the unions would be much more militant and markedly more autonomous vis-à-vis the state than in Mexico. In Brazil, state influence in the unions was facilitated by the 1940 Labor Code (based on Mussolini's Carta di Lavoro), but Getúlio Vargas's need for labor as a source of political support left open an important margin for labor mobilizations, and during the populist period (1950–1964) the state even tolerated the union activity of the illegal Brazilian Communist party. The reformist alternative also triumphed in Peru and Venezuela in the 1940s, laying the basis for

APRA control of the Confederación de Trabajadores del Perú and a clear predominance within the Confederación de Trabajadores de Venezuela of the Acción Democrática party.

The Colombian case was also characterized by a weakening of Left influence in the unions, but instead of the establishment of a relatively unified labor movement with the clear predominance of a single populist or reformist party the postwar period saw the consolidation of two union organizations at the national level, each identified with one of the traditional oligarchic parties. In the late 1940s, the majority Liberal party influence in the Confederación de Trabajadores de Colombia (Confederation of Workers of Colombia—CTC), together with a certain Communist presence within its ranks, led to a church-inspired initiative to create the Unión de Trabajadores de Colombia (Workers' Union of Colombia—UTC), identified with the Conservative party. The violent confrontation between the two traditional oligarchic parties in the late 1940s and 1950s helped to consolidate this division within the Colombian labor movement.

In all the above-mentioned cases, the drastic weakening of the Left in the labor movement coincided with the Cold War offensive and the concomitant U.S. pressure to root out left-wing influence in the hemisphere. Nevertheless, there were a few countries in which the Left managed to resist and succeeded in preserving its dominant position in the unions. The most outstanding case was Chile, where, despite the conflict between Socialists and Communists during the 1940s, the recovery of trade union activity in the 1950s was achieved on the basis of a joint Socialist-Communist hegemony within the Central Unica de Trabajadores (Single Confederation of Workers—CUT). The uniqueness of the Chilean experience was that this hegemony within the labor movement was accompanied by a solid and growing political presence that was to culminate with the 1970 electoral victory of the Unidad Popular candidate, Salvador Allende.

In Uruguay, the Communist party succeeded in maintaining its influence in the unions and in 1964 was able to promote the establishment of a unified national organization, the Convención Nacional de Trabajadores (National Convention of Workers—CNT), which it was to dominate from the outset. But in contrast to its counterpart in Chile, the Uruguayan Communist party lacked a significant presence in electoral politics. In both cases, however, the left-wing trade union leaders were obliged, as a result of the relative organizational weakness of the unions and the decisive weight of the state in labor relations, to rely on the parties as vehicles for a "political bargaining" similar to that employed by reformist parties in the continent.[5]

Finally, the other important example of continued Left influence in organized labor is Bolivia. There, the strategic importance of the tin miners was reflected in the adoption of a specifically socialist program in the famous 1946 Thesis of Pulacayo, in their central role in the 1952 revolution, and in their decisive weight within the Central Obrera Boliviana, and of the COB in Bolivian politics in subsequent years. During the administration of General Juan José Torres in 1971, the creation of a Popular Assembly dominated by the COB even raised hopes of revolutionary transformations spearheaded by the unions. The radicalized union movement in Bolivia exercised direct political influence while the left-wing parties were not only weak but fragmented and incapable of imposing any coherent political direction.

Whereas in the 1950s the Latin American Left struggled to hold onto its diminishing influence in politics and organized labor, the 1960s and early 1970s witnessed a revival of revolutionary expectations. The Cuban Revolution provoked important crises in many of the reformist and populist parties and put the socialist revolution on the agenda of the Marxist Left. At the same time, it placed in the forefront of debate the relationship between trade union struggle and the radical political transformations that appeared to be pending. This, in turn, intensified the clash between the rival political forces within the labor movement, leading to the expulsion of Communists and other Marxists from the reformist-controlled confederations: from the CTC in Colombia in 1960, leading to the creation of the Confederación Sindical de Trabajadores de Colombia (Trade Union Confederation of Workers of Colombia—CSTC), from the CTV in Venezuela in 1961, and from the CTP in Peru, with the subsequent creation in 1967 of the Central General de Trabajadores del Perú at the initiative of the Peruvian Communist party. These new organizations would lay the basis for important Left advances in the 1970s and 1980s.

The hopes of revolutionary breakthroughs in this period were nevertheless to be rudely shattered as popular advances were successively cut short by the installation of repressive military regimes in Brazil (1964), Argentina (1966, 1967), Bolivia (1971), and Uruguay and Chile (1973). The proliferation and consolidation of these military regimes in the Southern Cone placed the Left once again on the defensive and radically transformed trade union objectives. The working-class movements that had traditionally been most influential were subject to implacable persecution, and with the return to constitutional rule in the course of the 1980s they would find that the trade union environment had undergone fundamental changes.

An Overview of the Period 1973–1990

A discussion of the Left and the unions in Latin America since 1973 has to take into account the different national experiences just summarized.

At the same time, it needs to consider the ways in which the dynamics of capitalist development during the last two decades and the constraints inherent in the proliferation of repressive military regimes shaped the organizational capacity of the unions and influenced the priorities of the Left.

The prospects and the potential problems of the trade unions are inevitably conditioned in a profound way by factors that affect labor's general bargaining position in relation to capital and the state. Thus, for example, an understanding of the organizational advances since the 1940s or of the real gains that reformist unionism could claim during the period of populist predominance can hardly neglect the importance of the expansive dynamic that characterized the world capitalist system during the decades following World War II, the generally rapid growth of the Latin American economies, the industrialization process, and the subsequent consolidation of an industrial working class in the continent. Furthermore, it cannot fail to take into account the implications for labor's bargaining potential of a political context in which the populist forms of domination opened up the possibility of compensating for a structural weakness at the plant level by asserting political influence in the government.

In the same way, the trade union struggles that have characterized the 1970s and 1980s have inevitably been influenced by the global changes in the capitalist system: the so-called accumulation crisis in the developed economies, the gradual reduction in importance within world commerce of economies, such as those of Latin America, that are traditionally exporters of primary products, the dramatic increase in the financial drain aggravated by the debt, and, more recently, the overwhelming pressures in favor of the application of neoliberal economic policies.

The overall impact of these changes has recently been documented by the UN's Economic Commission for Latin America, which commented that "at the end of 1989, the average Gross National Product per person in the region was 8 percent lower than that registered in 1980 and equivalent to that of 1977. If we take into account that this deterioration was accompanied by greater inequalities in the distribution of income, it can be appreciated that, in terms of the general well-being of the . . . population, the eighties have been characterized by a deterioration of major proportions."[6] This process has been accompanied by a reduction in the supply of stable employment, increasing levels of unemployment, and a marked expansion of the so-called informal economy. These general tendencies have inevitably undermined the basis of the unions' traditional bargaining strength and are reflected in the falling rates of unionization in the private sector and, in particular, among industrial workers.

Within this general context, there are important distinctions to be made among individual Latin American countries in terms of both the moment at which the new correlation of forces was established and the impact of the policies introduced. For instance, in the Southern Cone (Chile, Argentina, and Uruguay) the neoliberal policies implemented by the military regimes in the mid-1970s, implied a process of deindustrialization that radically affected the potential recruiting base for the industrial unions, whereas in Brazil the policies adopted by the military in the late 1960s favored industrial growth and resulted in an important expansion of the industrial labor force, laying the basis for a reactivation of union militancy beginning in the late 1970s. Again, in the 1980s, while the overwhelming majority of Latin American countries stagnated or experienced negative growth rates, largely as a result of their debt problems, the Colombian economy continued to expand (thanks in part to the contribution of the illegal drug trade to its balance of payments), thus attenuating the pressure on the Colombian workers' movement.

Despite these differences, the general weakness of the trade union bargaining position undermined the mechanisms that had previously contributed to the hegemony of reformist unionism and might have been expected to favor a general radicalization of the union movement and a corresponding increase in Left influence. Before examining to what extent this was the case, we need to look at the way in which the changes we have been observing affected the political vision and objectives of the Left.

Since the early 1980s, the political influence of the traditional Left and, in particular, of the orthodox Communist parties, has clearly diminished. Not only has their electoral appeal been reduced but several have suffered internal divisions; the recent collapse of the Soviet bloc can only aggravate what appears to be a serious crisis of ideological identity. At the same time, however, there has been a parallel growth of a noncommunist Left, often clearly distinguishing itself from the Marxist-Leninist tradition. Furthermore, there has been an evident shift from the expectation of immediate revolutionary changes characteristic of the 1960s to a preoccupation with the consolidation of democratic institutionality in the 1980s.[7] As a result, union strategy can no longer be infused with optimism about the imminent modification of the global structure of society in a socialist direction. Given the relatively reduced expectations of the Left of gaining power and the general weakness of the unions, strategy is markedly more defensive, and the central dilemma is whether to defend the interests of the working class by signing pacts with employers and the state (concertación) or by resorting to militant, confrontationist tactics.

Contradictory Tendencies in the 1970s

During the middle and late 1970s, before the continent felt the full weight of economic crisis, two clear but contrasting tendencies called into question the traditional patterns of labor relations and presented a new series of challenges for the Left. On the one hand, the violently repressive military regimes in the Southern Cone, while reducing the Left to impotence, sought to extirpate once and for all what were considered the inherent vices of the populist heritage. The result was radical weakening of precisely the most highly organized and politicized labor movements in the continent. On the other hand, the decade witnessed the emergence in other parts of the continent of an altogether different threat to reformist hegemony in the labor movement: the development within the movement itself of a new, militant unionism that identified itself as class-oriented (*clasista*), was often more radical than the Communist-influenced unions, and placed new emphasis on grass-roots organization and autonomy vis-à-vis the state. This new phenomenon was not confined to the countries that had managed to maintain civilian rule. Indeed, its impact was most notable in Peru and Brazil, where military regimes had been in power since the 1960s, and in Central America, where the radicalization of union activity formed part of a popular movement with revolutionary overtones that would lead to the overthrow of the Somoza regime in Nicaragua and the regional crisis of the 1980s.

The military offensive against the unions and the Left in the Southern Cone hardly needs to be detailed here. For our purposes what should be emphasized is those aspects of the new policies that led to long-term modifications in the conditions for trade union struggle, anticipating problems that were to characterize the 1980s even after the return to civilian rule. These can be seen in their most dramatic form in the Chilean experience. The impact of the military regime since 1973 was felt in a sharp drop in unionization rates (from 27 percent in 1973 to less than 8 percent in 1983), a radical reduction of the unions' bargaining capacity, and the elimination of their political influence. Apart from the direct repression, the unions were affected by the imposition of an economic model that provoked high unemployment rates and cut industrial production. Furthermore, modifications in labor legislation drastically reduced the protection afforded to the union activist while a general ideological offensive sought to destroy the principle of collective solidarity in favor of a strictly individualistic logic.[8] These general tendencies were evident in the entire Southern Cone.

Although the emergence of a class-oriented unionism was most noticeable in Peru and Brazil, its influence can nevertheless be detected elsewhere in the region as the counterpart of the increasing difficulties that reformist unionism was experiencing as the economic crisis set in. It is reflected in the strengthening of independent unionism in Mexico in the mid-1970s, in Colombia's 1977 national strike, which unified the different union confederations behind a new radical tactic promoted by the Left, and in the support of competing confederations for the general strikes of

1975 and 1977 in Ecuador. The radicalization of union struggles in Central America was particularly marked in Guatemala and El Salvador well before the Sandinista Revolution had transformed the prospects of union organization in Nicaragua. Even in Venezuela, where the windfall resources from the oil boom helped consolidate AD control of the CTV, the late 1970s saw the emergence of an independent class-oriented leadership in the steel and textile industries.[9]

Although in some cases, such as Mexico and Venezuela, the advances were to be limited or ephemeral, there appeared to be clear indications of a potential recovery of leftist or militant influence in the continent. This impression was strengthened as the unions flexed their muscles in the struggle against the de facto military regimes: in the general strikes in Ecuador in 1975 and 1977 and in Peru in 1977 and 1978, in the overthrow of Banzer in Bolivia in 1978, and, above all, when the 1978 strike wave in Brazil added a new dimension to the liberalization process initiated by General Ernesto Geisel.

Of all these experiences, those that promised most in terms of a strengthening of trade union influence and of a genuine left-wing direction were those of Peru and Brazil. The dramatic upsurge of class-oriented unionism in Peru during the 1970s was clearly related to the particular characteristics of the military regime installed in 1968. During the period from 1968 to 1973, the Velasco government pursued a policy that facilitated union activity, especially as a result of the introduction of the Industrial Community Law and the Work Stability Law. The Communist-led CGTP, which supported government policy, experienced a rapid growth that enabled it to replace the CTP as the major national confederation. Identification with the regime proved a handicap for the PCP with the emergence of authoritarian tendencies after 1973, and this enabled other, more combative left-wing groups to increase their influence within the CGTP. With the overthrow of Velasco in 1975 and the definitive reversal of the reformist impulse of the military government, a hardening of labor policy, and a sustained fall in real wages, the CGTP would lead a wave of mobilizations to back the demand for democratic liberties and mechanisms for the resolution of labor problems. These massive popular protests, which culminated in the national strikes of 1977 and 1978, were led by the unions in repudiation of economic policies and clearly contributed to the end of the military dictatorship in 1980.[10]

The class-oriented unionism in Peru during these years placed new emphasis on the fight for worker rights within the plant, including work conditions and security. At the same time, it promoted active participation of the rank and file in the struggles and in union decisions in general, thus radically breaking with the traditional reformist style that had been imposed by the Alianza Popular Revolucionaria Americana. This preoccupation was reflected in the custom of organizing periodic general assemblies of workers and in the flowering of a worker press designed to keep the rank and file permanently informed. It also relied frequently on direct confrontational tactics, defending the necessity of radical policies that went beyond the mechanisms contemplated in current legislation. Union tactics were conditioned by a clear consciousness that the union struggle was part of a wider worker-peasant alliance backed by new social movements in the urban areas.[11]

The revolutionary perspective that informed union activity during these years meant that there was little temptation to enter into negotiations with the government. Indeed, in questioning the validity of "bourgeois legality" the union leadership paid little attention to the possibility of promoting legal reforms and did not concern itself with strengthening the central organisms of a notoriously atomized movement. For these reasons, the bargaining position of the unions was structurally weak. Finally, there was another characteristic of the class-oriented unionism that would prove a liability in the radically different context of the 1980s: the noncommunist Left, composed of a multiplicity of Marxist-Leninist groups, was marked by a particular way of participating in the union struggles. The militants, generally formed in the universities, concentrated their activities in the most important industrial centers and disputed the direction of the movement on the basis of a highly politicized discourse that, while reflecting the militancy of the rank and file, could hardly be said to represent its level of consciousness.[12]

As the influence of class-oriented unionism in Peru reached a peak in 1978 after a decade of continual advances, Brazil in the same year witnessed an unexpected and explosive strike wave that would lay the basis for a new unionism after well over a decade of forced quiescence. Despite the markedly repressive nature of the Brazilian regime, there had already been some indications of the emergence of new union demands in 1973–1974, especially in the metallurgical industry. In the "Declaration of São Bernardo" in 1974 the automobile workers demanded the recognition of union freedom, the elimination of the restrictions imposed by the labor law, and total freedom to negotiate collective contracts with the employers. As can be appreciated, the initial concern of discontented Brazilian union leaders was to escape the straitjacket imposed by corporatist labor legislation.[13]

Nevertheless, when the automobile workers of São Bernardo, led by Luís Inácio (Lula) da Silva, initiated the strike wave in May 1978, they did so in defiance of existing legal restrictions, and the movement assumed a dynamic that rapidly altered the general conditions for trade union struggle. In the face of worker militancy, the employers began to recognize the union's insistence on negotiating directly with the firm. At the same time, the government's failure to contain the walkouts led to a de facto achievement of the right to strike. The prominence of the metalworkers in the strike movement immediately raised a central question that had been absent in Peru: To what extent could the new unionism be characterized as class-oriented? In 1975 the new demands of the metalworkers of São Bernardo seemed to presage a style of unionism akin to that of business unionism: aggressive in the struggle for economic advantages but apolitical, firmly rooted in the plant but indifferent to the concerns of other sectors of the working class, capable of confronting the employer but without questioning the prevailing capitalist development model. Others, however, were to argue that the automobile workers, rather than constituting a labor aristocracy, were emerging as an effective vanguard of the working-class movement precisely because their location in the most dynamic sector of Brazilian industry offered optimum conditions for questioning the general wage policy of the state. Developments in the 1980s suggest that the emergent unionism would correspond more to this second vision.[14]

Confronting the Crisis in the 1980s

During the 1980s, the Left and the unions faced two fundamental challenges: first, to promote a return to civilian rule along with a restoration of basic democratic guarantees (whose importance for the Left had been sufficiently underlined by the experience of military rule); and second, once the basic guarantees had been restored, to respond to the deepening crisis and the neoliberal offensive. Cutting across the debates, of course, were the controversies inherited from the 1970s, especially with respect to the tactics most appropriate for furthering working-class interests.

We have seen in the case of Peru and Brazil how the struggle against the military regimes had favored the emergence and consolidation of a class-oriented unionism. Nevertheless, the implications for the Left were not the same in the two countries. In Peru, the class-oriented CGTP had been founded on the initiative of the local Communist party, which continued to dominate it during its period of rapid expansion in the 1970s and itself experienced a parallel growth in political influence. At the same time, the noncommunist presence in the CGTP was fundamentally influenced by a variety of Marxist-Leninist groups whose ideology was as traditional and orthodox as that of the PCP. In contrast, the emergence of class-oriented unionism in Brazil was not only *not* led by the Brazilian Communists but marked from the outset by a radical repudiation of the parties that had traditionally exercised influence on the Brazilian working class, including the two Communist parties (the Partido Comunista Brasileiro [PCB] and the Partido Comunista do Brasil [PCdoB]). The renovation movement initiated in 1978 evidenced strong "workerist" overtones, although it quickly recognized the need for a political party. But in this case it would be a new political party, the Partido dos Trabalhadores, clearly conceived as an alternative to the traditional Left and promising a new way of relating the trade union struggle to the complementary political struggle.

The Brazilian Communists, who were seriously weakened as a result of the military repression, questioned the class orientation of the new trade union leaders and suggested that the new militancy, especially among the metalworkers, reflected the interests of a labor aristocracy.[15] When the attempt to construct a single national trade union confederation broke down and the PT promoted the creation of the Central Unica dos Trabalhadores (Single Confederation of Workers—CUT) in 1983, the Communists refused to join it, preferring to work within the rival Confederacão Geral do Trabalho (General Labor Confederation—CGT), dominated by the more traditional leaders and still in control of a majority of the unions in the country. Not surprisingly, the Brazilian Communists had also repudiated the creation of the PT.

This clear polarization within the Left in Brazil occurred in the early 1980s, when the military regime had been liberalized enough to permit the Left an appreciable margin for maneuver—well before civilian rule was restored and basic democratic rights fully recognized. It is perhaps for this reason that the contrast between the positions of the PT and the Communists could be so clearly expressed. It appears that the Communists assigned priority to the task of fully restoring the democratic system. As a result, they were suspicious of the militancy of the relatively well-organized workers, fearing that it would provoke another wave of repression, and insisted on the necessity of a policy reflecting the interests of wage earners in general. Apart from opting to work within the CGT, the Communists also insisted on preserving the broad umbrella opposition movement grouped in the Partido do Movimento Democrático Brasileiro (Party of the Brazilian Democratic Movement—PMDB), resisting the PT proposal to create a class party. The PT, whose rapid growth was undoubtedly stimulated by its militant confrontations with the military regime, nevertheless refused to consider the return to democratic institutionality as the strategic aim. Its priorities were defined much more in terms of the necessary response of the working class to the crisis and to government that systematically passed on the economic costs to the workers.[16]

In Uruguay, the antidictatorial struggle was accompanied by similar confrontations involving the local Communist party, although the circumstances and the outcome were different. As in the rest of the Southern Cone, the intensity of the repression, which was directed above all at political militants, transformed the unions into privileged actors in the antidictatorial fight while, at the same time, it loosened the political-party tutelage to which unions had traditionally been subject. These circumstances seemed to be leading to a long-term modification in the relations between the unions and the Left parties similar to that which was taking place in Brazil.

The Uruguayan experience illustrates with particular clarity both the expectations that emerged in trade union circles and the difficulties encountered once civilian rule had been restored. The debates that had characterized the early 1970s had already led to a questioning of Communist party policy. While the Partido Comunista de Uruguay (Communist Party of Uruguay—PCU) apparently viewed the trade union struggle in classic Leninist terms and was careful to moderate conflicts in order to safeguard the democratic institutional framework, the Tendencia Combativa (Combative Tendency), many of whose members were influenced by the Tupamaros, rejected the tutelage of the PCU and considered the unions an instrument for promoting the economic and social changes announced in the CNT program. The different sectoral struggles were viewed as a direct contribution to the political transformations sought by the Left.[17]

With the weakening of the Communist presence in the unions during the military regime, a revival of union activity in the early 1980s was accompanied by an increased weight of the sectors that questioned Communist party strategy, although there was a clear consensus with regard to the desirability of an accelerated return to civilian rule. When the Plenario Intersindical de Trabajadores (Interunion Plenum of Workers—PIT) was founded in 1983, it was dominated by the noncommunist Left, which placed particular emphasis on union autonomy and on promoting ongoing contacts with the rank and file. Nevertheless, expectations of a profound reorientation of the Uruguayan union movement proved ephemeral.

Once civilian rule was restored and the CNT leaders had returned from exile, the Communist party managed to reassert its predominance in the central union organization, although its new denomination, "PIT-CNT," reflected the increased weight of the noncommunist Left within it. Nevertheless, the notion of a simple return to the predictatorial situation is misleading. The Left continued to control the labor movement and the Communists reasserted their hegemony, but the movement itself has been considerably weakened. The changes in the industrial structure of the country have visibly undermined the industrial unions and, in general, the mobilization capacity of the movement. An observer has commented that soon after the return to civilian rule "it became clear that the two rival tactics which had divided the Uruguayan union movement were proving equally incapable of achieving the central objective of restoring wage levels."[18] Indeed, President Julio Sanguinetti could rightly claim that he had successfully confronted the continuous strikes during his administration without making concessions and without losing the support of public opinion. Recently Left union militants have recognized that the union movement has been enormously weakened, has lost its former mobilizing capacity, and faces serious difficulties in its search for solutions to new challenges such as the introduction of new technologies and the growth of the informal sector.[19]

In the Peruvian case, the return to civilian rule in 1980 had already suggested that the military was no longer the most appropriate instrument for an antiunion offensive. The recessive policies introduced by the Belaúnde administration quickly revealed the fragility of the class unionism that had appeared so formidable in the later stages of the military regime. According to Jorge Parodi, "contrary to certain political predictions that a deepening of the economic crisis would lead to a greater solidarity between workers and a radicalization of their struggles, what happened is that the crisis tended rather to demoralize the workers, diminish their class identity, and promote a desperate search for individual solutions."[20] Furthermore, the requirements of parliamentary politics drained Left militants from the union front, especially in the case of the more radical noncommunist Left.[21]

As the economic crisis in Peru deepened during the course of the decade and wage and salary levels plummeted, trade union tactics became increasingly defensive. Accepting as inevitable the consequences of the crisis, many union leaders became concerned with preserving jobs on the basis of negotiations with the employers. In general, there was a return to the defense of sectoral interests as major structural changes, especially the dramatic expansion of the informal sector, robbed union struggles of their key role in the general popular movement. The general strikes that were organized lacked the political impact of those of the previous decade and became largely symbolic expressions of protest against a situation that the unions were increasingly incapable of influencing.[22]

The CGTP continued to dominate the union scene, but its relative importance for Left strategy had clearly diminished. During the latter years of the administration of Alan García, as hyperinflation threatened a collapse of the economy, certain sectors of the Left placed their hopes once again in the guerrilla movement; others looked increasingly toward the new social movements in the shantytowns; and many—among others the CGTP leaders—expected to achieve important changes following the 1990 elections. Disillusionment with the disastrous results of the elections for the Left was expressed by Valentín Pacho, secretary-general of the CGTP: "The CGTP has also been affected by the [electoral] repudiation of the Izquierda Unida because we supported this front. The leadership has always determined the line, and the masses have always respected it. We thought that despite the division [of the Left] the masses would not abandon the Izquierda Unida, but we miscalculated. . . . Nevertheless the union movement continues to support the CGTP, [as] it considers it the only remaining instrument."[23]

Perhaps the most dramatic reversal for the Latin American Left in recent years has been the COB's loss of political clout in Bolivia. With the return to civilian rule in 1978, the COB reemerged apparently with its traditional influence intact. It played a central role in frustrating the Natusch coup in 1979 and during the administration of Hernán Siles exercised a virtual veto over government policies. Between November 1983 and March 1985 it attempted to force the adoption of its own emergency plan for confronting the economic crisis, declaring seven general strikes during the period. But when Víctor Paz Estenssoro introduced radical neoliberal policies in 1985, the COB proved unable to block them and entered into a prolonged crisis that has markedly reduced its weight in the nation's politics.[24]

Several of the measures weakened the COB. The introduction of Decree No. 21060 limited important workers' rights: labor stability was suppressed, those with more than forty years of service were pensioned off, the workday was prolonged, and real wages were substantially reduced. The dictatorship exercised by the boss in the factory was reestablished by police vigilance within the plant; dismissals increased, union leaders were relocated, and, in general, the unions were disarticulated. The two general strikes called in 1985 to resist the measures were a failure, and the COB was subsequently wary of calling fresh strikes, particularly in the productive sector.[25]

Fundamental to the weakening of the COB, however, were the structural changes that had preceded the 1985 crisis, above all the dramatic fall of tin prices in the international market. The dismantling of the state mining company and a reduction by two-thirds of the mining work force over a period of two years forced the miners' union into a defensive posture concerned mainly with survival. This weakening of the working-class sector that had traditionally formed the backbone of the COB was accompanied by the development of alternative foci for popular organization, terminating its virtual monopoly of popular representation. With the emergence of other opposition organizations—such as the peasants, the regional movements, and the civic committees—the COB not only became just one of various channels of popular protest but also appeared to be no longer the most effective. It has even been argued that the working-class movement has become isolated from the other popular forces and, as a result of its internal decomposition, has totally lost the initiative.[26]

Colombia, despite the relative buoyancy of its economy during the period under study, by no means escaped the general tendencies that affected the other Latin American countries. Since the mid-1970s, government policies designed to adapt the Colombian economy to the new characteristics of the external market have accelerated changes in the structure of employment (diminishing the opportunities for stable employment, bloating the informal sector, and aggravating income inequalities) and, in general, led to a serious erosion of the living standards of the wage-earning population, despite a brief recovery in 1978–1979. The decline in unionization rates accelerated markedly in the early 1980s, rates falling from 14.5 percent of the economically active population in 1980 to 9.1 percent in 1984. This trend provoked an evident crisis of representation for the unions, which were increasingly exposed to an employer offensive and unable to respond through the traditional mechanisms of collective bargaining.[27]

In the face of this crisis, the traditional reformist confederations began to suffer defections; the pressure for the unified national movement that the CSTC had promoted in vain in the 1960s and 1970s culminated in the formation of the Central Unitaria de Trabajadores in 1986. This new organization immediately attracted unions that together represented about 65 percent of the organized working-class movement, notably increasing overall Left influence in spite of the heterogeneity of the affiliated unions. The prospects of the restructured movement are not yet altogether clear, but in recent years the militancy of the CUT has been reflected in its strike participation (84.5 percent of the total number) and in the remarkable ascendancy of political strikes (43 percent of the total for teachers, 56 percent in manufacturing, and 77 percent in agriculture). There has also been an upsurge of joint actions with other national labor organizations, including the 1988 general strike.[28]

While the working class was suffering the impact of the economic crisis and the unions were being forced onto the defensive in the Southern Cone, in Peru, and in Bolivia, the Brazilian unions were apparently more successful in defending worker interests. During the economic recession in Brazil from 1980 to 1983 the union movement was restructured on the basis of the two previously mentioned national confederations. The CUT, although the smaller of the two, grew at the expense of the CGT in the course of the decade and was consolidated as the primary point of reference for the Left. At the same time, the CUT attracted the more militant sectors of the Brazilian working class and was clearly distinguished from the CGT by its readiness to resort to strike tactics. Furthermore, it assumed an ideological definition clearly distinct from that of the political forces identified with the CGT.

The political posture of the CUT was expressed in its 1988 program:

The CUT represents a class unionism, combative, democratic, and an expression of the rank and file. . . . It represents a rupture with a populism that manipulates the masses on the basis of demagogic promises of social measures in order to support government policy. It represents a break with a reformism that contained demands and advances within the limits permitted by the government and the bosses. It represents a rupture with *peleguismo* [corrupt leadership] that lived at the expense of the government and of the working class. . . .

The alliance involving the reformism of the PCB and the PCdoB, the historic *peleguismo* and *neopeleguismo*, is sustained on the basis of a common interest in the maintenance of the union tax, the antidemocratic, bureaucratic union structure, and state control over union organization as the final card to stem the growing advances of the CUT in its struggle for union liberty and autonomy. . . .

The CUT, from the outset, is class-oriented and committed to articulating the immediate aims and the historic objectives of the working class . . . and encompasses socialism in its general perspective, continually attempting to incorporate the workers in general, including those who are not yet unionized. . . .[29]

At least until 1987, union struggle had proved relatively successful in defending wage levels.[30] Nevertheless, the hyperinflation of recent years has had a negative effect on the unions. It has also dampened somewhat the optimism of CUT leaders. Indeed, in a recent internal debate it has been argued that the CUT is reproducing the practices of the CGT, the PCB, and even Getúlio Vargas's workers' movement: "We introduce some changes in that we still issue bulletins and organize more assemblies, but in general our practice has not changed much."[31] Another leader maintained, "We are adapting our practice to the institutional union apparatus. . . . When we were in the opposition, we were oriented by the necessity to get rid of the *pelego* and overthrow the dictatorship. . . . The dictatorship has ended and we have lost our sense of direction. . . . we have become paralyzed and in effect are holding back the class struggle."[32]

Conclusions

The dilemmas that confronted the Brazilian CUT at the end of the 1980s illustrate the general difficulties faced by the Latin American Left in the field of trade union activity. Its influence within the union movement had grown, in countries such as Brazil, Peru, and Colombia dramatically, during the course of the economic crisis. At the same time, the 1980s had witnessed an unprecedented level of militancy, if measured by the impressive number of general strikes in the region.[33] Nevertheless, the crisis has undermined the traditional basis of union recruiting in the private sector and, in most cases, led to a weakening of the industrial unionism that has traditionally been the heart of the labor movement. The growth of union recruitment has been limited largely to the nonproductive sectors—among public employees and workers in the service sector (especially bank employees). This has inevitably strengthened the role of the state in labor conflicts.

As anchoring union organization within the plant and promoting rank-and-file participation became increasingly difficult, there were growing pressures to defend workers' interests by negotiating with the state. In some cases this has meant seeking to improve the union's bargaining position on the basis of reforms that would facilitate the organization of industrywide unions. In others it has involved backing reforms of existing labor legislation or even a new labor law. More generally, there has been a shift toward some form of "social pact" that might minimize losses. However, any attempt to negotiate the defense of workers' interests with the state aggravates a classic Left dilemma: To the extent that the national union leadership becomes involved in political negotiations without real bargaining strength, it runs the risk of losing contact with its rank and file.

Finally, the weakening of the unions, the dramatic increase in the size of the informal economy, and the emergence of new social movements have raised doubts as to whether the unions can be expected to continue to play as important a role in popular mobilizations or in Left strategy as they have up until now. What is all too clear is that as a result of the profound changes of the past two decades the unions and the Left are confronted with new challenges for which there are no ready-made answers.

Notes

1. Emilio Máspero, *América Latina: Hora cero* (Buenos Aires: Editorial Nuevas Estructuras, 1962), 31.

2. Between the 1930s and the 1950s, the only important noncommunist Marxist influences in the Latin American unions were Trotskyism in Bolivia and the Socialist party in Chile.

3. Dick Parker, *El sindicalismo cristiano latinoamericano en busca de un perfíl propio, 1954–1971* (Caracas: UCV, 1988), 22–24.

4. Rubén Katzmann and José Luis Reyna, *Fuerza de trabajo y movimientos laborales en América Latina* (Mexico City: El Colegio de México, 1979), 2–3: Enso Faletto, cited in Katzmann and Reyna, *Fuerza de trabajo*, 270, 280.

5. The concept of "political bargaining" was coined by James Payne in relation to the style of APRA unionism between 1956 and 1962.

6. CEPAL, *Transformación productiva con equidad* (Santiago de Chile: CEPAL, May 1990), 21, my translation.

7. Norbert Lechner, "De la revolución a la democracia: El debate intelectual en América del Sur," *Opciones*, 6 (May–August 1985):57–72.

8. René Cortázar, "Movimiento sindical y democracia," in Ignacio Walker et al., *Democracia en Chile: Doce conferencias* (Santiago de Chile: CIEPLAN, 1986), 231–232.

9. Iván Bisberg, "Política laboral y acción sindical en México (1976–1982)," *Foro Internacional*, 25, 2 (October–December 1984):169–171; Arturo Alape, *Un día de septiembre: Testimonios del Paro Cívico, 1977* (Bogotá: Ediciones Armadillo, 1980); Oswaldo Albornoz Peralta, *Historia del movimiento obrero ecuatoriano* (Quito: Editorial Letra Nueva, 1983), 96–101; Dick Parker, "Las organizaciones no-gubernamentales en la crisis centroamericana: El caso de los sindicatos," *Relaciones Internacionales*, 27 (segundo trimestre), 65–80; Steve Ellner, *Venezuela's Movimiento al Socialismo: From Guerrilla Defeat to Innovative Politics* (Durham: Duke University Press, 1988), 158–165.

10. Carmen Rosa Balbi, *Identidad clasista en el sindicalismo: Su impacto en las fábricas* (Lima: DESCO, 1989), 131–132; Nigel Haworth, "Political Transition and the Peruvian Labor Movement," in Edward C. Epstein, ed., *Labor Autonomy and the State in Latin America* (Boston: Unwin Hyman, 1989), 199–200.

11. Balbi, *Identidad*, 87–94, 113–115.

12. Jorge Parodi, "La desmovilización del sindicalismo industrial en el segundo belaundismo," in Comisión de Movimientos Laborales, *Sindicalismo latinoamericano en los ochenta* (Santiago de Chile: CLASCO, 1986), 329.

13. María Herminia Tavares de Almeida, "Desarrollo capitalista y acción social," *Revista Mexicana de Sociología*, 140, 2 (April–June 1978):468.

14. Tavares de Almeida, "Desarrollo capitalista," 489–491.

15. Hercules Correa, *O ABC de 1980* (Rio de Janeiro: Civilização Brasileira, 1980), 29–30.

16. María Helena Moreira Alves, "Trade Unions in Brazil: A Search for Autonomy and Organization," in Epstein, *Labor Autonomy*, 49–62.

17. Martín Gargiulo, "El movimiento sindical uruguayo en los 80: ¿Concertación o confrontación?", in Comisión de Movimientos Laborales, *Sindicalismo latinoamericano*, 170–172. In general on Uruguay see Martín Gargiulo, "The Uruguayan Labor Movement in the Post-Authoritarian Period," in Epstein, *Labor Autonomy*, 219–246.

18. Luis Alberto Quevedo, "Los nuevos desafíos del movimiento sindical en Uruguay," paper presented to the colloquium "La crisis del movimiento sindical de América Latina y las repuestas/propuestas alternativas," San Antonio de los Altos, Venezuela, November 27–December 3, 1988, 32, my translation.

19. Quevedo, "Los nuevos desafíos," 29; Emilio Mancilla and Osvaldo Melesi, comps., *El movimiento sindical en el Uruguay postdictatorial* (Montevideo: IFIS-CAAS, 1990), vii.

20. Quevedo, "Los nuevos desafíos," 27; Balbi, *Identidad*, 48; Haworth, "Political Transition," 209–216; Parodi, "La desmovilización," 332, my translation.

21. Balbi, *Identidad*, 167.

22. Carmen Rosa Balbi, "La crisis del sindicalismo en el Perú," paper presented to the colloquium "Crisis del sindicalismo en la sub-región Andina," Bogotá, October 22–28, 1989, 11, 48–51.

23. *ALAI*, 28, Quito, June 1990, 7, my translation.

24. René Antonio Mayorga, "La crisis del sistema democrático y la Central Obrera Boliviana (COB)," in Comisión de Movimientos Laborales, *Sindicalismo latinoamericano*, 199.

25. Francisco Zapata, "Crisis del sindicalismo," *Estado y Sociedad*, 4, 2 (1988):105, 107; Jorge Lazarte, "El movimiento obrero: Crisis y opción de futuro de la COB," in FLACSO-ILDIS, *Crisis del sindicalismo en Bolivia* (La Paz: FLACSO-ILDIS, 1987), 262.

26. Lazarte, "El movimiento obrero," 265; "El caso de la Central Obrera Boliviana," paper presented to the colloquium "Crisis del sindicalismo en la sub-región Andina," Bogotá, October 22–28, 1989, 16.

27. Alejandro Bernal, "La consolidación del crecimiento dependiente, sus impactos en la estructura del empleo y sus efectos en el sindicalismo: El caso colombiano," paper presented

to the colloquium "Crisis del sindicalismo en la sub-región Andina," Bogotá, October 22–28, 1989, 2, 54.

28. See Fernando Lopéz Alves, "Explaining Confederation: Colombian Unions in the 1980s," *Latin American Research Review*, 25, 2 (1990):115–133; Rocío Londoño Botero, "Los problemas laborales y la situación del sindicalismo en Colombia," *Revista de Planeación y Desarrollo*, 1–2 (January–June 1989); "Trade Unions and Labor Policy in Colombia," in Epstein, *Labor Autonomy*, 101–132.

29. CUT, "Pela CUT classista, de massas, democrática, de luta e pela base," *Notisur*, 13, 34 (December 1988):64–69, my translation.

30. Paul Singer, "La clase obrera frente a la crisis inflacionaria y la democratización en el Brasil," *Economía de América Latina*, 18–19 (1989):30–33.

31. Milton Rosa [president of the shoe workers' union in Novo Hamburgo and of the CUT in Vale do Sinos], *DisCUT*, 1, 1 (November 1989–January 1990):18, my translation.

32. Miguel Rossetto [president of Sindipole and secretary for union policy, CUT–Rio Grande do Sur], *DisCUT*, 1, 1 (November 1989–January 1990):16, 19, my translation.

33. For an overview of the general strikes in Latin America during the past decade, see *Latin American Labor News*, 2/3, (1990).

13

Something Old, Something New: Brazil's Partido dos Trabalhadores

María Helena Moreira Alves

To understand the debates about strategy, power, and government that have characterized Brazilian politics for the past two decades, it is necessary to examine the historical experiences that form the collective political consciousness of the Brazilian people. The events of two periods in particular have left an indelible mark on current politics: the populist period between 1946 and 1964, when labor politics was influenced by Getúlio Vargas's model of corporatism, and the period of the institutionalization of a national security state after the military coup of 1964.

The Legacy of Vargas

Getúlio Vargas first came to power through a military coup followed by indirect elections in 1934. A charismatic and able leader, Vargas was a nationalist who was determined to carry out rapid economic development based on state ownership of basic industry, in particular steel production and raw materials such as petroleum. An admirer of Mussolini, he used his power to institutionalize mechanisms of corporative participation to bring order into class relations. His Estado Novo was to leave a lasting mark on labor: a labor code copied from Mussolini's and trade unions tied directly to the state through the Ministry of Labor and special labor courts. The corporative nature of the Brazilian state and of state-civil society relationships was well established by the time the Estado Novo was overthrown by new democratic forces in 1945.

María Helena Moreira Alves is a founding member of the Partido Trabalhista.

225

The second important legacy of Getúlio Vargas was the Partido Trabalhista Brasileiro. The PTB was the symbol of populism: a political party controlled by leaders who exercised charismatic influence on the popular classes, organized vertically from the top down, and characterized by an effective strategy of mass mobilization. It won many benefits for workers—a legal work contract, an eight-hour day, paid vacations, pension funds, maternity leave, protection for women workers and child laborers—and because of this could count on the support of workers organized in the trade unions it largely controlled. Besides Vargas himself, whom workers referred to as the "father of the poor," the PTB was the party of two other historical leaders: João Goulart (who was deposed as president by the military coup of 1964) and Leonel Brizola (governor of Rio Grande do Sul in 1962–1964 and twice governor of Rio de Janeiro in the 1980s). In short, the period of bourgeois democracy that followed the end of the Estado Novo (1945–1964) was characterized by populist politics in which working-class organizations were used to provide political support for charismatic political leaders who championed nationalist economics and socioeconomic reforms as opposed to socialism.

The Legacy of the Partido Comunista Brasileiro

The Brazilian Communist party, one of the first founded in South America (1919), had the historical distinction of having organized an armed uprising in 1935. Prior to that, the PCB's secretary-general Luis Carlos Prestes had led a column of soldiers, workers, and peasants in a march from the south to the northeast of Brazil (close to three thousand miles), spreading revolt and gathering support along the way. These two events strongly grounded the PCB's reputation as a working-class vanguard party and established the legendary image of Prestes as the Cavaleiro da Esperança (Horseman of Hope). The PCB was for many years the main river into which various Left groups flowed. It competed with Vargas's PTB for working-class support, although in reality it often tended to establish electoral alliances with that party during pivotal elections. The PCB enjoyed only a brief period of legality after the overthrow of Vargas's Estado Novo and suffered considerable persecution throughout the populist period. The military in Brazil always considered the PCB dangerously marked by its early armed rebellion—a subversive force to be controlled or if possible eliminated.

Because of this history of clandestine action the PCB developed a highly centralized form of organization with strict internal discipline. Its decision making was similarly characterized by a rigid top-down structure of democratic centralism, with decisions being made only by a handful of members of the central committee. This verticalism has been a long-standing influence in the Brazilian Left. Most groups that broke from the PCB maintained its organizational design.

In 1964 a civil-military coalition took power in Brazil with the explicit agenda of deepening a dependent-capitalist model of economic development and institutionalizing state structures for central planning and governmental control of the population. The new power holders began the most widespread wave of repression against trade unions, community organizations, and political parties ever to be carried out in the country. Because members of left-leaning or progressive political parties were considered potential enemies, the clean-up operations targeted them most specifically.

Hurt by the violence of the repression, political parties began to discuss the alternatives available to them at that historical juncture. The debate over nonviolent versus armed-struggle strategies for bringing down the military government took place within Catholic social-action student organizations such as the Ação Popular (Popular Action—AP), and in the working-class Pastoral Operária (Workers' Pastoral). In 1968 AP opted for armed struggle and was joined by many Catholic militants citing the doctrine of the just war against torture and repression. The PCB supported nonviolence, and its central committee ordered members to join the bourgeois nonviolent opposition. In 1968 Carlos Marighela, one of the most important members of the PCB's central committee, openly broke with the policy and founded the Aliança de Libertação Nacional (National Liberation Alliance—ALN). Led by Marighela, the ALN developed the strategy of urban guerrilla warfare and rapidly became the most important organization of armed resistance. The PCB suffered several further divisions, and all of the emerging groups espoused armed struggle as the only possible route to the overthrow of the military dictatorship. Because of the Chinese-Soviet split, some of these splinter organizations became tied to the Soviet Union and others to China.[1]

The Negotiated Transition

By 1974 the Brazilian "economic miracle" was over. The results of the economic model were more and more evident: growing inequality in income and wealth, with large sectors of the population marginalized from the economy altogether. In addition, the military's borrowing policy had led to a rapidly increasing debt burden that suffocated the potential for investment. The bourgeois opposition grew stronger, and a class alliance was formed between the working class and the bourgeoisie for the purpose of delegitimating the military government and forcing a political opening.[2] This class alliance was based on two strategic points: First, the opposition would organize a widespread nonviolent mass movement focusing on violations of human rights, poverty and inequality, lack of electoral freedoms, and censorship of the press and calling for political amnesty. Second, the route to power would be electoral, working within the limited political system set up by the military and accumulating strength in time through electoral victories. There was only one legal political party, the Movimento Democrático Brasileiro (Brazilian Democratic Movement—MDB), and all efforts would be channeled through it.[3]

This consensual nonviolent position caused a resurgence of the armed struggle debate within the Left. Many militants argued that the armed-struggle organizations had made a major mistake in isolating themselves from the social movements, particularly the working-class ones—that their lack of rank-and-file worker support distanced their activities from the realities of the working class. Some militants also began to question the vertical and military organization of the armed-struggle groups. Finally, their defeat in the war against the national security state weighed heavily in the consideration of alternatives. Most of the organizations that had engaged in the armed struggle (such as the ALN) dissolved themselves during the liberalization period. Others, such as the pro-Chinese Partido Comunista do Brasil, maintained their organizational framework intact and joined the legally recognized opposition MDB, within which they worked as separate groups and even elected some of their members to local or congressional office.

The PCB continued to argue for the strengthening of the alliance with the bourgeoisie: not only should workers support nonviolence and an electoral route to change but they should refrain from organizing strikes that might undermine their class alliance with the national sector of the Brazilian bourgeoisie. The PCB believed that the Brazilian mode of production referred to as the "economic miracle" had developed a tripartite character, consisting of state-controlled companies largely concerned with building the necessary infrastructure for modern industry (roads, dams, electricity, telecommunications, ports, etc.), mining, and petroleum production; international capital concentrated in the more profitable durable goods sector, the most dynamic part of the economy; and national capital, dominating consumer goods production and a variety of smaller linkage industries that produced for multinational corporations. Hence, for example, the automobile industry's large assembly plants were dominated entirely by foreign capital, whereas automobile parts manufacturing was by law nationally owned. Because of this tripartite nature of dependent development, the PCB argued, there was at least a latent contradiction between national and international capital. Many important members of the Brazilian bourgeoisie felt displaced from political and economic decisions in the military government and were joining the opposition. Politically and strategically, therefore, it was important for workers to ally themselves with these national sectors in order to defeat their common enemy, the military and its international allies. For the PCB it followed that the correct practice was to avoid major strikes that affected national capital and support the bourgeoisie's effort to dialogue and negotiate a gradual opening in the transition to democracy.

Others argued for the resurgence of a social democratic and populist line. European-style social democracy had been espoused by many leaders of the opposition in exile. They argued that the class alliance being established naturally opened up the possibility of interclass negotiation of salary benefits, welfare policies of education and health, and other important social democratic gains for the working class. For them experience of European bourgeois democracy, including parliamentarism, seemed a viable alternative route for the Left in Brazil. Leonel Brizola, from exile in Portugal, began to organize a new PTB, reborn from the ashes of the out-lawed traditional populist labor party created by Vargas. This new PTB would be populist, capable of mobilizing masses of workers by recalling the memory of the "father of the poor." It would also build into its program many concepts taken from European social democracy. Thus, in the conception of the resurgent populists, the new party would benefit electorally from the PTB's tradition while including modernizing social democratic and even socialist ideas. Brizola established a solid connection with European social democratic parties and with the Democratic party of the United States, and the new PTB immediately became a recognized member of the Socialist International. When Brizola returned from exile after the amnesty of August 1979, however, he found his party divided: Getúlio Vargas's niece, Ivete Vargas, had also decided to build upon the legacy but in a more corporatist vein. Calling the social democratic ideology into question, she gathered supporters, and eventually split the party in two, between corporatists and social democrats. In addition, she petitioned in the Supreme Electoral Court for the right to use the traditional name of the party, Partido Trabalhista Brasileiro. It was assumed that the name itself would recall the image of the "father of the poor" and naive workers would vote for the *name* of the party rather than for a particular program. Because Ivete Vargas's proposal fitted much better with the plans of the military government for the transition, she easily won the suit.

In 1980, therefore, Brizola renamed his party the Partido Democrático Trabalhista and continued to organize support for a populist–social democratic alternative. The charismatic Brizola succeeded in gaining impressive working-class support in the two states that had been most historically bound to populism and Getúlio Vargas: Rio de Janeiro and Rio Grande do Sul. In other states populism was questioned and the image of Vargas himself had been erased by time. The PDT, in keeping with the historical framework of populism, was organized vertically, with the objective of *mobilizing* working-class movements rather than *organizing* workers autonomously. The PDT was also marked by the personality of its main leader. It was clearly Brizola's political party, dependent upon charismatic leadership to gain support and to govern. Brizola gave his image, his name, and his political expertise to the party and exerted unquestioned influence over its members, some of whom followed his directives with almost fanatical devotion.

The Emergence of the Partido dos Trabalhadores

In 1979, a large congress of trade unions was held in Rio de Janeiro to discuss strategies for building an autonomous workers' movement capable of breaking the tight regulations imposed by the military governments since 1964. The congress of the Confederação Nacional dos Trabalhadores na Indústria (National Confederation of Industrial Workers—CNTI) met in the wake of the huge strikes that had begun with the automobile workers of São Bernardo do Campo, in the state of São Paulo, and spread throughout the entire country in 1978 and 1979.[4] Tensions rose as workers were divided into three distinct groups: those who supported the military, those who led the nascent antigovernment "new trade union movement," and those who opposed the military but argued for a soft line on strikes because of the need to build interclass alliances with elite groups. At a certain point, expressing a multitude of frustrations, Luís Inácio (Lula) da Silva, the charismatic leader of the metalworkers of São Bernardo do Campo, shouted, "What we really need in this country is a Party of the Workers!"

Trade unionists who were connected to the Communist party (PCB) had been the major proponents of the interclass alliance with the national bourgeoisie aimed at defeating the military government. They believed that the traditional PCB was the one and only true "workers' party" and rejected Lula's plea. At the same time, Brizola, having just returned from exile, was concerned with reorganizing the populist–social-democratic alternative. Along with the Communists, he sought to persuade Lula and the "new trade unionists" to join in his effort to adapt social democracy to Brazil.

However, the plea for "a Party of the Workers" was deeply rooted in the desire of workers to move to the center of politics as primary actors rather than simply backstage organizers. Many workers were newly empowered by their decisive participation in social movements—in the new trade union movement, the grass-roots neighborhood associations, and the peasant movements. They were frustrated by the traditional Left parties' rigid disciplinary regulations, which left little room for internal debate. They increasingly insisted on participation in the development of political platforms and were blocked by established party bureaucrats. Having learned through their involvement in the grass-roots social movements to coordinate political action collectively, to make decisions collectively, to organize in a decentralized way, and to rotate leadership, workers now regarded the limitations of the traditional Left parties as political straitjackets that curbed their potential participation. The new "Party of the Workers" had to channel politically all of the experience gained in the years of organization of the grass-roots social resistance to the military governments. It would have to be a mass organization—flexible, dynamic, shifting, dialectically related to the grass-roots movements, and capable of changing with historical contexts without losing its crucial connection to those movements. It would also have to be deeply embedded in the workers' movements and to link levels of organization so as to remain strongly rooted in and never lose touch with the rank and file. At the same time it would have to maintain a *separateness* from the social movements so that their autonomy could be maintained and preserved.

Many working-class leaders felt that one of the lessons learned from the populist period was that grass-roots movements die when they become simply a base of support for politicians, easily manipulated through the co-optation of their leadership. Ultimately, as Lula told Brizola, "it was time for the people to learn where and how to swim by themselves." This is what the Partido dos Trabalhadores was meant to be from its founding.[5]

The PT has grown to be one of the most important parties in Brazil, having won mayoral races in São Paulo, Porto Alegre, and other key cities. That Lula, as the PT's candidate in the elections of December of 1989, came close to winning the presidency and received more than thirty-one million votes is an indication of how deeply its proposals have affected Brazilian society. Worker organizations and leaders have been catapulted to the front lines of politics and have achieved a hegemonic position within the Left. That this is a historic event is no longer denied even by the PT's most persistent opponents. Likewise, that the PT represents something new in Latin American politics is evident in the growing interest it now elicits.

The Novelty of the PT

The novelty of the PT lies in the nature of its relationship to social movements at the grass roots. Born of these movements, the PT interfaces with all kinds of organizations: in the urban areas it organizes in the trade unions, the neighborhood associations,[6] and the *favela* (shantytown) associations.[7] It is present in the struggles of the homeless for housing and of street children for recognition of their rights and in the mobilization for better health and education. In the countryside, it is the moving force of the rural unions of agricultural and migrant workers and those of the marginalized daily laborers (known as *bóias frias*) of the coffee and sugar plantations. The PT has also backed the struggle of landless peasants for land and of the rubber tappers of the Amazon to preserve the forest. Although it is not the only party of the Left to support the struggles of working people in Brazil for better living conditions, it has become the largest one in the social movements. In addition, it is active in the organization of women, in the black consciousness movement, and in the native people's organizations. What is of particular interest, however, is the manner in which it relates to these movements.

The PT does not have traditional "departments" or "party committees" for women, blacks, rural workers, rubber tappers, trade unionists, etc. Activists and militants are members of the different social movements and organizations *as well as* of the PT. Their militancy is different from that of the parties of the traditional Left. The PT does not decide the "party line" that will be imposed upon a particular trade union, for example, or in the women's movement. The militants are also not "party delegates" within social movements. They have a double militancy and are encouraged to keep the two separate as much as possible. Although members' connections to grass-roots bases are important for their standing in the party (in fact, active membership in a grass-roots movement is a requirement for PT membership), there are no formal mechanisms for molding militancy in the social movement to the positions of the party. The influence is *from the grass roots to the PT* and not the other way around. For example, militants of the black consciousness movement have been extremely important in shaping the PT's platform, in electing black people to public office, and in developing and coordinating concrete programs of government. Similarly, women permeate the PT, shape the platform on women's issues, exert considerable influence on the party, and are elected to a variety of public offices throughout the country. In the brief period of its existence, the PT has elected women as mayors of three major cities (Fortaleza, Santos, and São Paulo), a black woman from a favela organization as Brazil's first elected black congresswoman, and a number of other members of the black consciousness movement to state and municipal chambers. They represent their *social movements* within the PT but have no disciplinary mechanisms built into their militancy in the grass roots. In congresses and meetings PT members do not have to vote according to predetermined party directives in a formal manner, although naturally they tend to reflect the PT's platforms in their struggles at the grass-roots level.

Examples of this special relationship between the PT and the social movements abound. In 1986 the PT elected Congresswoman Benedita da Silva, of the Associação dos Moradores da Rocinha (Rocinha Residents' Association), as a state representative from Rio de Janeiro. Lula was also elected as representative from São Paulo, with more than eight hundred thousand votes, the most ever cast for a congressman in Brazil. The influence of social movements on the party was demonstrated by the laws and amendments proposed by the PT representatives. The law against racial discrimination introduced by Benedita da Silva was drafted in discussions with the black consciousness movement. The different constitutional articles relating to women's rights and the rights of women workers were drafted, in a similar manner, by groups active in the women's movement. Through the work of PT's representatives the nascent movement of the People of the Forest found an echo in Congress. The PT's defense of agrarian reform and the changes in the labor code were also the result of active participation of trade unionists, both urban and rural.

The autonomy of the social movements is considered too important to be threatened by the direct regulation of them by political parties. In the past, the experience of the grass-roots movements in Brazil with political parties had been largely negative. When parties worked in an organized manner within social movements they tended to become divided and debilitated. Party members would meet before regular meetings of the social movement to decide upon key issues. This practice was conducive to bitter political and even ideological divisions and to rigid positions that were often nonnegotiable within the movement because decision making came from outside. In addition, decisions were sometimes profoundly disconnected from the rank and file and the real needs of the organization. This blocked growth and effectiveness and, in the worst of cases, crushed the organization entirely. The imposition of party lines has divided and dissolved many important movements, particularly during the period of armed struggle, when the competing viewpoints were at times irreconcilable. As a corrective, the PT consciously encourages the autonomy of social movements vis-à-vis political parties. It does not want to become isolated from social movements, but it attempts to avoid co-opting leaders by tying them directly to party directives.

The preservation of the autonomy of social movements is intended to avoid an old problem: the co-optation of rank-and-file leadership to political posts to subordinate their organizations to the government. One of the criticisms put forward by members of the PT about the populist period was that co-optation and clientelism frequently characterized relations between reformist governments and the social movements. Co-optation increases the potential for clientelism and encourages dependent relationships that incorporate workers' organizations into a corporatist state. Since the PT was born out of a social movement deeply influenced by resistance to corporatism and clientelism, there is widespread concern within the party over the possibility of co-optation. In fact, the PT has often erred in the opposite direction. In virtually all of the experiences of government with a mayor elected by the PT, the social movements quickly became active critics, not even hesitating, as in Porto Alegre in 1989, to call a strike against the municipal authorities.[8]

Avoidance of the co-optation of leaders is difficult and complex. The PT has not always been successful in preventing a renewal of traditional forms of clientelism. Its first experiences in public administration in city governments were characterized by internal battles particularly over clientelist practices. In Diadema, where the PT was first elected to government in 1982, the problem was particularly acute. A plan to hire many leaders of the neighborhood and favela associations as civil servants[9] made the mayor and his staff the target of severe party criticism for clientelism that eventually led to their collective resignation. The chief concern was that, insofar as leaders became civil servants, especially when personally appointed by a politician in power, the line between autonomy and co-optation was inevitably blurred.

The Partido dos Trabalhadores is committed to preserving the role played by the organizations of civil society in keeping the government on its toes. One of its most cherished concepts is that power often turns the oppressed into the oppressor. Those who vote people into office should not simply relinquish power to them but remain watchful, suspicious, and critical. It is most important that a revolutionary government not co-opt its organizations and thereby deprive them of their primordial watchdog function.

The question that is difficult to resolve, however, is how to create mechanisms for preventing patron-client relationships, nepotism, and other improper forms of public conduct from developing. Because so many militants are critical and wary of "democratic centralism," concerned about guaranteeing internal debate, and anxious to avoid the dangers of "purge committees," mechanisms to sanction party members are always regarded with great suspicion. This has resulted in a high degree of inefficiency in all of the PT's "ethics committees." There have only been a few cases in which representatives have been expelled for unethical behavior or to enforce party discipline, and each such case has been a traumatic experience for the party. In fact, enforcing party discipline and keeping representatives faithful to the PT's program remains one of its most serious unresolved problems.

The PT's Internal Structure

The decision of the party founders to build a democratic and socialist mass party different from other experiences of the Left in Brazil had certain implications. First of all, it meant the abandonment of revolutionary theories of foquismo and strategies of armed struggle. The PT was not to be another clandestine party, with a secret and military organizational structure. It was also not to be a vanguard party based on the principle that a few people could ignite the revolution. Secondly, the PT was designed to be a legal party, organized on a mass scale and capable of competing with bourgeois parties for electoral office. Consequently, it had to comply with the electoral laws enacted by military governments. The difficulty lay in building a party that was both within the system and in opposition to it.

The Political Party Law of 1979 established a series of strict limitations on party organization. For example, it required that all members of a political party register with the Supreme Electoral Court. It also required a party to have a "top-down" structure in which the national executive committee (in which politicians already holding office were automatically included) named the members of all other party committees at regional and local levels. Similarly, candidates had to be chosen from lists named by the executive committees, and incumbents could run irrespective of party approval. Finally, local, regional, and national meetings and conventions had to be registered in writing and held in the presence of an officer of the Supreme Electoral Court. Records of meetings were to be permanently filed with the court. The entire body of legislation was designed to impede free political party organization and facilitate state control.

To exist as a political party and at the same time build a mass-based democratic party, the PT has developed two interrelated forms of organization. The first strictly complies with the law. The second, a parallel structure, allows the party to institutionalize mechanisms of rank-and-file participation and to establish its characteristic "bottom up" style. All aspects of the law are carefully fulfilled. Those who can withstand the political and job pressure sign the required membership forms issued by the court. Others, an equally active membership, sign mainly internal party records and participate in all committees, conventions, and meetings with equal rights. These are the *militantes,* some of whom are chosen as delegates for the preconventions. A third, more numerous group is connected to the party in more informal ways, providing financial support, working in electoral campaigns, distributing educational materials, etc., without participating in meetings, conventions, or committees. These are known in the PT as "sympathizers." By the 1989 elections the PT had approximately four hundred thousand officially registered members, slightly more than one million militantes, and more than four million sympathizers.

The PT regularly holds local, regional, and national conventions that comply strictly with the law and are overseen by the court. Members of executive committees and boards are named, and candidates for political office are chosen. In reality, however, these official conventions simply sanction decisions previously made at preconventions held at local, regional, and national levels. They are the culmination of a democratic internal party decision-making process that is alive with membership participation. The preconventions are part of the other, parallel structure of the PT.

The PT is made up of units known as the *núcleos* (nuclei) established either in neighborhoods or in the workplace. People organize wherever they work, much in the same manner as the factory committees described by Gramsci in his *Ordine Nuovo* articles. They also organize núcleos in their neighborhoods, streets, and then electoral districts. As a militante of the PT, for example, I belong both to the núcleo of the University of the State of Rio de Janeiro, where I teach, and to the núcleo of Laranjeiras, where I live. In turn, the neighborhood núcleo of Laranjeiras is part of the sixteenth Electoral Zone, which includes other nuclei as well. A prerequisite for joining the PT is membership in at least one núcleo, although it is unnecessary to belong to both a workplace and a neighborhood organization. The requirement is meant to ensure that only those who are in fact involved in social movements become members of the PT. Those who apply must have the support of their workmates or most immediate neighbors.

The voting system of the PT also establishes its difference from traditional political parties in Brazil. Internal democracy is exercised through a complex system of proportional voting in all the preconventions. The membership of the PT includes members of the progressive Catholic church, progressive Protestants, members of Marxist-Leninist groups, including those that had engaged in the armed struggle, independent socialists, and Trotskyists. In order that their ideas may be properly debated and their positions reflected in the party, the PT has institutionalized a mechanism whereby each group may form an organized sector in the party (known as a *tendência*) and advance proposals and field candidates for party posts and electoral office. The proposals that receive majority backing at the preconventions are approved.[10] For party posts a tendência may organize a slate and will receive seats in proportion to its voting strength. For example, if a Trotskyist tendência gets 10 percent of the votes in a municipal preconvention, it will have the right to name 10 percent of the members of the municipal executive committee. The same holds true in choosing candidates for political office.

The proportional system of voting encourages internal party debate and maximizes representation of the rank-and-file membership at all levels of the organization. It also allows for a much greater degree of control by the rank and file over the choosing of candidates for political office. On many occasions the rank-and-file vote in the preconvention goes against the desires of the top PT leadership. Two recent examples illustrate this point. The Executiva Estadual of São Paulo as a whole supported the candidacy of Congressman Plinio de Arruda Sampaio for mayor. However, when the preconvention was held in 1988, the rank-and-file groups supported the candidacy of Luiza Erundina, who was deeply involved in the homeless movement and the struggle for housing in the city, and she became the candidate and was elected mayor. Another example of decision making from below occurred at the national preconvention with the selection of the vice-presidential candidate on Lula's slate for the presidential election of 1989. Lula himself campaigned within the PT for the president of the Green party with a view to forging an alliance. The rank and file, however, eventually chose Senator João Paulo Bisol, of Rio Grande do Sul, as the candidate in recognition of his work in favor of workers' rights in the Constituent Assembly.

There is an enormous amount of rivalry among tendências, and the unwary visitor to a PT convention may be surprised by the off-the-record negotiation between groups, shouting debates in the plenary sessions, and even organized cheering at the time of voting. Once it is all over, however, rivalries are set aside, and militantes cheer and wave the PT's flags. At campaign time all work together "taking to the streets" (in the PT's terminology). This element of campaign militancy is what makes political analysts say that the PT is a "party of arrival"—meaning that the PT has won surprising victories at the last minute through the zeal of the millions of militantes who flood the streets everywhere to talk individually with voters.

The PT's Program

The PT defends national sovereignty with a program of control of multinational investment according to guidelines aimed at limiting profit remittance and over- and underpricing, eliminating tax subsidies, regulating working conditions, maintaining standards with regard to health and occupational safety, monitoring salary levels, and guaranteeing job security. Because the PT sees Brazil as immersed in the international capitalist economy, it attaches much importance to problems stemming from the investment patterns of multinational corporations, taking into account their different standards of salary and benefits for workers in rich nations versus Third World ones. The program therefore seeks to ensure that similar benefits be provided to workers in the Brazilian affiliates of multinationals. Workers' control in the form of factory committees with representation in the negotiation of workplace conditions and eventual provisions for joint management and profit sharing is also proposed. Because the Brazilian economy is approximately 40 percent state-owned, the PT has developed a detailed program for the rehabilitation and democratization of the state companies. The program is based on an analysis of the state sector's economic difficulties that suggests that privatization is no solution. Instead it calls for joint management and workers' control of public companies.

The defense of national sovereignty also involves the postponement of interest payments on the foreign debt. The PT advocates the immediate suspension of payments coupled with an auditing of the debt itself to determine its makeup. It would deduct that part of the debt that has already been paid as a consequence of unilateral floating interest rates that rose from 6 percent in 1974 to 14 percent by 1984 and then renegotiate the rest in terms adapted to the needs of the Brazilian people.

In the long run, the PT strives to build socialism from the day-to-day struggles of working people in Brazil. Democratic socialism, in its view, is necessarily historically rooted, dialectically related to the ongoing requirements of social movements. The incorporation of workers into the decision-making apparatus of the state—at all levels—must be coupled with the institutionalization of mechanisms of worker participation in the workplace. Democratic socialism involves the democratizing of economic and political life not simply in the distribution of production but also in the redistribution of political, social, and economic power. Within the conception of planting the seeds of socialism in the day-to-day struggles of the workers, the PT organizes factory committees, workers' councils in the workplace, neighborhood committees, health, education, and transportation councils, and other citizen committees to develop collective programs and find solutions to problems.

In the political sphere the PT has been the backbone of the Movement for Popular Amendments, which organizes group discussions to present formal amendments to the Constituent Assembly. Some of these popular amendments, such as the agrarian reform, have been supported by more than six million voters' signatures. As have other social and economic reforms put forward by the Partido dos Trabalhadores, the party's agrarian program has been drafted with the participation of representatives from social movements in the countryside and the Amazon region, and therefore it reflects the priorities of those most directly concerned with the issues. For example, the PT defends different solutions for agrarian reforms that take into account the diversity of the regions of Brazil. A rural estate of more than five hundred hectares that is left largely idle in the south and southeast would be considered unproductive for purposes of redistribution, but rural property of up to fifteen hundred hectares left idle in the Amazon region would not be considered unproductive because the People of the Forest Movement, the rubber tapper unions, and other peasant movements have argued that idleness should be encouraged in forest areas. Productivity of land would similarly vary, with very specific regulations for the preservation of the Amazon forests of the central and northern parts of Brazil. All of the detailed economic and social proposals of the PT were drafted in a similar manner and reflect the day-to-day participation of those directly concerned with the issues being addressed.

The Presidential Elections of 1989: Building Alliances

The Left and popular movements in Brazil have traditionally been limited in presidential elections to opting for the lesser of two evils, none of the candidates having ever defended far-reaching socioeconomic change. All of this came to an end with the military coup of 1964, in which the class alliance that supported the national security state became apparent. Then in 1989, for the first time in Brazilian history, the country's eighty-three million voters had before them real choices. Political parties that embraced widely different ideologies presented distinctly class-based programs, from the extreme Right, both rural (Ronaldo Caiado) and urban (Paulo Maluf), to the Left (Lula), the new Right (Fernando Collor de Mello), the social democrats (Mário Covas), and the populists (Leonel Brizola). The differentiation of candidates and political programs was evidenced in the debates as well as in the free political-party spots aired on television and the radio. For the entire three months preceding the first round of the presidential elections of November 15, citizens watched the parties present their proposals on television and avidly discussed the different approaches. The results of the first round showed a nation divided: Collor received the most votes; right-leaning voters had rejected the more extreme positions of Caiado and Maluf. On the opposite side, the votes were divided between the prosocialist PT (Lula), the populist PDT (Brizola), and the social democrats (Covas).

The runoff elections were to be held on December 17. This was the first time that citizens freely considered the question of class relations in politics—not simply through the debates but in terms of the possibility of choosing for president a leader who came from the working class and presented a clear program for socioeconomic transformation. For the first time, the Left was capable of taking over state power on its own rather than being reduced to choosing among candidates of the bourgeoisie. The forging of an interparty alliance to support Lula for president became the most important point on the political agenda of all leftist and progressive parties. The Frente Brasil Popular (Brazilian Popular Front—FBP), which had supported Lula/Bisol in the first round, was committed to the concept of an interparty alliance that refrained from assigning hegemony to any party.[11] This was the first successful experience of the tactical unity of the Left and was based upon an explicit programmatic recognition of

the different positions of each party. For the second round it was necessary to broaden the Frente's appeal to include the populists, the social
democrats, the PCB, the Center (represented by the MDB), and
the Greens. The decision to join the alliance was made by the rank-and-
file memberships of the various parties in conventions organized immediately after the first round. The experience of discussing political programs
and electoral unity in a public convention held in the midst of the most
important presidential campaign in Brazilian history forged a practical
unity of effort. Having temporarily laid aside the Left's characteristic
intense rivalry, militants covered the streets of the nation with the
campaign slogan that emphasized the alliance: "Now it is Lula."

Discussions among the various parties were aimed at synthesizing
diverse proposals. The PDT, represented largely by Brizola, argued that
the program should include its concept of public education, based on the
Centro Integral de Educação Psico-Social, which had been a trademark of
Brizola's government in Rio de Janeiro. The Partido Social Demócrata
Brasileiro of Mário Covas insisted that the program be more moderate in
terms of the foreign debt and the agrarian reform so as to conform to the
social democratic ideas it had advanced in the first round of the elections.
Thus the program of the alliance to support Lula for the second round
was substantially toned down and modified to incorporate social democratic and populist ideas.

The PCB, which had become legal in 1979, had fielded its own candidate for the first round, Congressman Roberto Freire of Pernambuco. In
the conversations about the alliance to support Lula in the second round
the PCB made no particular programmatic demands. The very small percentage of votes received by the traditional Communist party had led
members to consider joining the efforts of the PT and even to move
toward dissolution in the postelection period.

The nonhegemonic character of the Frente was embodied in the in-
structions it passed on to its affiliates: militants should always campaign
in the shirts of their own parties; they should carry the flags of their
parties in all demonstrations and in door-to-door canvassing; the political
programs of the Frente on television and radio would be produced by
representatives of all the parties in the campaign; leaflets and other materials would carry the names, colors, and symbols of all the parties; artists,
actors, and other well-known public persons of each party would always
appear in their own party clothing and carrying their party's flags; and
the differences between the parties that composed the Frente would be
accepted by all campaign workers at all times.

These directives were strictly and willingly followed by the militants.
Clearly, people felt free to demonstrate their support for Lula in the

second round because their own political beliefs had been preserved by the nonhegemonic character of the Frente. The campaign came to be characterized by a multitude of colors, symbols, and flags. The last rally, in Rio de Janeiro, drew close to one million people waving their parties' flags and applauding the speeches of their main leaders. When Lula appeared flanked by Brizola, Mário Covas, and Miguel Arraes—symbols of the PDT, the PSDB, and the PMDB—the crowd exploded with joy. Clearly, the policy of building alliances based upon the recognition of differences struck a responsive chord among voters. The second round of the elections ended with Collor, leading an alliance of Right and Center-Right parties, receiving 35,089,998 votes (53.03 percent), and Lula 31,076,364 (46.97 percent).

In the gubernatorial elections of November 1990, the policy of building alliances based on programmatic points was applied in each state. Much as in the year before, not all parties joined the alliance for the first round, some preferring to field their own candidates. For the second round, however, progressive parties formed coalitions to support the candidate with the most votes among them. Thus a broad-based alliance of Left and Center-Left parties was built to endorse candidates of the different parties in each state where a progressive ran against a right-wing candidate— among others São Paulo, Rio de Janeiro, Rio Grande do Sul, Minas Gerais, Bahia, Amazonas, and Acre. Affiliation with the Frente meant not a loss of the party's distinctiveness but rather a reinforcement of the most important common points for campaign purposes. Leftists are thus beginning to learn to build upon common programs in order to acquire sufficient strength to counter the Right's economic and political control. This policy of alliance formation is feasible not only during periods of national elections but also in Congress, particularly in order to prepare for the next presidential race in 1994.

Notes

1. Of these organizations, perhaps the most important was the Vanguardia Popular Revolucionária (Popular Revolutionary Vanguard—VPR), which was led by Captain Carlos Lamarca and carried out the most effective rural guerrilla operation in the Amazon area of the Araguaia River.

2. See my "Interclass Alliances in the Brazilian Opposition," in Susan Eckstein, ed., *Power and Popular Protest: Latin American Social Movements* (Berkeley: University of California Press, 1989).

3. In 1965 the military government abolished all political parties and created two new ones, the Aliança de Renovação Nacional (Alliance of National Renewal—ARENA), which represented the military government, and the MDB, which became the officially recognized opposition party. The MDB became an "umbrella" organization for a variety of opposition parties which had been driven underground. Only in 1979, with a newly promulgated party law, did other political parties receive legal recognition.

4. For more information on the strikes and the development of the "new unionism" in Brazil see my *State and Opposition in Military Brazil* (Austin: University of Texas Press, 1986) and "Trade Unions in Brazil: A Search for Autonomy and Organization," in Edward Epstein, ed., *Labor Autonomy and the State in Latin America* (Winchester: Mass: Unwin Hyman, 1989).

5. Partido dos Trabalhadores, "Declaração Politica," São Bernardo do Campo, October 13, 1979, cited in Margaret Keck, *Change from Below: The Workers' Party in Brazil's Transition to Democracy* (New Haven: Yale University Press forthcoming), 151.

6. Neighborhood associations are registered as nonprofit organizations by specific districts or areas of cities. Residents organize to defend community interests, pressure government agencies for the delivery of services, and develop cooperative self-help projects. They became particularly important during the period of military rule, when residents of poor neighborhoods banded together for protection. In some major cities there are thousands of such associations, and they are joined by federations at city and even state levels.

7. Favela associations organize collective self-help projects among shantytown residents. They maintain a strong community identity and exercise considerable political influence.

8. The mayor, Olivio Dutra, had been president of that city's bank workers' union and a member of the executive committee of the Central Unica dos Trabalhadores, which represents eighteen million workers in Brazil. The majority of the members of the CUT are also members of the PT. In spite of this interconnectedness, when Dutra decided that local owners of public buses deserved an increase in fares the CUT, of which the bank workers' union is one of the most important affiliates, called a protest strike against the city government to force a change.

9. For a more detailed discussion of events in Diadema, see Keck, *Change from Below,* 337–341.

10. The tendências have more recently become associated with the different Trotskyist groups within the PT that have organized themselves as political parties. They view the PT as an umbrella organization, maintain their individual, usually highly centralized, political-party organizations, and act as pressure groups to get their positions accepted and to occupy political-party posts. This has created deep divisions in the PT and provoked an internal debate on how to prevent tendências from working as "parties within the party"—or, in the terminology of the PT, "wearing two shirts, one on top of the other."

11. The Frente Brasil Popular was composed of the PT, the PCdoB, and the Partido Socialista Brasileiro (Brazilian Socialist Party—PSB).

About the Book

Recent developments in Europe, including the collapse of communist governments in Eastern Europe, the electoral decline of most Western European communist parties, and a pronounced rightward shift in social democratic movements, have elicited assertions that the historical evolution of the Left is at a standstill. The evidence from Latin America, however, suggests that the Left is far from being marginalized. Gains on the electoral front and in labor movements, for example, indicate there exists a close connection between a new unity within the Left and its greater emphasis on the struggle to achieve and deepen democracy.

In eight country studies, contributors examine the lessons drawn from the failure of guerrilla strategies in the 1960s, the challenge to the traditional Left posed by the emergence of new social movements, and the new emphasis on democratic reforms over socioeconomic change. They also analyze how the Left has responded to the erosion of U.S. influence in the region and discuss whether the Left has benefited from the mobilizations and protests generated by IMF-imposed austerity programs. In a final section contributors explore issues of regional significance, including the trade union struggle and guerrilla warfare, and evaluate prospects for the future.

About the Editors
and Contributors

Barry Carr is Reader in History at La Trobe University, Melbourne, Australia. His research has dealt with the history of the workers' movement and the Left in Mexico. He is the author of *El movimiento obrero y la política en México 1910–1929* (1979), and *Marxism and Communism in Twentieth-Century Mexico* (1992). He is currently researching the impact of the Great Depression (1928–1935) on worker and peasant mobilizations in Cuba and Central America.

Marc W. Chernick is Assistant Director of the Institute of Latin American and Iberian Studies and teaches in the Political Science Department at Columbia University. He has been a Fulbright Scholar in Colombia and Visiting Professor at the University of The Andes in Bogotá and the National University of Colombia. He is the author of several articles in English and Spanish on Colombian politics and violence, including a forthcoming book on the Colombian peace process.

Ronald H. Chilcote is Professor of Political Science and Economics at the University of California, Riverside. He is the author of and editor of nine books, including *Theories of Development and Underdevelopment* (Westview, 1984), (with Joel C. Edelstein) *Latin America: Capitalist and Socialist Perspectives of Development and Underdevelopment* (Westview, 1986), and *Power and the Ruling Classes in Northeast Brazil* (1990). He is a founder and currently managing editor of *Latin American Perspectives*. His research has focused on Portuguese-speaking Africa, Brazil, and Portugal.

James Dunkerley is Professor of Politics at Queen Mary and Westfield College, University of London. His books include *The Long War: Dictatorship and Revolution in El Salvador* (1984), *Rebellion in the Veins: Political Struggle in Bolivia, 1952–1982* (1984), *Power in the Isthmus: A Political His-*

tory of Central America (1988), and *Political Suicide in Latin America and Other Essays* (1992). He is currently preparing a historical monograph on the Bolivian Revolution of 1952.

Steve Ellner is Professor at the Universidad de Oriente in Puerto La Cruz, Venezuela, where he has been teaching economic history and labor studies since 1977. He is the author of *Venezuela's Movimiento al Socialismo: From Guerrilla Defeat to Innovative Politics* (1988) and the short monographs *The Venezuelan Petroleum Corporation and the Debate over Government Policy in Basic Industry, 1960–1976* (1987) and *Generational Identification and Political Fragmentation in Venezuelan Politics in the Late 1960s* (1989).

Richard Gillespie is Senior Lecturer at the University of Warwick and coeditor of *The Journal of Communist Studies*. His publications include *Soldiers of Perón: Argentina's Montoneros* (1982), *The Spanish Socialist Party* (1989), and *Cuba After Thirty Years: Rectification and the Revolution* (1990).

Nigel Haworth teaches in the Department of Management Studies and Labor Relations at the University of Auckland. He is the author of numerous articles on twentieth-century Peruvian labor history and politics and has edited (with Jean Carrière and Jacqueline Roddick) *The State, Industrial Relations, and the Labor Movement in Latin America* (1989). Recent articles include "Political Transition and the Peruvian Labour Movement 1968–1985," in E. Epstein, ed., *Labor Autonomy and the State in Latin America* (1989).

Donald C. Hodges was schooled in Argentina from 1919 to 1942 and returned there for several months each in 1971, 1976, and 1985. A professor of philosophy and former chairman of the Department of Philosophy at Florida State University, he is also an affiliate professor of political science at FSU. Among his dozen books on Latin American politics are two on Argentina: *Argentina, 1943–1987: The National Revolution and Resistance* (1988) and *Argentina's "Dirty War": An Intellectual Biography* (1991).

Michael F. Jiménez received his Ph.D. from Harvard University in 1985 and currently teaches in the Department of History at the University of Pittsburgh. He has written extensively on social movements, class politics, and peasant resistance and is the author of the forthcoming book *Red Viotá: Power, Authority, and Rebellion in the Colombian Andes*.

Brian Loveman is Professor of History at San Diego State University. He is the author of numerous books on Chilean and Latin American history, including *Struggle in the Countryside: Politics and Rural Labor in Chile* (1976), *Chile: The Legacy of Hispanic Capitalism* (1979), and *The Politics of Antipolitics: The Military in Latin America* (1989, 2nd ed.).

Tommie Sue Montgomery is Associate Professor of Latin American Studies at Agnes Scott College in Atlanta, Georgia. In addition to *Revolution in El Salvador: Origins and Evolution* (Westview, 1982), she is author of numerous scholarly and popular articles on El Salvador, the church in Central America, and U.S. policy in El Salvador. In 1991 she carried out research on Salvadorian refugees in Belize under a Fulbright Research Grant.

María Helena Moreira Alves holds a Ph.D. in political science from M.I.T. She is Professor of Political Economy at the Universidade do Estado do Rio de Janeiro. One of the founders of the Workers' Party (PT), since 1985 she has been a member of the Union Education Department of the CUT, which represents eighteen million Brazilian workers. She organizes courses for trade union members in the state of Rio de Janeiro.

Dick Parker has been teaching in the Department of Sociology of the Universidad Central de Venezuela since 1975 and is the director of its workshop "Movimiento Obrero Latinoamericano." Among his several books is *El sindicalismo cristiano latinoamericano en busca de un perfil propio (1954–1971)* (1988).

Index